THE TRACKER'S FIELD GUIDE

A Comprehensive Manual for
Animal Tracking

Third Edition

JAMES C. LOWERY

FALCONGUIDES

GUILFORD, CONNECTICUT

FALCONGUIDES®

An imprint of Globe Pequot, the trade division of
The Rowman & Littlefield Publishing Group, Inc.
4501 Forbes Blvd., Ste. 200
Lanham, MD 20706
www.rowman.com
Falcon and FalconGuides are registered trademarks and Make Adventure Your Story is a
trademark of The Rowman & Littlefield Publishing Group, Inc.

Distributed by NATIONAL BOOK NETWORK

Copyright © 2022 James C. Lowery

All photos by James C. Lowery unless otherwise noted.
Maps by Melissa Baker © The Rowman & Littlefield Publishing Group, Inc

British Library Cataloguing in Publication Information available

Library of Congress Cataloging-in-Publication Data available

ISBN 978-1-4930-6703-9 (paper: alk paper)
ISBN 978-1-4930-6704-6 (electronic)

♾™ The paper used in this publication meets the minimum requirements of American
National Standard for Information Sciences—Permanence of Paper for Printed Library
Materials, ANSI/NISO Z39.48-1992.

The authors and The Rowman & Littlefield Publishing Group, Inc. assume no liability
for accidents happening to, or injuries sustained by, readers who engage in the
activities described in this book.

To those who devote their lives to habitat protection

CONTENTS

Contents

ACKNOWLEDGMENTS

Threads from every part of this book lead back to Tom Brown Jr., who introduced me to tracking and who showed that the hard-to-imagine is possible. The complete dedication to the learning process and the honoring of the track's maker above all are lessons I will always carry with me.

For the third edition's conversion and improvement of photos, I am indebted to help and coaching from Rhanna Nyman; she and Rowan Nyman are also responsible for cover design elements. I am very thankful for Kim Cabrera's help with the Resources appendix stemming from her vital role connecting trackers with one another.

Doug Gaulke made the book's completion possible through his substantial help with illustrations and knowledge about mammals outside my area, such as the gray wolf and white-tailed deer. Paul Rezendes, Mark Elbroch, Matt Gray, Renee Robison, and Dick Newell also contributed essential photos. Marge Erickson merged her extensive tracking background with professional editing skills in proofreading the manuscript.

Thanks go to the first edition manuscript reviewers for their suggestions and encouragement: Don Mitchell, Wanda DeWaard, Roseann and Jonathan Hanson, Carl Olmstead, and Steve Montgomery. Tom Lowery designed an attractive and flexible layout concept for the original book development.

Invaluable help in field research as I sought tracks of specific mammals was provided by Curtis Bjurlin and Alexander Brown of the Endangered Species Recovery Program at California State University, Stanislaus, who released grasshopper mice and pocket mice onto my tracking boards; Patty Quickert and Laura Patterson of the California Department of Water Resources, who did the same with harvest mice; and Elizabeth Jozwiak of the Kenai National Wildlife Refuge, who helped with snowshoe-hare tracks and signs. Alice Koch helped with pronghorn, badger, and kit fox tracks on the Carrizo Plain and Larry Lambrecht helped find elk tracks in Arizona.

I am indebted to the owners and managers of the natural areas where we have conducted classes and collected track information for this book. The importance of Windy Springs Preserve, and my appreciation of its late owner and steward Tom Drummond, cannot be overstated. Also I acknowledge the

Acknowledgments

Desert Studies Center, Zzyzx, California; the University of California James Reserve; the Dunes Center in Guadalupe, California; Wind Wolves Preserve; the Carrizo Plain National Monument; the Palos Verdes Peninsula Land Conservancy; and Lone Juniper Ranch in Gorman, California. Special thanks go to Steve Martin and the staff of Working Wildlife, where we were able to conduct animal-movement workshops and study tracks of captive wild animals, and to Rose Berger of SunWolf Farms for her very professional and enthusiastic help with horses and their gaits.

The groundwork laid by dedicated tracking teachers over the past thirty years has benefited all of us who study and teach the art. I would like to acknowledge especially the pioneering work of Tom Hanratty, Charles Worsham, Jim Halfpenny, Paul Rezendes, Jon Young, Susan Morse, and Mark Elbroch. More recently the contributions of CyberTracker evaluators and instructors toward expanding the tracking audience and its expertise continues to be especially important.

I cannot list all of the dedicated Earth Skills tracking students who accompanied us as we learned. Many of these people field-tested early drafts of this guide in classes and gave suggestions and encouragement. You know who you are—thank you. Our First Nation friends Robin, Terry, and Barbara, along with their extended family, helped to keep us humble and thankful. Scott Cunningham's music was more important than he knows.

I am grateful to Globe Pequot Press and Falcon Guides for continuing to make this book widely available.

Finally, the sacrifice and support I received from my wife, Mary, toward this book cannot possibly be described and can be understood only by those who know her. From carefree exploration to times of crushing focus, she was my constant companion. She is a true tracker because she always finds what is necessary. This project and my life have been blessed by her.

1
INTO THE ANIMAL'S WORLD

If you are already a tracker, you know what novice trackers will learn in their first day: The animal whose tracks you just identified is going to call you out. Where am I going, it will say. Why am I traveling alone? Why did I bypass this perfectly good food? How recently was I here? Why did I take this side trail?

The tracks won't answer everything, but they do tell you more than you probably think. Mood, posture, speed, and personality. The reason for a choice of a bedding site. The current place in this year's rearing of young. Deliberate avoidance of another of its species. An exploratory urge or hungry focus.

Most importantly, the tracks begin the conversation between you and the animal, the animal leading the way because it's the one with the answers. You don't need to be an accomplished tracker to hold up your end of the conversation, but it's best to know how to read what else is in the tracks besides the identity of its maker. And, it's essential to bring in biology and behavior too.

With these principles in mind—learned from my own fieldwork as well as from teaching hundreds of tracking workshops—I wrote this book to help you identify tracks confidently and efficiently, and then to step into the animal's world toward a rich and often surprising journey of discovery.

There are a lot of tools here: extensive notes about the biology of each animal, many examples of track interpretation, and "Track Windows" suggesting how your exploration can access an animal's unique personality and biology. If you are a beginning tracker, you will grow into some of these tools over time. If you are an advanced tracker, you will find useful ones not found in other references.

Remember that the opportunity to interact with the animal you are tracking, whether it be a chipmunk or an elk, is special and sacred. The animal passed here, in this way, only once. It left behind the signs of its body language, signs of choices about food and travel, evidence of when it rested and where it ran. Each of these threads draws inward to the animal's mood and outward to its whole ecology. From them, patterns emerge that captivate and astound, and a story with many levels is carried away.

To bypass the opportunity is not only to miss a good story, it is to reject that dose of humility and sanity that the animals give us. We humans talk too much to each other, and so I will be disappointed if you don't use this book to reach out and touch the four-leggeds. The tools are here, and amazing encounters are within your ability.

The Tracker's Triangle

From your first to your last day of tracking, you will pay attention to three elements. They will be important in track identification, but they will also lead beyond it to track interpretation. These elements are:

Single prints. The raw material of tracking, these are to be studied, measured, and remembered. Chapter 2 gives some tips about evaluating them for field identification. Throughout the Mammal section, careful drawings and photos of single prints will guide you. Summaries of prints are given at the back of the book.

Track patterns. Patterns help to identify tracks because each species has evolved with distinctive ways of moving most naturally. Chapter 3 provides a nuts-and-bolts introduction to track patterns and gaits that will help the beginning tracker, while chapter 5 discusses more advanced pattern interpretation and gait visualization. The mammal section includes examples of track patterns from my field notebooks. Summary track patterns are found at the back of this book.

Soil movement. Every physical movement of an animal creates a disturbance in the track, which Tom Brown Jr. calls "pressure releases." The beginning tracker can notice and interpret soil movement within the first few hours in the field. While the thorough study of pressure releases is beyond the scope of this book, chapter 4 shows how noticing soil movement contributes to track identification, and chapter 6 provides some tips about using pressure releases to interpret tracks.

A beginning tracker will learn to go back and forth among these three elements as she or he identifies a track. Usually, no one element will do the trick because animal gaits and the substrate in which tracks are made are so variable. For more experienced trackers, dancing among the clear print, the pattern, and the pressure releases becomes second nature. The process leads to an understanding of the animal's mood and body language, and this in turn prompts questions about its biology.

The journey into an animal's biology through tracks and signs is incredibly rich. In writing this book, I learned from the specialists who spent countless days and months in the field studying how an animal used its habitat, how it traveled, where it fed or hunted, how it bred and raised its young, and how it survived. From the more than 900 articles and books I read, covering field research from the 1920s to today, I distilled the "Notes for the Tracker," which should give your tracking some valuable focus and perspective. A "Recommended Reading" list of the most useful of these sources is included for trackers who want to go beyond this book.

2
CLEAR PRINT IDENTIFICATION

Track identification is a process of going back and forth between the **clear prints** and the **track pattern** so that all information is brought in and all possibilities are considered. This systematic approach simplifies track ID for the beginner and becomes a habit that leads directly to track interpretation for the advanced tracker.

When you encounter tracks, begin studying whichever element gives you the best information, narrowing down the choices, and then go to the other element. In mud or dust, clear prints are usually the starting point, and in soft snow or soft sand, the track pattern might be studied first. **Soil movement** might be brought in to illuminate the animal's speed and to shed light on using the track pattern for identification.

Knowing the mammals in each family that occur in your tracking area helps immensely, because the number of choices in each group is really pretty small. Obtain a local mammal list from a nature center, natural history museum, or fish-and-wildlife office. Regional or state mammal guides also help. (Note that this guide does not include all mammal species in North America. Consult appendix A for coverage.)

This chapter introduces clear print identification; chapter 3 covers track patterns.

In the clear prints you're looking at, try to find both front and hind tracks; this is not always possible, especially when the hind tracks cover the front ones. **Look at the number of toes, the shape of the tracks, and whether you see claws**. Then use the summaries at the back of this book (or look at the chart on page 6) to find out which mammal family the tracks might belong to. If you can't easily tell which are front and which are hind tracks, at least try to match the ones that look similar to each other. You can often get to the correct family even if you temporarily confuse front and hind prints.

Look really carefully and also keep an open mind as you do this. Sometimes claw impressions do not show when you expect them to. Sometimes a track's inside toe can't be easily seen. Sometimes an animal's movement may distort the shape of the track. Be ready to revisit your hypothesis if other information doesn't make sense.

Next, **measure the front and hind tracks,** or at least the hind ones if the front are not available. It's important to measure the actual size of the animal's foot that created the track, i.e., the *bottom of the track,* not the track distortion (see page 7). Measure to at least $\frac{1}{16}$ of an inch or 1 mm accuracy, or the measurements will be meaningless when you compare them to track averages in this book. For the length of a track, don't include the claw impressions in your measurements. When an animal is diagonal walking with a direct register (see chapter 3), be careful to measure just the hind track *inside* the whole compression.

Finally, **pay attention to detail** because where there is overlap in track size among species, fine details often do the trick. Look at the exact shape of the heel pad, the shape and positioning of each toe, and the relative depth of different parts of the track. Consult photographs and drawings for the relevant species in this guide.

Remember that the track pattern (chapter 3) and soil movement (chapter 4) should always be considered in track ID. Using three elements will become second nature and will actually simplify the process.

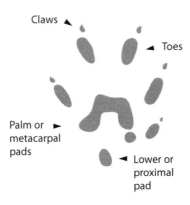

Claws

Toes

Palm or
metacarpal
pads

Lower or
proximal
pad

Clear Print Identification

Group	No. of front toes	No. of hind toes	Shape	Claws	Notes
Cat	4	4	round	no	Some house cats have 5+ toes.
Dog	4	4	egg	yes	
Rabbit	4	4	egg	maybe	
Rodent	4	5	toes long	maybe	Many kangaroo rats have 4 hind toes.
Weasel	5	5	boxy	maybe	Inside toe small
Raccoon	5	5	human	maybe	
Opossum	5	5	spread	maybe	
Bear	5	5	human	maybe	
Insectivore	5	5	tiny	maybe	
Ungulate	2	2	heart	no	Horses, mules, and burros have 1 toe.

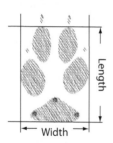

Length

Width

Measuring a track. Measure the width to the outermost points of the toes. Length should not include claw marks. Track width is often more useful than track length for comparison with averages in this guide, because forward motion may distort the length of the track. Measure to $\frac{1}{16}$ in. or 1 mm.

Measuring tracks in soft soil. A coyote made these two right hind tracks about 7.6 meters (25 ft.) apart, the top one in wet sand and the bottom one in dry sand (the bottom track is a single impression from a slow walk). The photos are reproduced at exactly the same scale to show how the track in soft soil would need to be measured to get a true reading of track width. With practice, a tracker can learn to measure collapsed tracks consistently to within less than ¹⁄₁₆ inch. Making test thumbprints helps to read how much the soil collapses.

Clear Print Identification

A

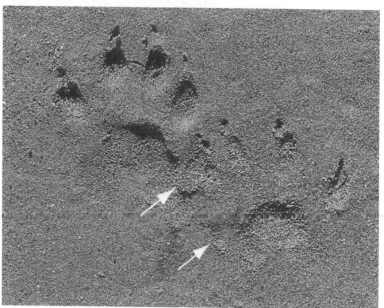

B

Examples of working through clear print ID.

A: If the very faint inside toe (arrow) of this ringtail track isn't recognized, this "four-toed" track still couldn't be a cat's because of its overall shape, couldn't be a dog's because the heel shape isn't right, couldn't be a rabbit's because the pad area is clear, not furred, and couldn't be a rodent's front track because the toes aren't elongated. This leads to a re-evaluation of assumptions and closer examination by the tracker.

B: The process of elimination begins by noticing the faint inside toes (arrows). The next pair of tracks (out of the photo's range) is similar, so this is a "5 + 5" animal. Considering each "5 + 5" family methodically, track size and/or the local habitat in this instance eliminates all but opossum, raccoon, river otter, and badger. The lack of an opposable thumb rules out opossum, the lack of very long, prominent claws rules out badger, and the small size of the inner toe rules out the river otter. Even though this raccoon creates confusing tracks by walking up on the ball of its hind foot (left) and the tips of its toes, there is really no other animal the tracks can belong to.

3
TRACK PATTERN BASICS

While animal gaits and track patterns are quite variable, they are enormously important in confirming the identity of tracks and should *always* be studied during the identification process. This chapter describes some of the most common track patterns, with which you can find your way with the majority of tracks you see. In the beginning you need not visualize precisely how an animal moved: You just need to recognize the patterns and associate them with mammals that commonly create them. Eventually, being able to picture, or to "role-play" in your mind, how a track pattern was made will not only give you greater success, it will lead to "becoming" the animal, which is the very essence of tracking. A more detailed treatment of gaits and track patterns appears in chapter 5.

"Alternating" Pattern (Diagonal Walk)

This consists of fairly equally spaced double prints, with the hind track superimposed over the front one on the same side. If you see this pattern, first confirm that these are double prints, and, by noticing soil movement, that the rate of speed is slow. If so, then the pattern almost always belongs to a member of the **cat**, **dog**, or **hoofed animal group**, or it belongs to an **opossum**, a **ringtail**, a **muskrat**, or a **badger**.

If you see this pattern, narrow down the choice of the mammal group by counting toes (if prints are clear) and noticing the shape of the track. Then, bring it down to the species by measuring the size of the tracks and the stride (see "Measuring Track Patterns for Interpretation" in chapter 5). Often, just eyeballing the stride helps because in this walking gait, the length of the stride approximates a little less than shoulder-to-hip distance for that animal. (For example, a 53-cm/21-in. stride could belong only to a hoofed animal, gray wolf, or mountain lion.) *But be careful:* Many alternating walkers overlap in stride, so

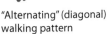

"Alternating" (diagonal) walking pattern

use the *actual* track size and shape rather than just the stride for your most accurate reading.

Noticing whether the hind tracks are directly superimposed on top of each front track (**direct register**, left photo) or overlap a little behind each front track (**indirect register**, right photo) also helps identification.* This reading must be done on fairly even ground because on uneven ground a "direct-registering" animal may alter its foot placement. If you see consistent direct registering in an alternating track pattern, the track pattern will

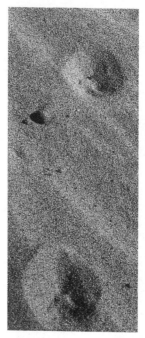 

Direct register   Indirect register

have been made almost always by a wild member of the cat family (bobcat, mountain lion, lynx) or a fox (kit fox, red fox, gray fox). Ringtails sometimes direct-register also.

All other alternating walkers—hoofed animals, coyotes, wolves, domestic dogs, and domestic or feral cats—indirect-register when they produce an alternating track pattern. In certain soils it is very hard to see that each print in a direct-registering alternating pattern is actually two tracks, but often the "shadow" of the front track beneath will show very subtly, since for all these animals, the front track is larger than the hind. In contrast, an indirect-registering pattern will usually show the overlapping front and hind tracks pretty clearly.

Exceptions and cautions. Occasionally you might find a left-right-left-right track pattern that is not an alternating or "diagonal" walk. Two kinds of trots and one kind of stretched-out gallop may create such a pattern. You can quickly eliminate the gallop and one trot because in these gaits, the

---

*In this book the terms *direct* and *indirect register* apply only to slow-moving (walking) track patterns and are meaningless when applied to faster-moving gaits such as trots.

left-right-left-right prints are single tracks rather than doubles. And all three patterns will show much more "action" in the tracks because of higher speed; see chapter 4 on soil movement. With a little examination, there will be no problem verifying whether an alternating pattern was really created by a walk.

With regard to the direct register, remember that in deep snow or tall grasses, even indirect-registering walkers often approximate a direct register due to efficiency of walking in their own footsteps. Even then, though, the register is often slightly off.

If your alternating pattern has double prints and shows a lot of soil movement, it is likely not a walk but rather a fast walk or trot. In this case the tracks are still likely to belong to a member of the cat, dog, or hoofed-animal groups. But we can also add some other possibilities such as voles, introduced rats, and pocket gophers, which all commonly trot, as well as a host of other mammals that do so occasionally.

"Bound" Pattern

This is a track pattern appearing to be pairs of impressions, one usually a little behind the other as shown at right. The "pairs" are actually four tracks, because the hind feet land on top of where the front had previously landed. When you see this bounding pattern, it will have been made almost always by a member of the weasel group, which includes the marten, fisher, river otter, mink, black-footed ferret, short-tailed weasel, long-tailed weasel, and least weasel.

All of these weasel family members have long, tubular bodies and short legs, enabling them to alternately stretch and compress their bodies, inchworm-like, to create their bounding track pattern. Habitat, the presence or absence of webbing in the tracks, track size, toe details, and trail width will usually narrow the identification down to one or two possibilities.

Exceptions and cautions. The "canid trot" (see chapter 5) also produces pairs of impressions, one set back from the other, but each print is a single and not a double track; also because one track in each pair is a front and one a hind, the two impressions are different sizes. Kangaroo rats also create pairs of tracks, sometimes with one set slightly behind the other, but the impressions are not double ones because the kangaroo rat bounds on only its hind feet. If you are uncertain whether a pattern

Bound pattern

was created by one of the weasel family members listed above, follow the trail until you can get a reading of track detail. With bounders, the terrain and the animal's speed create subtle variations in foot landing, often revealing parts of the front tracks beneath the hind. Note that the term "bound" is used differently by some other tracking instructors.*

"Gallop" Pattern

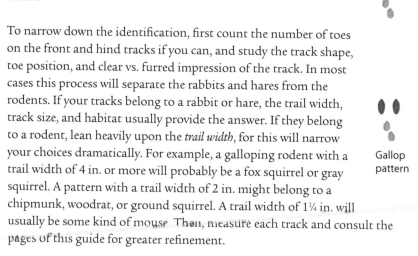

This pattern is characterized by groups of four tracks with the hind tracks positioned ahead of the front ones in each group. Though almost every North American mammal can "gallop," there are certain groups that characteristically create the pattern shown at right. If you find a regular gallop pattern as shown here, it will "almost always" have been made by a rabbit or hare, a mouse, chipmunk, ground squirrel, tree squirrel, woodrat, or shrew.

To narrow down the identification, first count the number of toes on the front and hind tracks if you can, and study the track shape, toe position, and clear vs. furred impression of the track. In most cases this process will separate the rabbits and hares from the rodents. If your tracks belong to a rabbit or hare, the trail width, track size, and habitat usually provide the answer. If they belong to a rodent, lean heavily upon the *trail width*, for this will narrow your choices dramatically. For example, a galloping rodent with a trail width of 4 in. or more will probably be a fox squirrel or gray squirrel. A pattern with a trail width of 2 in. might belong to a chipmunk, woodrat, or ground squirrel. A trail width of 1¼ in. will usually be some kind of mouse. Then, measure each track and consult the pages of this guide for greater refinement.

Gallop pattern

Note that I recommend relying on the trail width, rather than stride measurement, to help most with identification of gallopers, because the former relates to the animal's body width while the latter may vary widely with speed.

The relative placement of the front and hind tracks in a gallop pattern also helps with track identification. Front tracks placed next to each other (left

---

*Some consider a "bound" to be any gait in which the front legs and/or the rear legs move simultaneously, resulting in numerous track patterns. This book holds a narrower definition. See chapter 5.

photo) are generally characteristic of white-footed mice (*Peromyscus* genus), pocket mice, chipmunks, red squirrels, and, to a lesser degree, gray squirrels. Other gallopers usually form patterns with the front feet angled in relation to one another (right photo).

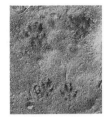

Gallop patterns with lateral (left) vs. diagonal (right) placement of front tracks

As always, be careful and study the clear prints because many other mammals besides rabbits, rodents, and shrews may occasionally gallop.

"Overstep" Pattern (Pace Walk)

In this pattern there are pairs of tracks on each side of the trail, the hind track positioned ahead of the front track on each side. This is created by the hind leg swinging beyond the position of the front track in a walk (an "overstep"). If you confirm that the pattern you see is a walking pattern, then it probably belongs to a bear, skunk, porcupine, beaver, or marmot. (Hoofed animals in the camel group, such as llamas, also create the overstep pattern, and mountain lions often use the gait.)

A special case is the common raccoon gait, in which the hind leg steps so far beyond the front's prior position that it lands next to the opposite front track (drawing at right).

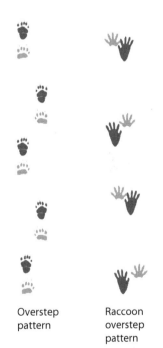

Overstep pattern

Raccoon overstep pattern

Exceptions and cautions. A very common trot also creates a pattern identical to the overstep or "pace" walk, so be certain that you look at soil movement to distinguish the two. If the front and hind tracks are reversed (the hind one landing *behind* and not *beyond* the front one), the gait is a slow walk. Both of these might have been created by animals not in this "overstep" group.

4
SOIL MOVEMENT AND TRACK IDENTIFICATION

In tracking, soil movement is the study of *pressure releases*—Tom Brown Jr.'s term for disturbances left behind by the moving foot.* (To be accurate, we should actually say "substrate movement" since pressure releases also occur in snow, leaves, and other substrates.) In chapter 6 we provide suggestions for learning how to read tracks for motion.

Practically, a tracker should begin to notice soil movement in his or her first day, because it plays into track identification as well as the classification of the track pattern. The most obvious application will occur in distinguishing similar track patterns that can cause confusion in track identification.

The photo at right shows a trail that a novice tracker might consider to be an alternating ("diagonal") walk pattern. The shape of the track, the heel-pad shape, and the number and position of the toes all argue for the cat family, and track measurements would allow for a domestic cat or small bobcat. The stride measurement falls outside the usual range of walking strides for a domestic cat and within that of a bobcat, and furthermore the track pattern appears to be a direct register—suggesting bobcat. However, the soil

This domestic cat's trotting pattern resembles a diagonal walk, direct register.

---

*Tom Brown Jr., *The Science and Art of Tracking,* New York: Berkley Publishing Group, 1999

shows a lot of "action"; there are prominent disk fissures behind the toes, and soil is pushed up ahead of the tracks in plate fissures. The gait must then not be a walk but a trot, thus invalidating comparisons with walking strides. This trail was made by a feral cat. In the same way, soil movement can be used to distinguish another kind of trot from an overstep ("pace") walk.

The other application of reading soil movement is to adjust or qualify measurements of a clear print when the track is distorted because of balance or speed. While this may seem to be self-evident, I have seen students make an identification error in this way.

5
TRACK PATTERN INTERPRETATION

Your goal in interpreting a track pattern is not just to label it but to *visualize* the animal's movement that created the pattern. This chapter describes how to begin visualizing leg movement from track patterns. The reading of soil movement or pressure releases, which should go hand-in-hand with this, is touched upon in chapter 6.

Learning to visualize a moving animal from a track pattern will require, first, that you store images of animals using various gaits in your memory. You must watch animals move, over and over again, noticing every detail you can. Study domestic animals: horses, dogs, cats. Study wild animals when you see them: deer, raccoons, rabbits, skunks, squirrels. Study nature programs that show animals moving. Record them and watch the movements many times over. Take advantage of resources on the Internet, in books, and on video that describe and show animal movement.

The second requirement is to form a habit of visualizing how sets of tracks were created. Begin with a general idea of the animal's leg movement, then allow the tracks themselves to confirm and refine your visualization. Notice the spacing of the tracks and compare it to the animal's leg length. Postulate which feet touch the ground at the same time, then study those tracks to see if soil movement is similar in those pairs or groups of three. Also study pressure releases to understand speed and perhaps posture. Role-playing by moving on all fours helps immensely, especially with the slower-moving gaits. Remember that there is always only one motion that can have created a given set of tracks! Grit your teeth and work through a puzzle until you have understood all you possibly can.

The following sections provide some guidance in how to approach track pattern interpretation.

Alternating or Diagonal Walk Patterns

The sequence of leg movement in a walk is left hind–left front–right hind–right front. Virtually all of the "alternating" or "diagonal" walk patterns will have been created by this movement sequence.

About Gait Terminology

Gait and track pattern terminology is quite inconsistent in the field of tracking. Some terms, such as "trot," describe general leg movement that can create numerous track patterns. Others, such as "bound," primarily describe leg movement but have been used by different trackers to label different track patterns. "Lope" and "gallop" may also be applied variously, and some terms may be understood differently by trackers and equestrians. While confusing to the beginning tracker, these inconsistencies, when encountered in reading and when working with other trackers, will present no problem to the advancing tracker, who with experience can easily move beyond terminology to the precise visualization of gaits.

You will notice as you role-play this sequence yourself that most of the time, two legs are in motion at any one time, except for a brief moment in which only one leg is moving and the three others are on the ground. In part of each cycle, the two diagonally opposite legs (e.g., right front and left hind) move simultaneously, and in part of the cycle the two laterally placed legs (e.g., right front and right hind) move simultaneously, if only momentarily. If you study the movement of many "diagonal walker" species, you realize that some show a greater percentage of each cycle in diagonal leg movement, and some a greater percentage in lateral leg movement. Differences may occur even among individual animals and at varying times with one animal.

From an alternating track pattern, it is not always easy to read the *precise timing* of foot movement because some of the required evidence, namely the front tracks, are partially or, in the case of a direct-register walk, almost completely covered by the hind ones. (Reading the timing of leg movement comes into play when you are reading a motion such as a head turn and need to confirm your reading by knowing which feet touch the ground at any given moment.) Yet alternating patterns do offer some good interpretative possibilities. Slowing or hesitation can cause one or more pairs of front/hind prints to be spaced more closely together. And pivots, stops, or head turns may cause a variation in pitch (inward or outward rotation) of front or hind tracks that stands out dramatically from the regular pattern. (See the "Spotted Skunk" pages for an example.)

Diagonal or alternating walk

Overstep or "Pace" Patterns

To visualize an overstep or "pace," imagine a gait in which the two laterally paired legs (e.g., left front and left hind) move simultaneously. Pacers such as llamas and camels show this motion most classically. In North America most species that create pacing or overstep patterns—for example, bears and skunks—indeed spend the greatest portion of each walking cycle in laterally paired leg movement, but their gait is often somewhat of a hybrid between this "pace" and the "diagonal" walk described above. That is, a small portion of each cycle may be devoted to diagonally paired leg movement.

Nevertheless, we can say about pace walkers that as each hind leg swings forward, it moves *beyond* the location of the previously created front track on the same side. This overstep is made possible by the increased stability of the two legs on the opposite side supporting the overstep walker. But other factors are also in play such as the longer hind legs of some pacers such as raccoons. (Note that when a bear walks uphill and shortens its rear stride, it will create an alternating track pattern while technically "pace walking.")

Overstep or
pace walk

Because this gait is slow, and because tracks are separate, an overstep track pattern can be read very precisely for the exact timing of leg movement, as long as the track substrate is good. Begin with the general knowledge of leg sequence, pick a section of the trail, and begin role-playing. In general, the front and hind feet on one side of the body are on the ground at the same time, but there is usually some offset with native North American pace walkers. Pay attention to the pitch of each track and to pressure releases that show shifting balance from track to track; a clear picture of the leg sequence as well as shoulder orientation may then emerge. (See the "Striped Skunk" pages for an example.) When you interpret overstep patterns, try to visualize body language. Some mammals may posture to others using a pace walk. A running pace may be seen among ungulates, raccoons, or other mammals.

Slow Walk and Fast Walk Patterns

In a slow walk, the typical walking sequence described under "Alternating or Diagonal Walk Patterns" above is modified only in timing; legs move more independently of one another, and there is a greater percentage of each cycle in which the animal is supported on three legs. In the most extreme slow walk, or "stalk," each leg is moved and planted before another leaves the ground. Because the hind leg does not move forward as far as with a normal speed walk, a slow walk creates the pattern shown at left, with the hind track falling *behind* the front one on the same side.

Slow walk   Fast walk

Results of a very stable gait, slow walk patterns may offer opportunities to read an animal's mood. If the animal is sniffing the ground or browsing, all four tracks will show greater depth at the toes. If it is alert with its head up, there will be more pressure toward the rear of the tracks. A stalking cat sometimes pinches its toes from excitement, leaving a raised area between the toes and the heel pad.

In a fast walk the animal moves the diagonally opposite legs simultaneously. This gait is essentially a trot (described below), except that the animal maintains contact with the ground at all times. For this to occur, there is a slight offset from pure diagonal leg movement. A fast-walk track pattern is an alternating pattern with a longer stride. There is also more "action" expressed in the tracks. (See the "Domestic Cat" pages for an example.)

Trot Patterns

In a trot, the animal moves diagonally opposite legs simultaneously and is momentarily airborne between the times each pair hits the ground. Trots vary in speed and posture. Some are used to move quickly through an open area, some are used for leisurely long-distance travel, and some are showy displays to other animals, for example. Trotting patterns are a fruitful raw material for track reading. The four patterns shown here are seen most often, but there are many other variations.

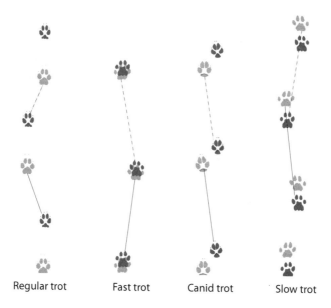

| Regular trot | Fast trot | Canid trot | Slow trot |

Begin the interpretation of a trot by marking which front-hind (F-H) pairs hit the ground simultaneously (as shown with the dotted and solid lines in the illustration above). The distance of this pair to the opposite pair that hits next will show relative speed, and the distance between the F and H tracks that hit the ground at the same time will show whether the animal's legs are stretched out or gathered somewhat under the body, as in a slow, "bouncy" trot.

Next, look at soil movement in the tracks. Because the animal is airborne between steps, the feet will "dive in" as they land, often pushing soil up in front of the tracks; there will also be a push-off evident as the feet leave. Look for differences in these pressure releases that may show you the animal's posture. Elk often trot stiff-legged with their heads held very still in order to see danger, while a coyote's slow trot may be more fluid, for example.

Finally, study the opposite F-H pairs of tracks and compare them to one another. Because each pair is created by feet moving simultaneously, the two tracks should *usually* mirror one another in pitch and major pressure releases. Reading similarities and differences in the opposite pairs (RF-LH [right front-left hind] and LF-RH) may clearly show the animal's shoulder orientation. (See pages on the "Mule Deer" and "Pronghorn" for examples of trot-pattern interpretation.)

One trot, called the "canid trot" or "side trot," is familiar to watchers of domestic dogs and is also commonly seen with wolves, foxes, and coyotes.

The track pattern shows front tracks on one side and hind tracks on the other. While the classic posture that creates this pattern is a sideward tilting of the shoulders (see the "Domestic Dog" pages), a canid might also create it with shoulders barely tilted and the spine flexing back and forth instead.

Bound, Lope, and Gallop Patterns

The bound, lope, and gallop are related gaits in which the front legs move together or in quick succession, followed by the hind legs moving together or in quick succession. The exact timing of this leg movement, and the place where each foot lands, will determine what the gait is called. But even within the same system of terminology, the borderline between any two of these gaits may be shady, and indeed two trackers watching an animal move in real time may have different opinions about what label to apply to what they have just seen.

Fortunately, the track patterns themselves allow us to go beyond labels to visualize the gait exactly. The tracks should answer these questions: What is the sequence of footfalls? Which feet touch the ground at the same time? When is the animal airborne? How fast is the animal moving? What is the animal's posture?

A **bound pattern** is created by the two front feet landing in quick succession, then exiting before the two hind feet land in quick succession more or less on top of the front tracks. Weasels and martens are classic bounders, with long slender bodies that allow compression and expansion like an inchworm as they move. But fishers, mink, ringtails, and spotted skunks sometimes create this classic bound pattern as well. By generalization, we might also use "bound" to refer to any pattern in which the two front feet land close together and the two hind feet land parallel to them, as a slow-hopping squirrel might do.

Because classic bound patterns are so regular, nuances stand out and allow interesting interpretation. A change from its normal right or left lead, or a different pitch or positioning of a track, can lead to visualization of hesitations or increased alertness, for example. (See the "Marten" pages for examples.)

Bound

A **lope pattern** may be considered a slight extension of the bound. In a lope the front feet land one-two, with a greater difference in timing and space than is shown in the bound. Then the hind feet land one-two with essentially the same timing; one of the hind feet lands either between the front track impressions or on top of the farthest one, while the other hind foot lands beyond the two front tracks. The lope is an easygoing gait regularly used by weasel family members such as skunks, otters, fishers, and wolverines, but it is also seen sometimes among cats, dogs, and ungulates.

Several details may be noticed from loping track patterns. First, the characteristic rocking motion from the animal's weight shift in each cycle is reflected regularly in pressure releases. Second, the pattern will show whether the animal is using a "transverse lope" with the same front and hind leads (e.g., LF-RF-LH-RH) or a "rotary lope" with alternate front and hind leads (e.g., LF-RF-RH-LH). Third, the animal's shoulder orientation can be read by the position of front and hind tracks and pressure releases within them. (See the "Raccoon" pages for an example of lope pattern interpretation.)

Lopes

Finally, speed can be read from the distance between groups of four. A classic horse canter or slow lope is a "three-beat" gait, in which one F-H pair hits the ground together in every cycle. The feet that would land together would be the last hind in one group of four and the first front in the next group. Visualizing the leg reach of your animal will tell you whether the track pattern you are analyzing could have been created by a three-beat lope.

In a **gallop pattern**, the two front feet land and the two hind feet move *beyond* the front tracks. Rabbits, hares, and many rodents are built to gallop easily, their hind legs placed more widely than the front ones, allowing the back legs to move easily around and beyond the front ones. But the vast majority of North American mammal species gallop some of the time. We can call any group of four tracks with the sequence F-F-H-H a gallop pattern.

As with lopes, the footfall sequence in a gallop may be "transverse" or "rotary." Also notice the degree to which the two front legs land simultaneously and

Cottontail gallop

Kit fox gallop group

notice the same with the hind legs; this will say something about speed as well as posture. A gallop usually has one or two periods of suspension that can be deduced from the tracks. The galloper is usually airborne between the hind feet exiting and the next front ones landing; but there may also be a suspension between the front and hind feet. (See the "Black-Tailed Jackrabbit" and the "Snowshoe Hare" pages for gallop interpretation examples.)

Interpretation of a Trot

Accurately interpreting motion in a track pattern requires that you can visualize exactly which feet touch the ground at any moment. In this red fox's trotting trail, alternate pairs, e.g. right front and left hind, move, land, and exit simultaneously, so the tracks created by these feet are "read" together. In the left diagram, solid and dotted lines indicate the legs that move together while the right photo shows detail of one of these track pairs. As it should be in a trot, these two tracks look almost identical. Among other things, both show deeper internal pitch to the right and soil movement created by a rotation of the rightmost toes (arrows) undoubtedly caused by the fox's hard look over its right shoulder. The fox also slowed momentarily in this step, indicated by the shorter distance between these tracks compared to the other pairs in this sequence.

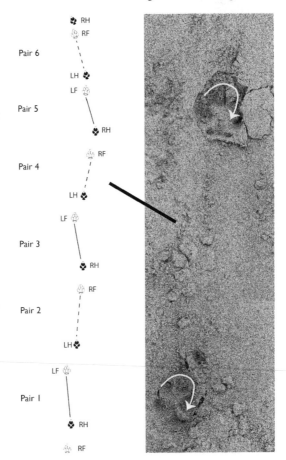

Pair 6 — RH, RF, LH, LF

Pair 5 — RH, RF

Pair 4 — LH, LF

Pair 3 — RH, RF

Pair 2 — LH, LF

Pair 1 — RH, RF

Measuring Track Patterns for Interpretation

Following are common track measurements and their significance for interpretation.

A: Trail width is measured from the outermost points of a trail. For gallopers and bounders, trail width helps in species identification. For other mammals, it can help identify individual animals of a species.

B: Stride, for alternating and overstep walkers, is measured from the toe of one hind track to the toe of the opposite hind track. Stride helps in species identification, and recording left and right strides helps to distinguish the tracks of individual animals of a species apart from one another because these measurements tend to be unique. For gallopers and bounders, stride is less useful for species identification because it can vary with speed.

C: Straddle measures the inside of a track pattern. Especially for alternating walkers, straddle helps distinguish individual animals; a mammal's straddle may also change as it approaches adult size. A change of gaits might also produce a straddle change. If left and right tracks overlap over the center line, the straddle is negative.

D & E: Group and intergroup measurements for gallop and lope patterns can help with track identification because it relates to a mammal's leg length and reach. These measurements change with speed.

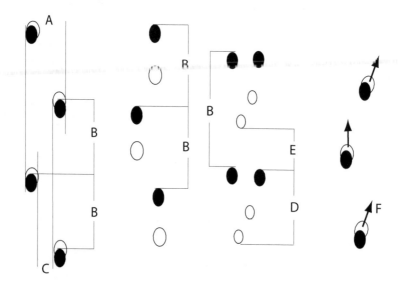

F: Pitch measures the outward or inward orientation of an individual track away from the direction of travel; pitch may be positive or negative. When recurrent in the same track (e.g., right front), pitch may help identify an individual animal, or it may point to an ongoing action such as carrying something in the mouth. If pitch occurs incidentally, it may be associated with a temporary action such as a look.

Visualizing an Animal's Size

Among other useful applications of track measurement, tracks can show an individual animal's body length as long as you know which feet are touching the ground simultaneously in the track pattern you are studying. In a bear's pace walk, the same-side feet are planted at the same time as shown in the left photo. So, measuring the "reach" of this juvenile brown bear from hind toes to front toes (dark line) equates closely to its shoulder-to hip length (white line). A black bear's "reach" in the right photo can be similarly calculated. This method can be used with diagonal walk patterns too. However, the ratio of reach-to-body-length will vary among species somewhat due to different species' leg lengths and body design, so it's best to study photos and videos of various species to be accurate.

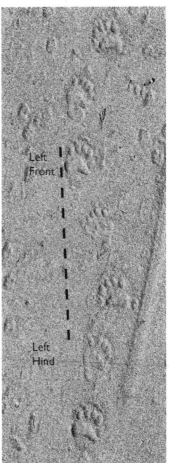

Left
Front

Left
Hind

6
USING PRESSURE RELEASES FOR INTERPRETATION

The ability to read soil movement or pressure releases (Tom Brown Jr.'s term) is an essential tool that brings track interpretation from the general to the very specific and accurate. It not only confirms the precise identification of an animal's gait but also allows you to develop a vivid picture of motion and posture, leading to an understanding of mood and personality.

There is a paradox in learning track reading. While it makes tracking more accurate, the process itself takes the tracker away from the concrete and scientific—for example, measurements and comparisons with field guides—to a place where the tracker is, shall we say, alone with the animal. No outside reference can confirm a track reading because each instance—with its soil texture, moisture, and ground slope, not to mention a host of other factors—is completely unique. Answers can be sought only here, at the point of contact between animal and earth, and the tracker must rely on his or her experience as well as on experimentation and role-playing. Understandably, some trackers used to grounding in "facts" become uneasy here, and many others are overwhelmed.

It's important, then, to realize that accurate track reading is definitely achievable. I have seen sixth graders who had never studied a track in their lives interpret human tracks quite accurately in their first hour of tracking (though honestly it will likely take years of work to develop the experience and confidence to do it consistently). An interesting test of accurate track reading comes out of the 1990s. Biologists in Namibia observed the behavior of numerous groups of wild animals including five carnivore and seven ungulate species in various interactions. Native Ju/'Hoan trackers were then brought in and tested for their ability to identify, from the tracks left behind, the species, sex, age, individuality, and detailed behavior of each animal, along with the timing of events. Of 569 track reconstructions, the Ju/'Hoan trackers got 98% of the answers right.

A solid introduction to reading pressure releases is beyond the scope of this book. The serious tracking student should take a class in track reading (primarily through Tom Brown Jr. or his students). Also, Brown's book *The*

Science and Art of Tracking is an excellent reference, which nevertheless points out as I do that track reading must be learned primarily by individual practice. Following are some pointers.

Learn What Is Evidence

Even beginning trackers can usually see a great amount of detail in tracks, but they don't know what to do with it. A soil disturbance may have been caused by a speed change, head turn, stumble, change of direction, an individual quirk, or by compensation for the slope or soil texture. How is one to learn exactly what caused a pressure release?

First, you must study various motions by animals and people in controlled circumstances (using even, fine-grained soil on level ground) so that you can begin to build a vocabulary of soil disturbances. For example, study how head turns, at different speeds and in different directions, appear in tracks, or how a change of direction manifests itself. Don't expect to develop a list of

pressure releases that have a one-to-one correspondence to a cause. Rather, develop a sense of how much pressure is required to create certain soil disturbances. In time, these insights can be applied dynamically to track reading; for example, you will know that a huge plate crumble to the side of a track was probably caused by some major action such as a stop-and-pivot, not by a curious head turn. As you do these studies, keep a pressure-release journal.

Next, expand your study from controlled experimentation to practicing with fresh tracks in the field on level ground and in fine dust or wet sand. Here, you can

Shallow trays filled with wet sand allow controlled studies of pressure releases.

be certain that anomalies in the tracks were caused by bodily motion and not by compensation for soil or uneven terrain. Deer, foxes, and bobcats are excellent candidates; their walking trails are usually very precise, and body movements that are out of the ordinary will stand out. Use the track analysis technique described below and make thumb impressions in the soil to re-create how quickly and severely a foot had to move to create a given pressure release.

Track Analysis Technique

A methodical approach really helps in reading tracks so that you take in as much information as you possibly can. Follow these steps:

1. Mark which tracks are right and left, front and hind, in the sequence you're studying. This may take some role-playing, especially if there are extra tracks, for example from a gait change or stop.

2. Role-play or visualize until you hypothesize the exact timing of leg movement and justify which feet touch the ground at the same time.

3. Analyze the details of an individual track. Temporarily shelve any preconceptions you have about what the animal did, and instead *just picture how the foot moved.* Some trackers like to draw flow lines, showing the direction and intensity of motion throughout the track; even if you don't draw this for every track you study, get the picture in your head.

4. Expand your visualization from the moving foot to the animal's body, and picture how the body might have moved to create this foot motion.

5. Confirm your reading by studying companion tracks that were on the ground at the same moment. Role-play a sequence until you're confident of your reading. Justify everything you see.

Remember that *there is only one correct reading* of a set of tracks. Eliminate every wrong possibility until only the right one remains. Initially, the process may take as long as several hours for a set of tracks, but there is a rich payoff in your experience.

Human-track reading, while different from animal-track study, provides valuable, transferable information and skills. Because humans momentarily balance their entire weight on one foot while moving, evidence of motion and balance are concentrated in single prints. Read motion in people tracks from heel to toe (assuming the person is moving forward), and confirm your reading with signs of anticipation and compensation both in the track you are reading and in the previous and following tracks. You can also ask a companion to make tracks while being videoed, you not looking of course, allowing you to read the tracks and then confirm your accuracy—a big boost to your track-reading skill!

Attitude

Reading motion in tracks requires a holistic approach drawing upon analysis, visualization, role-playing, and memory. All things, from the finest detail to the broadest view of the landscape, are considered until a moment of clarity is reached.

While determination, analysis, and focus are required to accomplish it successfully, track reading most of all requires a childlike innocence. At times in the process, you have to unburden yourself from preconceptions and rules that cloud your vision, and approach the track as though you have never seen anything like it before. This opens the window to the animal and allows your awareness to take in more than your analytical mind can readily explain.

Eventually you will now and then glance at some tracks and without analysis jump immediately to an image of the animal's movement. These experiences are gifts that cannot be taken for granted. The humble tracker, always learning, will confirm the image by track analysis to keep the process going.

7
MAMMAL PAGES

Mammals are arranged alphabetically within groups, beginning with those that show four front (F) and four hind (H) toes in tracks, moving to the five-front-/five-hind-toed mammals, and ending with ungulates. Space did not allow coverage of all mammal species in North America. To be certain of track identification, consider other mammals in your area that are not covered in this guide. Consult appendix A and compare it to lists of local mammals from wildlife agencies and nature centers.

Track averages here are biased toward the western United States; species may show different averages in other regions. Consistently recording measurements in your own area will not only aid in track ID but over time will also help you distinguish males, females, and juveniles of many species from their tracks. I include usual ranges where I had enough measurements.

Track windows, based on each animal's particular biology, offer many reference points from which to study a mammal's behavior from tracks and signs. Remember that there are many more possibilities for each animal, so keep an open mind!

Species names are taken from American Society of Mammalogists taxonomy lists current as of 2020. The number of subspecies listed within each species, however, come from the ASM *Mammalian Species* series as well as Feldhammer (2003) and may not reflect the most recent taxonomic changes.

Range maps, depending upon the species, are adapted from George Feldhamer, *Wild Mammals of North America* (2003), and various individual accounts in the Mammalian Species series published by the American Society of Mammalogists. (See appendix B for citations.) Because species' ranges are constantly in flux and because data is never exhaustive, your own field observations may well contribute to knowledge about mammal ranges. Start by acquiring the most accurate mammal range maps you can for your local area from your state wildlife or biodiversity office, and make sure you communicate confirmed track sightings to offices or organizations promoting habitat protection.

A mammal's **home range**, listed for each animal in "Social Habits" under "Notes for the Tracker," should be applied to your local area with caution. Definitions as well as methods of measuring home ranges vary by study, and home ranges themselves vary widely by habitat. Nevertheless, the figures here provide a starting point and an idea of relative size. Home ranges given here are in the metric system (hectares and square kilometers); consult appendix C to better picture home-range sizes and to convert these measurements to acres or square miles.

CATS

BOBCAT Track ID

TRACKS Asymmetrical; third toe from outside (F and H) is farther ahead than second toe.

Claws rarely show.

Hind smaller than front but more elongated

Dip on top of heel pad and three lobes on bottom (F and H)

LEFT FRONT

LEFT HIND

COMMON GAITS

A: Diagonal walk, direct register (most common)

B and C: Trots (common)

D: Slow walk (often seen when hunting or stalking)

E: Pace walk (occasional)

Front

Hind

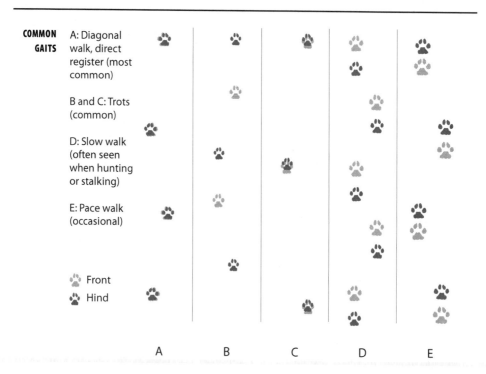

A   B   C   D   E

TRACK MEASUREMENTS	Average, inches	Average, cm	Usual range, inches*
Front width	1¹¹⁄₁₆	4.3	1½ to 1¹⁵⁄₁₆
Front length	1¹¹⁄₁₆	4.3	1⅜ to 1¹⁵⁄₁₆
Hind width	1⁹⁄₁₆	4.0	1⅜ to 1⅞
Hind length	1⅝	4.2	1¼ to 2
Trail width	3⁹⁄₁₆	9.1	2⅛ to 5¾
Stride**	12⅛	30.7	7¼ to 16

*More than 97% of my measurements fall within this range.   **Diagonal walk

34

A: Direct register print, showing rear on top of front

B: Common pace showing F-H-F-H (bottom to top)

Vs. other cats: On the small end, 15% of my bobcat rear-track measurements overlap with those of domestic or feral cats, and strides also overlap considerably. Look for consistent direct register in the bobcat's diagonal walk pattern vs. irregular indirect register in domestic cats. Also, the bobcat's rear track is more elongated than the house cat's. On the large end, overlap with small mountain lion tracks would be very rare. **Vs. gray fox:** In soft sand, gravel, or other difficult soil, a small bobcat track would be easily confused with a gray fox's, which also shows direct register and may overlap in track size, stride, and trail width. Fox tracks also rarely show claws. The telling difference is the heel pad's shape: tall and wide for the bobcat (photo C) vs. short for the fox (see photo D on page 69). The rear track of a gray fox is also more egg-shaped than the bobcat's.

FINE POINTS

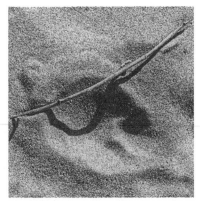

C: Heel pad shape distinguishes bobcat from gray fox in absence of other detail.

Bobcat tracks are windows to **a very habitual animal**, giving you the opportunity to know its territory like your house cat knows its neighborhood. Resting spots, hunting areas, and routes are used over and over again. When you find a trail, settle down to study the tracks carefully, taking measurements and noticing indicators that are unique to this animal. Very likely the next time you come to this very place, your bobcat will be there again. Learning the "baseline" of habitual routes allows you to study nuances of change dictated by season, weather, and prey habits. The female, whose range is sometimes very small and who is even more habitual than the male, may bring her new young along the same trails every spring, allowing you to follow generations and to notice when a daughter eventually takes over the very same travel routes she learned from her mother. And once you get to know the habits of a resident female, the tracks of a male passing through will stand out clearly.

Habitual resting spots might include sunny places in cooler weather and shady places in hot weather. These and well-hidden denning sites are requirements for bobcat habitat. Rearing dens are well marked by many uncovered scat piles in the vicinity. Look for denning and resting spots, but do not approach dens closely during birthing and rearing time, because the necessity of moving a litter may cause stress on the mother and her young. Scent marking is important; pay attention to distinctive cat odors on bobcat trails.

Another window to bobcat behavior is **the way it uses the landscape**. Bobcats are ambush hunters. You may find a "pass-through" corridor through which your animal travels fairly directly, until it comes to a hunting area. Look for changes in its route and for ambush and stalking sites. How is it using cover and wind direction to enter a hunting area? How do the trails and runs of its prey, such as cottontails, dictate its routes? Sometimes bobcats are out in broad daylight, taking advantage of a break in poor weather or the rhythms of activity of their prey. Be alert for very fresh tracks.

Detail in bobcat tracks provides another entry point. Notice gait changes such as slow walks or stalks and sudden sprints that may be ambushes. A stalking bobcat sometimes pinches its toes in excitement while the rest of the foot moves ever so slowly. Because its diagonal walking and trotting patterns are usually exact, you can read subtle changes in them such as head turns. Bobcats take their prey to a secluded feeding site, and you can sometimes read the carrying of prey from changes in the regular walk or trot pattern.

The round tracks and the diagonal walk, direct-register pattern characterize a bobcat's trail. This female travels this route regularly in the coastal dunes of California.

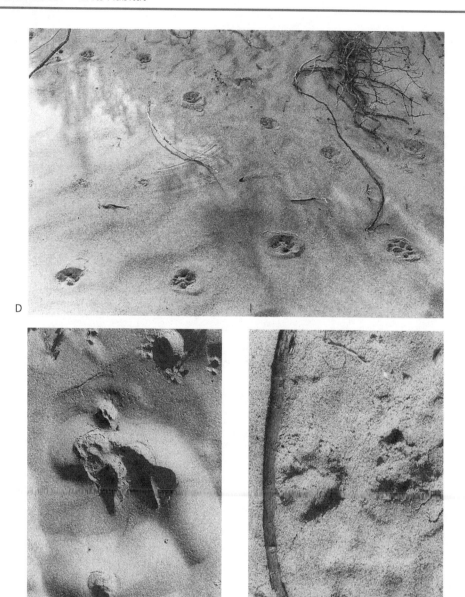

Track reading in a bobcat's territory:
D: Mother's and kitten's trails converge.

E: At the top of a sand dune, a tired kitten stops and rests, sitting back on its haunches.

F: The kitten stops and looks over its left shoulder toward its mother's trail. This twisting motion is read through pressure releases and internal pitch.

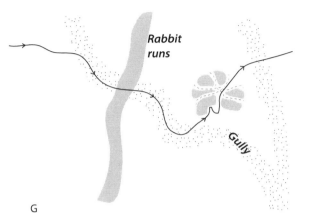

Rabbit
runs

Gully

G

G: An adult moves down a gully to climb up
to a hunting area, stopping behind cover and
downwind before it enters the area with rabbit runs.

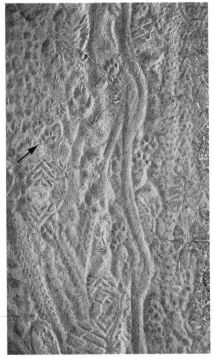

H

H: Using a wide-stance pace walk, a female
bobcat drags a rabbit between its legs to
a feeding spot, accompanied by her kitten
(arrows).

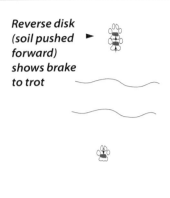

*Reverse disk
(soil pushed ►
forward)
shows brake
to trot*

*Disks on
F and H
throughout
gallop*

*Explode-off
with ►
acceleration
to gallop*

I

I: Pressure releases show an
acceleration from a trot to a
gallop, then a brake after the
bobcat misses an opportunity.

SPECIES AND WEIGHT   *Lynx rufus*

10 subspecies in North America

3.8 to 31 kg
(8 to 39 lb.)

Male about 33% larger than female

HABITAT   Varied from desert to mountains to forests, except cultivated areas and highest mountains. In mountains, migrates to areas of lower snow cover in winter. Territory usually includes rocky ledges, dense bogs, or thickets for denning and resting. Ambush hunting requires cover and abundant medium- to large-size prey within territory.

BREEDING   Most mating December through April, though likely earlier in warmer and more arid locations and may occur throughout year. Males, and females when necessary, violate territorial boundaries to seek each other out, then stay together for several days. Ambushes, parallel running and bumping, and pursuit are part of mating behavior; pair may also hunt together. Gestation about 63 days; litters 2 or 3. Females breed in second spring; male maturity relates more to body mass.

DEVELOPMENT   Blind for 3 to 11 days, young are raised by mother alone, weaned by 7th to 8th week. Female may hunt away from den for 24 hours. Young explore surroundings by 4th week, follow mother on short excursions after 8th week, accompanying her thereafter. May travel alone in mother's home range after 4 months. After 7 months, dispersing young stay in female's home range for a while, then gradually move farther away. Natal dens used for many years; 1 litter may have up to 5 auxiliary dens within a few kilometers of natal den.

SOCIAL HABITS   Female home ranges usually don't overlap with one another; male ranges overlap several females', but little contact among adults. Range size depends upon food availability, from less than 1 km² to 95 km², males' larger than females'. Residents, especially females, have regular travel corridors between resting and hunting sites. Females have regular resting sites used for days at a time, males less so. Transients, especially yearlings, have nomadic lifestyle and are usually part of a local population. Female ranges shrink during breeding and rearing period, male ranges expand then.

Solitary hunter depends upon locally abundant rabbit or medium-size rodent populations as mainstay, though also eats small rodents, birds, fish, reptiles, and amphibians. Larger bobcats in the North and East kill deer. Ambush hunter, stalking within pouncing distance or lying in wait. Drags prey to inconspicuous feeding site. Sometimes eats grasses. May be active during the day as well as dusk, dawn, and night, often dependent more on temperature than light.

Juveniles may succumb to starvation or predation by owls, red foxes, or coyotes; first-year mortality may approach 70%. Stress from intrusion during birthing and rearing young causes movement of den sites. Metabolism doesn't change seasonally, requiring selection of sunny and warmer sites to survive colder winters. Mountain lions may kill adult bobcats. Lifespan 10 to 14 years.

Both males and females scent-mark range with scats, urine, and anal glands. Scats 7/16 to 7/8 in. diameter, constricted usually with blunt ends and lacking large bone fragments. Scats covered 50% to 60% of the time. Males also urinate on scrapes of debris made with hind feet. Females leave many uncovered scat piles near natal and especially auxiliary dens where young are reared. Larger prey remains often covered. Larger birds are plucked. Resting sites in steep, rocky terrain or under brush piles, overhanging roots, or rock piles. Males use scent posts.

J: Bobcat scrape in Joshua Tree, California, covering scat

K: Bobcat scat

L: A bobcat hind-feet scrape without scat.

CATS

TRACKS

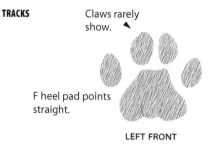

Claws rarely show.

F heel pad points straight.

LEFT FRONT

Top of heel pad may or may not show a dip (F and H).

Hind smaller than front; both tracks round in shape

LEFT HIND

COMMON GAITS

A: Diagonal walk, indirect register (most common)

B: Trot (common)

C: Trot (occasional)

D: Gallop (lower 4 tracks) to lope (upper 4 tracks) (occasional)

E: Pace walk (rare)

Front

Hind

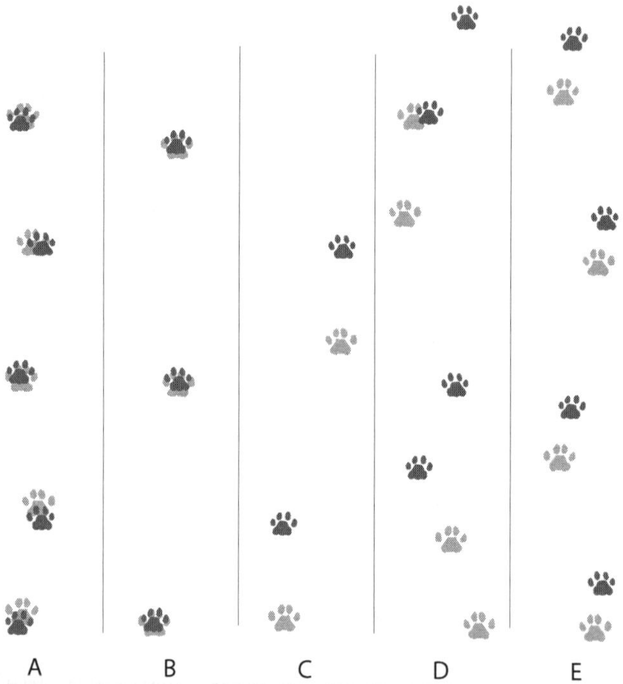

A   B   C   D   E

TRACK MEASUREMENTS

	Average, inches	Average, cm	Usual range, inches*
Front width	1⅜	3.5	1¼ to 1½
Front length	1⅜	3.5	1⅛ to 1½
Hind width	1⁵⁄₁₆	3.3	1³⁄₁₆ to 1⁷⁄₁₆
Hind length	1⁵⁄₁₆	3.4	1³⁄₁₆ to 1½
Trail width	3¼	8.2	2¼ to 4
Stride	9⅝	24.4	6⅝ to 12¹⁵⁄₁₆

*More than 95% of my measurements fall within this range.

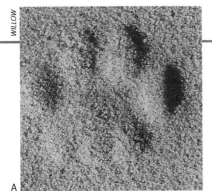

A

FINE POINTS

Note that five-toed cats are not uncommon (photo C) and six- and seven-toed cats may even be found. Feral cats may roam miles from human habitation and even share trails with bobcats. **Vs. bobcat:** Though track size, trail width, and stride may overlap with small bobcats, domestic cats normally diagonal-walk with an irregular indirect register (photo B) vs. the direct register of the bobcat. (A trotting pattern as shown in figure B on opposite page may resemble that of a direct-register walking bobcat, but soil movement in front of the heel pad and around the toes [see photo D] reveals this to be a fast-moving gait.) Also, the cat's front heel pad is not angled outward as is the bobcat's, and the space between the heel pad and toes on the hind track is less in a cat's track (photo A) than a bobcat's track. **Vs. gray fox:** Track size and shape are similar, but the tall heel pad of the hind track differs greatly from the fox's shorter one, and the fox usually direct-registers while walking.

A: Hind track

B: Diagonal walk, indirect-register pattern

C: Five-toed domestic-cat track

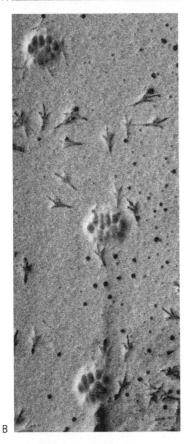

B

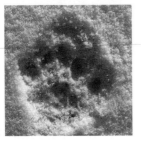

C

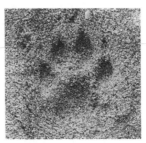

D

D: In the trot shown in fig. B, previous page, a cat's track pattern may resemble a walking bobcat's direct register, but soil pushed in front of the heel pad shows this to be a fast-moving gait, not a walk.

A mere 9,000 years removed from its wild African ancestor *Felis silvestris,* the domestic cat retains virtually all of its wild behavioral genes, giving the urban- or rural-bound tracker a rich opportunity to **study hunting habits and strategies** of a "wild" carnivore close to home. The instincts to hunt, catch prey, play with it, and eat it can be expressed independently of one another and are unaffected by human feeding. A cat naturally gravitates toward "transition areas" where it hunts by stalking or ambush. Hone your landscape-reading skills by identifying a cat's hunting areas and the corridors between, where it is less aware. Individual cats, based on their experience as kittens, may become specialists at hunting certain prey, and this may affect their routes.

 More fascinating still is the domestic cat's **social adaptability**. It easily slips into its ancestor's role as a solitary hunter, living by itself except in breeding or rearing season. In this case, it resembles a miniature mountain lion or bobcat in its home range and resource use. But where food sources are abundant and "clumped," cats also form dense feral (wild) or semiferal colonies more analogous to those of African lions. In this case, female/juvenile groups are headed by a dominant female. A "central" such group, determined by lineage, dominates a given area, while one or more "peripheral" groups compete for resources. Meanwhile, males drift among these female-headed groups, competing for sexual dominance. You can uncover the local cat social structure by reading tracks and signs. If you find a colony, look for primary and secondary bedding and feeding areas, as well as communal latrines used in colonies. In a fluctuating cat community, scent marking is widespread, especially the rubbing of prominent spots with glands on their faces and tails. Look for cat-high marking places, well-used trails that skirt the edge of such places, and scratching posts. Patient observation of tracks and the cats themselves may reveal clan relationships maintained by many physical gestures including rubbing and mutual grooming.

 Besides offering an easy study of gaits by simple observation, the cat gives us something else: **a rich expressiveness in body language** that is especially feline. The slow deliberate stalk, the low-slung running stalk, and the high-stepping fast walk all express different moods. Study the track patterns, pressure releases, and toe movement, which is especially revealing about mood. Towards other cats, dogs, or humans, a cat also shows a variety of aggressive or defensive postures, which can also occupy the tracker's curiosity.

E

E: A communal latrine in a feral cat colony

F

F: Cat at a ranch in central California drags a killed rabbit between its legs, creating a wide walking stance.

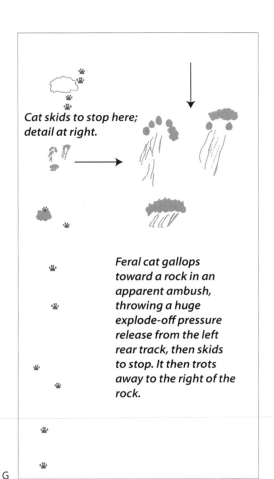

Cat skids to stop here; detail at right.

Feral cat gallops toward a rock in an apparent ambush, throwing a huge explode-off pressure release from the left rear track, then skids to stop. It then trots away to the right of the rock.

G

G: Cat hunting at a beach in Southern California

H

H: A feral cat's high-stepping fast walk is revealed by fracture lines in the sand and crumbles at the toe area.

MOUNTAIN LION Track ID

TRACKS

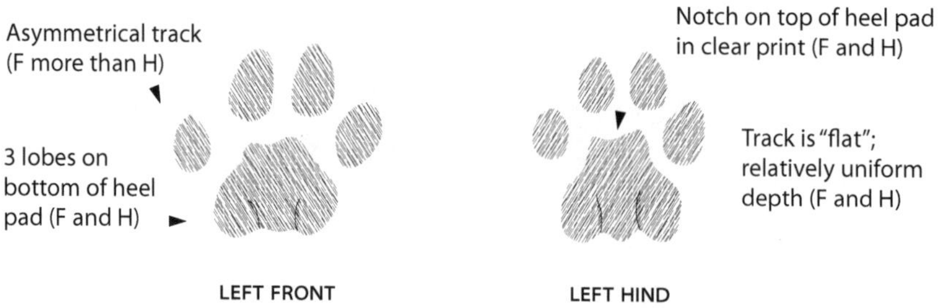
Asymmetrical track (F more than H)
3 lobes on bottom of heel pad (F and H)
Notch on top of heel pad in clear print (F and H)
Track is "flat"; relatively uniform depth (F and H)
LEFT FRONT
LEFT HIND

COMMON GAITS

A: Diagonal walk, direct register (common)

B: Pace (common)

C: Fast trot (occasional)

D: Slow trot (occasional)

E: Slow walk (occasional)

Front
Hind

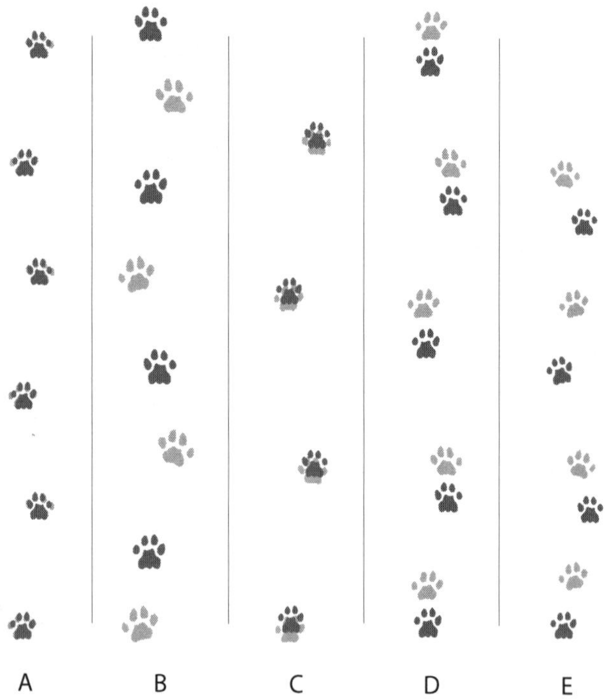
A
B
C
D
E

TRACK MEASUREMENTS

	Average, inches	Average, cm	Usual range, inches*
Front width	3⅜	8.7	2¾ to 4⅛
Front length	3⅜	8.7	2⅝ to 4⅛
Hind width	3	7.6	2½ to 3¾
Hind length	3¼	8.2	2½ to 4¹⁄₁₆
Trail width	6⁹⁄₁₆	16.7	4¼ to 9⅜
Stride**	19⅛	48.6	14 to 24½

*More than 95% of my measurements fall within this range. **Diagonal walk

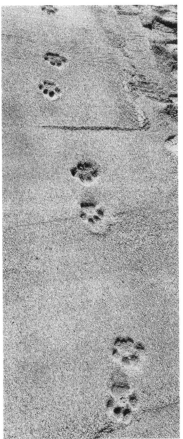

A: Pace walk of captive cougar

A tracker realistically might confuse mountain lion tracks only with those of a lynx or a large dog. **Vs. other cats:** Bobcat tracks are smaller, and though there might be overlap between a bobcat's and a tiny lion kitten's tracks, the latter would be extremely rare to find in the field. A lynx's tracks might overlap both in size and stride length with a lion's but show much more open space between the heel pad and toes than the lion's. **Vs. dogs:** Some large domestic dogs make tracks quite similar in shape and size to mountain lions', and large dog tracks sometimes lack conspicuous claw marks. Look for the three lobes on the bottom of the lion's heel pad versus usually two lobes on a dog's track. Also, a cougar's toes are more asymmetrically placed than a canid's. If confusion persists, try to isolate which are the rear tracks. Though a dog's front foot might resemble the round shape of a lion's, its rear foot is almost always egg-shaped.

FINE POINTS

B: Left front track

C: Left hind track

47

Fresh mountain lion tracks put you in the presence of **the perfect large predator**, powerful and very possibly aware of your presence in its territory. Funnel the excitement of this discovery into increased alertness of your own, and of course, exercise necessary precautions in mountain lion country. Then settle down to follow the lion's trail for as long as you can. Especially if you've had tracking experience, don't stop to analyze the tracks so often; just follow the trail and allow the lion's extraordinary alertness to influence your own.

 A fascinating window to the mountain lion's world is its **hunting strategy**. Because the lion is so well adapted physically to ambush hunting (achieving perhaps an 80% success rate once it is in position to take a deer or elk), it spends most of its time finding exactly the right place and time to make a kill. Places are well known to a resident lion; they are rocks or medium-density brush near regular prey trails and feeding areas. But timing is everything, so a mountain lion spends hours on the hunt, walking slowly, skirting open areas, and staying out of sight. From time to time it stops for many minutes to listen, smell, and look for its opportunity. Then it may take a long time to stalk into position before its ambush. If you are lucky enough to find a lion's hunting trail, patiently follow it and try to read how cover was used and where the prey was located. But even if you are in lion territory without a fresh trail, begin looking for deer as a lion might. Notice active deer trails, their direction of travel, browse areas, and convenient cover. You'll begin to understand the lion's behavior and may even find a lion trail because of it.

 As solitary hunters with a need for a large kill every seven to ten days, mountain lions depend upon proper spacing from each other to survive. Their home ranges tend to be very large, and where they overlap, lions avoid contact with each other through scent marking and general alertness. You can begin to understand this **"land tenure system"** by identifying individual lions in a given area and noticing how many lions of what size travel through well-used corridors. Carefully measure each set of tracks that you find, recording track size, left and right stride, and trail width. But don't depend entirely upon this: Notice unique placement or pitch of each left or right rear foot, for example, and if you have learned to recognize indicator pressure releases, use these also. Look for scrapes left by a resident male, which are signposts to lions of both genders. More than one lion traveling together usually means there is a resident female with cubs, who stay with her for about a year and a half. Study their tracks to discover how many lions share an area.

Finding a fresh mountain lion track, like this one in Rose Valley, California, boosts one's alertness and offers a glimpse into the world of a perfect predator.

D: Tracks of a female mountain lion with three yearlings were encountered in the Sierra Nevada. The mother with two of them (dark lines) headed toward a meadow frequented by mule deer, while one male (light line) made an exploratory loop investigating the territory.

D

E: Every pair of trotting tracks in this sequence showed a deep heel-pad impression and pinched toes on the front track (bottom) and a highly compressed heel pad with almost no toes showing on the rear track (top). This suggests this mountain lion was leaning back, perhaps from carrying the weight of prey in its jaws.

E

F (detail)

F: In an awesome sprint, a mountain lion gallops with 1.2 to 1.5 meters (4 to 5 feet) between each footfall in a gallop pattern, throwing explode-off pressure releases in each track (detail above).

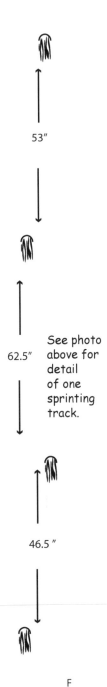

53"

See photo
62.5" above for
detail
of one
sprinting
track.

46.5 "

F

G

G: To mark its territory, a resident male mountain lion scraped a pile of debris with its rear feet, in the direction of the arrows. The strongly planted front feet created deep impressions and broken pine needles (out of the photo's range).

SPECIES AND WEIGHT   *Puma concolor*

11 subspecies in North America

36 to 120 kg (80 to 265 lb.)

Male up to 45% larger than female

HABITAT   Sea level to 4,267 meters (14,000 ft.) in desert, chaparral, forest, and swamps, usually in terrain broken by vegetative or topographical cover allowing for stalking and ambushing large prey. Avoids open shrubless deserts and grassland. May cross open country to disperse or to move between summer and winter range where deep snow persists. Prefers access to deer, elk, or bighorn sheep but may adapt to smaller prey.

BREEDING   Breeding possible throughout the year, primarily by established residents. Polygamous, though stable home ranges may produce consistency. Male seeks out female and the pair may stay together 2 to 6 days, on rare occasions sharing a kill. Gestation around 93 days, litters 1 to 6, averaging 2 or 3. Birthing at any time, with peaks in spring, summer, or fall, depending upon region. Natal den not modified, usually in dense underbrush away from animal trails. Sexual maturity at about 24 months; resident females breed every 2nd year.

DEVELOPMENT   Kittens remain at natal den site for first 40 to 70 days; after about 2 weeks the mother may sleep 0.5 to 1.5 km (⅓ to ⁹⁄₁₀ mile) away from them. Young weaned at 2 to 3 months; mother may lead them to a kill as early as 7 or 8 weeks. When older they may be left at a kill for days while the mother hunts, then brings them to new kill. Young stay with mother for 10 to 26 months (average 15) and may separate from her for days at a time as they get older. Dispersal usually alone, not with siblings, up to 275 km (171 miles), and lasting up to many months.

SOCIAL HABITS   Except during breeding and rearing, lions are usually solitary, usually avoiding others of either gender. Males' home ranges often overlap several females' but not each others'. Female ranges often overlap. Where territory is shared or a lion explores another's range, contact is normally avoided. "Transients" (dispersing young or displaced old) may occupy numerous temporary areas for months at a time until finding a home range or displacing another lion from one. Home ranges depend upon prey density and habitat, and range from about 50 to 1,300 km² (20 to 500 square miles). Lions enforce their temporal and spatial distance from one another by scent marking and possibly auditory cues.

FEEDING

Large prey including deer, elk, or bighorn sheep make up core diet, a lion killing 1 every 7 to 10 days on average (females with large kittens 1 every 3 days). Rabbits, porcupines, beavers, ground squirrels, and other medium-size mammals are also eaten, especially by young lions. Coyotes, badgers, and bobcats may be taken opportunistically. Solitary ambush hunter, stalking to within 15 meters (50 ft.) of prey and attacking from the ground with a few leaps. Usually hunts at time of prey activity, especially around dusk and dawn but throughout the night. When hunting, alternates between slow movement and waiting/listening. Drags kill up to 137 meters (150 yards) to secluded spot and feeds for up to several days, covering the kill with debris in between feeding. May travel 9.7 km (6 miles) per night hunting.

SURVIVAL

Sources of nonhuman mortality include injury by prey when hunting, killing of young kittens by adult males, fights among adults, and old age. Insufficient habitat for adequate dispersal of young and automobile collisions are prevalent near population centers.

SIGNS

Scats usually segmented, sometimes containing bone and fur, sometimes smooth and dark, may be covered with soil or left in open. Scat piles frequent near kills. Resident males, and rarely females, make scrapes with hind feet, usually off a trail; piles of needles, leaves, dirt, or snow are 15 to 30 cm (6 to 12 in.) wide, 15 to 25 cm (6 to 10 in.) long, and 2.5 to 5 cm (1 to 2 in.) deep, sometimes containing scat or urine. Kill sites show stomach and intestines removed, most of carcass eaten. Kill sites with kittens show much disturbance from scratching, playing, and wrestling. Natal den very inconspicuous in dense brush, without prey remains or scats. Scratch marks on trees.

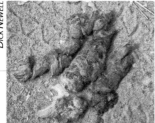

H: Uncovered mountain lion scat

H

DOGS

DOGS

TRACKS

Middle toes smaller and shallower than outer toes in clear prints

Claw marks usually narrow, outer ones often not showing

Hind heel pad often registers only the center circle, without the "wings."

LEFT FRONT

LEFT HIND

COMMON GAITS

A: Diagonal walk, indirect register (common)

B: Canine trot (common)

C: Slow trot (common)

D: Slow walk (occasional)

E: Lope (occasional)

Front

Hind

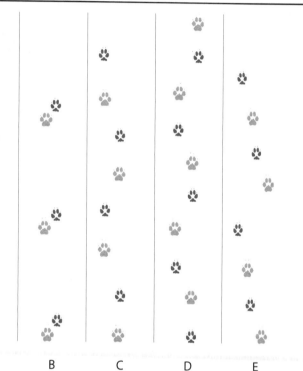

A   B   C   D   E

TRACK MEASUREMENTS

	Average, inches	Average, cm	Usual range, inches*
Front width	2	5.1	1½ to 2⅞
Front length	2⅜	6.0	1¾ to 3¼
Hind width	1¹¹⁄₁₆	4.3	1⅜ to 2⅜
Hind length	2¹⁄₁₆	5.2	1⅝ to 2⅛
Trail width	3⅞	9.8	2⅝ to 5½
Stride	16⁷⁄₁₆	41.8	11 to 21¾

*More than 95% of my measurements fall within this range. Note: Eastern coyote is larger.

A B

D

A and B: Coyote front and hind tracks, respectively

C: A diagonal walk pattern shows an indirect register, but placement of the pairs is usually quite regular from one to the next.

D: When a coyote trots with its head down or is going downhill, the middle toes may appear larger; notice plume ahead of rear foot, caused by "drag-out."

C

FINE POINTS

Once the canine family is recognized, coyote tracks can be easily distinguished from wolf and gray-fox tracks by size (wolf's are larger and gray fox's smaller). Red-fox tracks are of similar size but show the clear chevron-shaped heel-pad depression (page 93). That leaves domestic dogs, some of whose tracks are coyote-sized. Without a reservoir of coyote track images to call upon, a tracker should look at a combination of clues, no one clue being adequate: a) The coyote's inner toes are shallower and often shorter than the outer ones, the opposite being true for a dog; b) Its feet usually do not scuff the soil like a dog's; c) In a walk the indirect-register placement of rear on top of front is usually regular, not variable like a dog's; d) The claw marks are sharp and not blunt like a dog's; and e) The overall trail is usually efficient and direct, not meandering. Fortunately, if a dog's track resembles a coyote's, it is usually only the front *or* the rear, so look at both carefully.

That howling you hear at night leads you right to the **coyote's territorial structure** and the tracking that can help illuminate it. The "pack" is most often a family group of three to five, including the breeding pair of a territory and their offspring. They sing a "group yip-howl" not upon making a kill but when they are about to separate to hunt for the night or when they regroup; the howling is led by a dominant coyote. If responded to with a distant group howl, another "pack" is announcing where its territory is. Ironically, the tracker will most often find trails of single coyotes or of a breeding pair traveling together because of a dispersed hunting style. Try following or backtracking a trail until you find a rendezvous point, or make some good track measurements to determine how many coyotes are in the local group. A lone coyote with a very long trail is likely a transient, a subdominant animal who disperses from the family group and wanders more widely.

In their search for food, coyotes are the **consummate opportunists**, coursing through their home range, alert for the sudden movement or smell that will mean a meal. Large prey such as adult deer or elk are attacked rarely, only when this prey is at a great disadvantage. Mostly, a coyote will look for a rabbit to flush or may spend time in a meadow pouncing on voles or listening for gopher movement. It may make an entire meal of grasshoppers, trot off to eat chokecherry or manzanita fruit, or kill and eat a gopher snake or rattlesnake. Easily found scat piles, often in groups, give the tracker answers to what's been eaten. Pick apart scat (using tweezers and washing your hands afterward) and look for bones, fur, whiskers, and claws of prey animals. Scat remains of fruit usually show intact seeds, which can lead you to the location of the coyote's meal, and thus to regular travel routes.

You could call the coyote **"the dancer"** for the way it moves nimbly through its terrain, and indeed you'll find more variations in trots, lopes, and walks than you will for any other predator. Even if you've filled your tracking notebook for years with gait drawings and think you understand, for example, the four basic trotting patterns, the coyote will keep showing you some new steps. Not only are there many variations in foot placement in a coyote's gaits, but pressure releases also reveal whether the coyote was gliding leisurely, stepping stiffly, listening with the head up, or sniffing with the head down. When you find a coyote trail, get out of the comfort zone of what you're familiar with and really study the track pattern. Record foot placement and visualize or imitate the gait as precisely as you can. Try reading body posture and mood in the pressure releases. You'll likely be captivated by the coyote's dancing.

The consummate opportunist, a coyote patrols its wide territory ready to investigate every potential food source whether it be plant, mammal, or insect.

E

E: A coyote family rendezvous site

F: Near a desert campsite in California, a female coyote has scent-marked on a cigarette butt recently dropped on her regular travel route. Arrows point to her hind tracks.

G: Though resembling an overstep walk, this coyote track pattern reveals itself as a slow lope with repeating groups of F-H-F-H tracks.

F

G

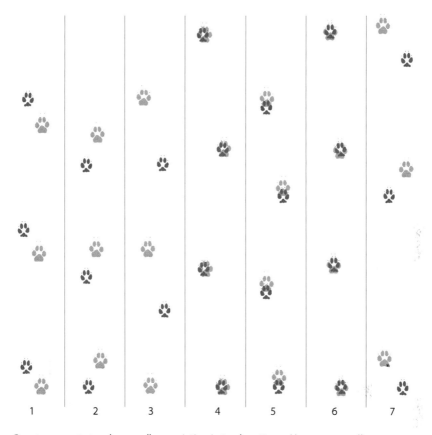

1   2   3   4   5   6   7

Coyotes seem to teach an endless variation in track patterns. Here are some I've recorded:

1: The "side trot" depicted in pattern 1 is a common gait for many North American canids, especially domestic dogs and coyotes. The pattern reveals a momentary sideward tilt of the shoulders that causes all of the rear feet to land to one side of the front tracks. (The trot does not necessarily mean the animal is looking in the direction of the tilted shoulders, however!)

2 and 3: The coyote also creates two other "side trot patterns" rarely found with other canids.

4: This fast walk also shows the sideward shoulder tilt.

5: In this diagonal walk the rear feet land a little farther behind the front track than is usually seen, and the ridge behind the toes is higher than usual, suggesting a more deliberate, "showy" walk.

6: At first glance this pattern looks like a diagonal walk, direct register, in which the rear tracks superimpose directly on top of the front ones. But the long stride, as well as a disk pushed forward in front of the heel pad, indicates this is a high-stepping trot instead.

7: A running pace pattern

DOGS

SPECIES AND WEIGHT	*Canis latrans* 11 subspecies in North America 7 to 20 kg (15 to 44 lb.) Male slightly larger than female

HABITAT   Desert, grassland, forest, chaparral, and borders of urban areas, from Central America to northern Alaska; range has expanded with disappearance of wolves. Local populations limited by absence of open areas.

BREEDING   Courtship may begin 2 to 3 months before mating, which is usually in February or March. Numerous males may follow a female in heat. Breeding pair may mate in successive years but not necessarily for life. Gestation about 63 days, litters average 5 or 6, varying directly with food supply and inversely with coyote density. Coyote-wolf hybridization probable, especially in northeastern United States; coyote–domestic dog hybrids may occur, but survival in the wild after first generation would be very unlikely due to shift in breeding time.

DEVELOPMENT   Pups emerge from den at 2 to 3 weeks. Dominance hierarchy of pups determined within first month. First female, then male brings regurgitated food. Male may stand guard within sight of den. Pups' "training time" from May through July; den abandoned by early July. Dispersal of young from 6 to 9 months, but most dominant pups may stay with parents. Adult weight reached at about 9 months. Maximum age in wild 13 to 15 years.

SOCIAL HABITS   Coyote "packs" are usually a breeding pair and their offspring, averaging 3 to 5 individuals. Group usually separates to hunt and forage. Breeding group defends territory, especially at breeding and rearing time, through scent marking, group howling, and, if necessary, chasing off intruders. Solitary nonbreeding coyotes may overlap areas with breeding groups. Where large prey sources (e.g., carrion) are available, especially in winter, larger coyote groups may aggregate for feeding only, when they may make hierarchal displays. Home range may be from 8 km² to 40 km² or more.

Meat from rabbits, rodents, and ungulates makes up 80% to 90% of diet. Insects **FEEDING**
including grasshoppers and Jerusalem crickets in summer, and fruits including
manzanita berries, chokecherries, coffee berries, elderberries, and cultivated fruit
in summer and fall are important supplements. Coyotes may kill deer fawns in
spring and summer, with bites to head or neck. Larger prey such as adult deer
and elk may be killed when vulnerable, such as when weakened or in deep snow,
usually by 2 coyotes attacking rear legs. Most adult deer and livestock eaten by
coyotes are encountered as carrion. Coyotes use visual cues, then auditory and
olfactory, to locate prey; a single coyote may pounce on meadow voles or mice,
or a pair may flush and catch a jackrabbit. Ultimately an opportunistic feeder
eating a huge variety of foods.

Pups vulnerable to raptors, mountain lions, and other coyotes; mortality rate **SURVIVAL**
more than 40% in first year, about 20% in second. Does not compete well with
wolves. Responds to human management practices by producing larger litters.

Scat gray to brown, about 1.6 to 1.9 cm (⅝ to ¾ in.) diameter, often with fur and **SIGNS**
bones; tail sometimes tapered. Some scats entirely fruit seeds and remnants,
insect remnants, or (in early summer) grasses. Often deposited in groups, at trail
junctions, or on prominent raised surfaces. Scratches in dirt by rear feet after
urinating, primarily by dominant male, most often on the periphery of territory
and most frequently in breeding season (Dec–Mar). Natal den excavated primarily by female beginning in December. Group howls and yip-howls initiated by
dominant coyote before separating to hunt and when reuniting; also a response
to other groups to ensure territorial spacing. Lone coyote may howl when separated from group.

H

H: Coyote scat containing juniper-
berry remains

I

I: Typical coyote scat shows gray color; fur
and bones of prey are visible.

DOGS

TRACKS Claw impressions usually prominent and blunt

There is no "generic" domestic dog track due to wide variation, but these examples illustrate some often-seen traits.

Top of heel pad comes to a rounded point, isn't flattened or dipped (F and H).

Middle toes are usually noticeably larger than outer toes (F and H).

LEFT FRONT

LEFT HIND

COMMON GAITS

A: Diagonal walk, indirect register (common)

B: Canine trot (common)

C: Pace walk (occasional)

D: Gallop (common)

E: Lope (occasional)

 Front

Hind

A   B   C   D   E

TRACK MEASUREMENTS

Domestic-dog tracks may overlap in size with all wild North American wild canids (from kit fox to wolf). However, measuring tracks is not irrelevant—where there are no wolves present, domestic-dog tracks are often larger than those of all the other wild canids, including foxes and coyotes.

Domestic-dog tracks usually stand out because of the irregular placement of tracks, the scuffed texture of the soil, large blunt claw marks, and the size differential between the middle toes (larger) and outer toes (smaller) of each track. Even when a dog moves quite regularly, as in a trot, and the feet do not scuff much, the tracks are usually distinguishable from wild canid tracks by studying the overall track shape, including the heel pad, and comparing it to drawings and photos of wild canid tracks of similar size. Also look for unnatural outward or inward pitch of some of the feet.

FINE POINTS

A

B

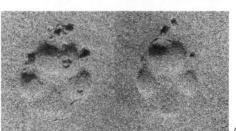

C

A: A dog's walking pattern often shows irregular foot placement.

B and C: Pairs of F and H illustrate variability of track shape.

D: Occasionally a dog track shows three lobes on the back of the heel pad.

E: Large middle toes and blunt claw marks are common.

F: Random foot motion often creates a scuffed impression.

D

E

F

DOGS

Domestic dogs are walking teachers of those trickiest of tracking funda-
mentals to learn, **the gaits**. Every dog from small to large can show a lot
about body posture, mood, speed, and foot placement reflected in tracks,
but honestly, the best subjects are the more long-legged, athletic dogs
because they can perform the largest variety of trots, lopes, gallops, and
paces, and their movement most closely corresponds to what you might
find when tracking coyotes, foxes, or wolves. Use your own dog, or borrow
a friend's, to do an afternoon's experiment in a large tracking box, at the
beach, or in some playground sand. Begin by just watching leg movement
and foot placement in a trot; then study different types of trots. Don't
be in a hurry to study tracks until you've got some good visual images
of motion and posture (for example, the differences in body language
between a showy, bouncy trot and an extended trot). Eventually study the
tracks and see how track patterns and foot placement correspond to different speeds and posture, and then move on to lopes and gallops. People
who show dogs professionally pay a lot of attention to a dog's posture and
efficiency of motion; find one of these people to spend some time with,
or find the American Kennel Club's video *Dog Steps*. Milton Hildebrand
studied dog gaits in the 1960s and his articles (see "Appendix B: Recommended Reading") can fill you with knowledge about the subject.

Of course, where there are track patterns, there are also **pressure releases**,
and your own dog can also help you understand these. A warning, though:
Many dogs show a lot of sloppy, random foot movement, so you have to
account for this "action" in the tracks as you read them. Nevertheless, a
dog can show you how a head turn, nose to the ground, or pulling on a
leash, for example, is reflected in the track. Study these motions, and also
look at pivots, accelerations, and braking. Spend an hour or two with a
dog and a stick or Frisbee and you'll really begin to get the feel of track
reading!

Every true dog person notices the **unique traits of each breed** and indeed
of each individual dog, and the passionate tracker will find a lifetime of
potential study, not only of different track shapes but of stride, straddle,
and walking style of different breeds and individuals. Try to associate
walking-stride length with the length of the dog's legs and therefore its
height; use the straddle to help with shoulder breadth. Then begin to
notice from the tracks the unique walking personality of your own dog
or of a neighbor's; this ability will transfer to the reading of personality in
wild animal tracks.

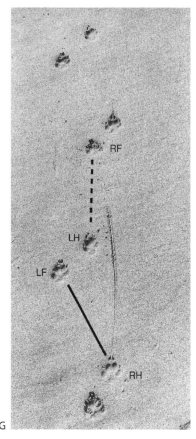

G: In a common canine trot, a domestic dog has its shoulders angled significantly to the left. The angle of the shoulders can be pictured by noting which pairs of feet hit the ground simultaneously (dotted and solid lines), as shown here.

H: Just unleashed, a dog digs in and accelerates from a standstill to a full gallop. The first front track digs in as the dog puts its head down. The next front track shows less acceleration, and the first hind less still as the head comes up.

I: This domestic dog has an injured left hip, causing her to lope on only three legs, with the injured leg dragging slightly in the snow. Because of the injury, she always paces when walking.

DOGS

TRACKS   Semi-retractile claws
rarely show (F and H).

Much open space
between heel pad
and toes (F)

H track less round
than F

Narrow, 3-lobed
hind heel pad

LEFT FRONT   LEFT HIND

COMMON   A: Diagonal
GAITS   walk, direct
register
(common)

B: Canine
trot
(occasional)

C: Trot
(occasional)

D: Lope
(occasional)

E: Slow walk
(occasional)

Front

Hind

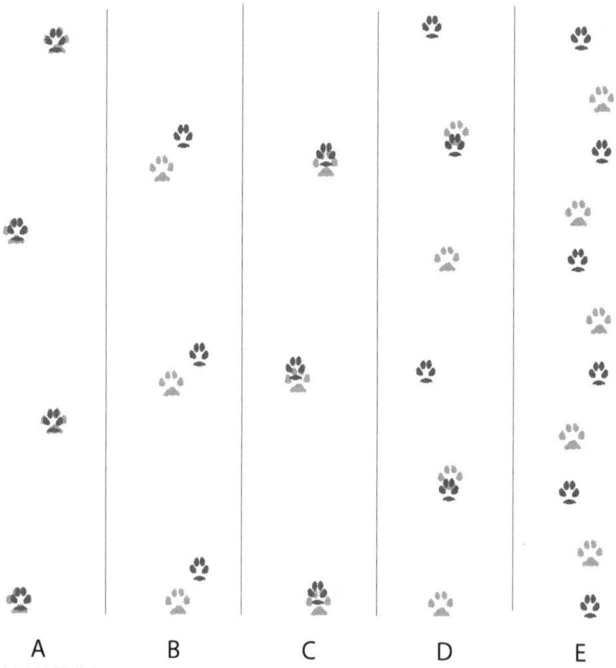

A   B   C   D   E

TRACK
MEASUREMENTS

	Average, inches	Average, cm	Usual range, inches*
Front width	1⁷⁄₁₆	3.6	1¼ to 1⅝
Front length	1⅝	4.1	1³⁄₁₆ to 1⅞
Hind width	1³⁄₁₆	3.1	⅞ to 1⁹⁄₁₆
Hind length	1⁷⁄₁₆	3.7	1¹⁄₁₆ to 1¾
Trail width	2¹³⁄₁₆	7.2	1³⁄₁₆ to 4¼
Stride	10¹¹⁄₁₆	27.1	6⅛ to 14¾

*More than 97% of my measurements fall within this range.

68

DOGS

A

B

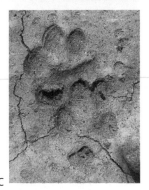

C

D

FINE POINTS

Because gray-fox tracks rarely show claw impressions outside of snow and mud, they most resemble cat tracks, and further, the fox's direct-register walking pattern could be confused only with that of a **small bobcat** (not a house cat, which usually indirect-registers). Though the gray-fox front track is round like a cat's, check the shape of the hind track, which is more oval, and especially study the shape of the heel pad, which is short and small in a fox and tall and big in a bobcat (compare photos here with the bobcat's on page 35). Only a juvenile-red-fox track would overlap in size with a gray fox's but would show the chevron-shaped depression in the heel pad (see page 93). Where they share habitat, gray-fox tracks may be mistaken for **kit fox** tracks, and indeed these overlap in track size, trail width, and stride. First, know the habitat, and then look for telltale claw marks, which you are much more likely to see in a kit fox track. Also, the gray fox's front track is much rounder, with more open space between heel pad and toes, than the kit fox's.

A: Front (left) and hind tracks

B: Direct-register diagonal walk pattern

C: Tracks in mud do not always show claws.

D: Small heel pad helps distinguish gray fox from cat track where print is otherwise indistinct.

If you can imagine living in the shadows while thriving with confidence and adaptability, then you have begun to understand the world of the gray fox. The fox is therefore an extraordinary teacher about **your own awareness**, for most people, indeed many trackers, walk right past its trails even while they are seeing ample evidence of coyotes, bobcats, rabbits, or raccoons. The ten-pound fox's prints are distinctively delicate, usually in a perfect direct-register walk, but because the fox likes the byways rather than the main routes, its compressions really have to be looked for. Once you recognize the tracks, begin to follow a trail as far as you can. You may expect to track a fox to its den or resting site, but will probably reach your own physical limitations instead, as the fox leads you under brush, over boulders, up steep slopes, and even up trees. Nevertheless, after a few days of fox tracking, you'll begin to see its tracks in almost every habitat, even in areas where biologists haven't recorded them—a secret you now share with the fox.

When you find a straight-line fox trail, it often leads to a foraging or hunting site where the fox then zigzags, backtracks, and generally skirts the edges of things. Here you can learn of its **foraging adaptability**: The fox may wander down to the ocean shoreline to feast on crabs, head for a desert mesquite bush with ripe pods, hunt for voles in a meadow, skirt chaparral brush to ambush a rabbit, pluck cactus fruits from a prickly pear, dig up sleeping potato bugs, or as one man observed, climb a peach tree and bat the fruits down to the young foxes below. You can understand a fox's seasonal and daily preferences by tracking and by scat analysis. Look for distinctive small scats deposited on rocks or stumps; their content may lead you to current foraging or hunting areas. After foraging, a fox usually takes a direct route to its day bed in brush, on a boulder, or in the crotch of a tree. If you find this kind of trail, be very quiet and use your stalking skills.

Gray-fox tracks also provide a window to its **family life**. Once you've discovered good gray-fox habitat, schedule some tracking trips there in June and July because that's when you'll likely find tiny juvenile fox tracks, and even the tracks of two parents and several little foxes traveling together single file. At this time the little foxes are 2½ to 4 months old and weigh 1.6 to 2.3 kg (3½ to 5 lb.). When you find a family's tracks, take careful measurements and then mark the prints of each individual fox, identifying the adults and how many juveniles are together. By fall the young are the size of small adults and begin to forage and hunt on their own, and by January the surviving young foxes will likely breed.

A gray fox wanders at the base of Frazier Mountain, California.

E

E: Along a gray fox's route, three scats point to its varied diet. One contains fur and a claw, and the two others contain seeds from different native shrubs.

F: A gray fox's foraging trail was backtracked for 300 meters in the southern Sierra Nevada through thick stands of sagebrush and rabbit-brush. The fox changed direction constantly, circling and investigating, climbing over and through brush, never walking more than half a meter in a straight line.

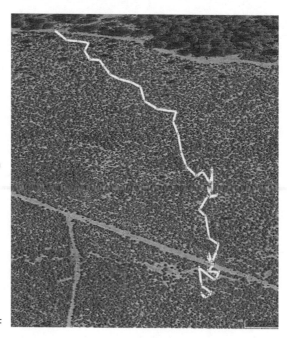

F

 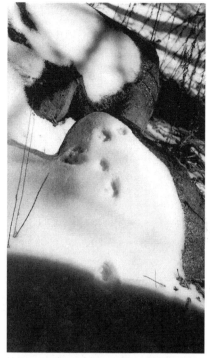

G: In the sparsely vegetated high desert of California, a gray fox bed can be a simple windbreak among rock outcroppings.

H: In a northern Arizona canyon, a fox has climbed on a rock for a vantage point.

I: Gray foxes offer good tracking study because they commonly visit tracking stations baited with a little scent of food.

DOGS

SPECIES AND WEIGHT
Urocyon cinereoargenteus

7 subspecies in continental United States

3.5 to 5.5 kg (7 to 12 lb.)

Male 7% to 20% larger than female

HABITAT Brushy, rocky, and forested habitats from sea level to 2,438 meters (8,000 ft.) including chaparral, oak woodland, deciduous forests, piñon-juniper woodland, riparian areas, and deserts. Prefers broken habitat more than the red fox but will hunt in meadows and on the outskirts of agricultural areas. Adapts to areas near human habitation if there is enough cover.

BREEDING Most breeding late January through February, gestation about 53 days. Females sexually mature at 10 months; most females breed in their 1st year. Litter size averages 4, usually 3 to 5.

DEVELOPMENT Pups remain at den until about 10 weeks; mother may rest away from the den, and father may also rest nearby. Female's home range may shrink to as small as 20 hectares (49 acres) while nursing. Young begin to accompany parents on foraging trips in June or early July, when they are about half adult size, family often staying together. Pups reach adult size at 5 or 6 months. Young foxes forage by themselves in September; family bond breaks up by December. Dispersals from a fraction of a mile to 80 km (50 miles) have been recorded.

SOCIAL HABITS Home ranges generally 1 km² to 3 km², often overlapping. Territories not aggressively defended. On a given night a gray fox usually uses a fraction of its home range for foraging, and effective home ranges shift somewhat with season and food availability. Gray foxes are probably monogamous, but high mortality causes pairs not to be long-lasting. The vast majority of a local population is under 2 years of age, most of these yearlings.

FEEDING

Diet variable depending upon habitat and season. In arid areas of Southwest, fruit such as coffee berries, juniper berries, manzanita berries, and cactus fruit comprises much of diet especially in fall and winter, but mammals including voles, rabbits, mice, woodrats, and ground squirrels are often caught also. Insects including grasshoppers, crickets, beetles, and Jerusalem crickets are eaten in great numbers especially in spring and summer. In the northern and eastern part of its range, the gray fox eats primarily mammals, especially rabbits and voles, supplementing the diet with fruits and insects. In all areas foxes may take songbirds and ground-nesting birds, as well as lizards or snakes, opportunistically. Grasses may be eaten in spring and summer, probably as a purgative. Except when raising a family, foxes tend to forage alone. Hunting and foraging activities may begin an hour before sunset and peak 1 to 4 hours after sunset, with another peak before sunrise. Foxes sometimes hunt in morning or late afternoon and may change resting spots midday.

SURVIVAL

Adult mortality of greater than 50% keeps local population young, but foxes could survive to 15 years. Golden eagles, coyotes, and bobcats may take some foxes. Legal trapping for pelts in many states is probably the greatest contributor to mortality.

SIGNS

Scats usually 1 to 1.6 cm (⅜ to ⅝ in.) diameter, sometimes with tapered tail, deposited along trails, often on top of logs, rocks, or other raised surfaces; usually found singly but occasionally in groups of several. Scat may contain fur, bones, feathers, insect remains, grasses, or often seeds and other fruit remains. Daytime resting spots in dense brush, in crotch or limb of tree, or on top of boulder. Natal den in brush pile, hollow log, rock outcrop, or underground burrow dug by another animal; sometimes found as high as 7.6 meters (25 ft.) in tree hollow. Dens generally not excavated but do have leaves or bark added for bedding.

J: These gray fox scats contain numerous insect parts.

GRAY WOLF   Track ID

TRACKS   Slightly asymetrical track, with third toe from outside more forward (F and H)

▲ Length greater than width (F and H)

LEFT FRONT   LEFT HIND

COMMON GAITS

A: Diagonal walk (common)

B and C: Trots (common)

D: Lope (occasional)

E: Gallop (occasional)

Illustrations D and E are smaller scale.

Front
Hind

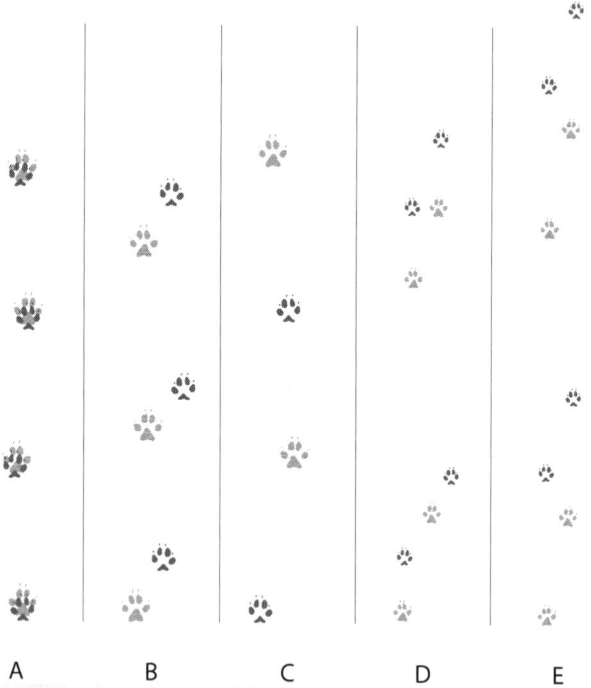

	A	B	C	D	E

TRACK MEASUREMENTS

	Average, inches	Average, cm	Usual range, inches
Front width	3⅜	8.5	2¾ to 3¾
Front length	3⅞	9.8	3⅜ to 4⅜
Hind width	2¹⁵⁄₁₆	7.5	2½ to 3½
Hind length	3¹¹⁄₁₆	9.3	3⅜ to 3⅞
Trail width	4¹⁵⁄₁₆	12.5	
Stride*	21¹⁵⁄₁₆	55.7	

*Diagonal walk

DOGS

Doug Gaulke

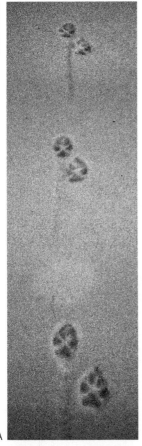

A

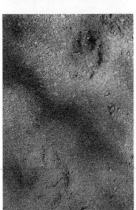

B

While gray-wolf tracks on average are larger than other wild canids', they may overlap somewhat with those of eastern coyotes (which probably have wolf genes intermixed). It will take some field experience to distinguish the tracks; you need to take into account behavior, group size, and habitat use, as well as look at stride lengths and individual track characteristics. **Vs. domestic dog:** Shape of front and hind tracks, and stride length, will weed out many domestic dogs whose tracks are as large as wolves'. If identification is still tricky after examining the regularity of the track pattern (efficient and regular for wolf, sloppy and more random for dog), you may have to follow the trail, looking at behavior as well as location. Wolves are more cautious than dogs, and their trails are generally goal-directed, revealing an intimate knowledge of a very large territory.

FINE POINTS

C

C: Left front and left hind tracks in a canid trot

A: Common canid trot pattern

B: Front (at bottom) and hind tracks

77

DOGS

It is one thing to track a lone predator and quite another to access the awe-inspiring **group dynamic of a wolf pack** that is supremely aware, adaptable, and intelligent about its territory. Because packs may move many miles each day, the first task is to find where the wolves are. You can patrol likely routes such as dirt roads and cutoff trails. Remember that pack members often split apart, even for several days, so your group of tracks may not represent a whole pack. If tracks go single file, follow the trail until individuals split off, then take measurements, and begin to notice qualities that might distinguish pack members from one another: size of tracks, stride lengths, and gaits. The alpha male or female in a pack usually takes the lead while traveling, and younger wolves are often more cautious, for example, when encountering a new scent. Dedicated study of each track set can help you zero in on individual personalities. Though all members of a pack periodically scent-mark by "squat urination" and defecation, only dominant wolves, primarily the alpha male and female, mark with "raised-leg urination," so the perpetrators' tracks can be singled out. Wolves are always marking with scents, in fact, often every few minutes. While we can scarcely imagine the richness of that scent world, we can deduce some things about a pack from the marks that we can see or smell. Wolves mark a lot more frequently at the outer edges of their territory and upon encountering another pack's sign. Also, breeding season around February brings an increase in the raised-leg urination as well as scratching the soil. Look for double scent marks of the alpha pair especially in the weeks leading up to breeding. Lone wolf tracks may also be encountered; these dispersers are common in all wolf populations and may travel hundreds of miles seeking a mate and a new territory. Loners go out of their way to be inconspicuous, leaving few scent marks. However, they are constantly investigating other wolves' scents, and you may find frequent nose marks where they do so.

A pack's **hunting technique** is as variable as the terrain and the prey but always shows an impressive knowledge of the land. A pair of wolves splits up, one traveling through the brush to flush out prey and the other moving along the road to ambush it. A pack takes a route downwind from a moose bedding area so that a resting moose can be sensed, flushed, and chased. A pack circles toward a beaver lodge, knowing that deer come there to feed on the beavers' stored branches and are vulnerable close to the ice. A pack chasing a moose splits, one wing driving the moose downhill and the other circling to intercept the moose in the valley. A pack charges headlong into a musk oxen herd to scatter them and isolate a vulnerable calf. A pack patrols the edge of a lake, knowing that younger, more vulnerable elk prefer that area to deeper snow. When you trail a pack, expand your awareness beyond the tracks to include the matrix of prey activity in its territory, as well as wind direction and terrain. When you encounter tracks of a hunting scenario, take time to study it; a pack's next kill may be many miles away.

DOGS

DOUG GAULKE

D: A deer carcass eaten by wolves shows rib bones entirely crushed.
E: Raised-leg urination site (arrow) along a wolf trail

D

DOUG GAULKE

E

DOUG GAULKE

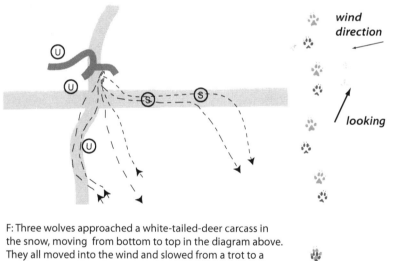

F: Three wolves approached a white-tailed-deer carcass in the snow, moving from bottom to top in the diagram above. They all moved into the wind and slowed from a trot to a walk or slow walk as they crossed a dirt road. The last wolf to approach, a female, was most cautious, going from a diagonal walk to a hesitating slow walk as shown in the detail at right; pitch of the tracks as well as internal pitch showed her looking toward the carcass. In the diagram urination and scat are marked with U and S, respectively. The darker line shows where the wolves dragged the carcass away from the road to feed on it before they departed.

F

DOGS

SPECIES AND WEIGHT   *Canis lupus*

5 subspecies in
North America

23 to 80 kg
(50 to 176 lb.)

Male larger than female

The coyote hybridizes with the eastern but not western gray wolf.

HABITAT   In North America, gray wolf habitat is currently restricted to mountains, forests, and tundra where ungulates provide enough food and where large home ranges free from intensive human interference are possible. (Previously, wolves lived in many habitats throughout the lower 48, including deserts and grasslands.) Reintroductions and range expansions have occurred in recent years in the Rockies; Arizona has seen the reintroduction of the Mexican wolf.

BREEDING   Breeding usually January to early April depending upon latitude. Alpha male and female are primary breeders and may actively suppress breeding activity by subordinates in the pack, though this sometimes occurs. Lone pairs that have dispersed also breed. In weeks leading up to breeding, both alpha wolves increase scent marking ("raised-leg urination"); blood is sometimes visible in these marks up to 6 weeks before estrus. Natal den usually in underground burrow, log, or other crevice, sometimes prepared several weeks before birthing. Gestation 63 days, litters 1 to 11, usually about 6, born late April to June.

DEVELOPMENT   Pups emerge from den at 3 to 4 weeks, weaned at 7 to 8 weeks. Adults hunt away from den and regurgitate food to pups upon return. Pack may move pups to a new den. Throughout summer, pack uses numerous "rendezvous sites" where pups are left as adults hunt; sites may change every few weeks. These are usually open areas with much matted vegetation from pups' play, well-used runs, scat piles, and aboveground beds nearby. By early fall young begin to travel with adults.

SOCIAL HABITS

Packs, usually 5 to 12, generally consist of a breeding pair and offspring from 1 or more litters, but larger packs occur. Exclusive territories are maintained by constant scent marking through scats and squat urinations (which all pack members do) and raised-leg urination (done primarily by the dominant pair). The alpha male or female usually, but not always, leads when a pack travels together, and makes choices about travel routes; an alpha wolf also often leads a chase during the hunt. Social hierarchy is reinforced by dominant/submissive body language toward one another and in frequent group "greeting ceremonies." Howling is a group expression as well as a mechanism to communicate when the pack is spread apart. The entire pack may not always travel together; some members may lag behind for up to several days. A pack's home range depends upon the terrain and prey density and is commonly several hundred to more than 1,000 km². Especially in early spring and late fall, some pack members, especially yearlings but also some pups and adults, may disperse to seek a new territory or to join another pack. Lone wolves are inconspicuous, leaving fewer scent marks and leaving them in less conspicuous places; however, they often investigate other wolves' scent marks. For lone wolves, dispersal distances of 15 to 886 km (9 to 551 miles) from their pack territory have been reported.

FEEDING

Ungulates make up wolves' primary food, including deer, elk, moose, bison, caribou, musk oxen, mountain goats, and mountain sheep. Prey may be attacked close to a bed, flushed out of a standing or traveling group, or merely encountered on a trail; scent as well as visual perception is used. Prey attacked in convenient place (flanks, neck, or head) by lone wolf or by several wolves using group hunting techniques. Large kills made usually every 2 to 10 days depending upon pack and prey size. Kills usually consumed within a day or two. Other prey including hares, beavers, and small rodents taken opportunistically or in between large kills. Some packs modify or extend their territory seasonally to follow prey.

SURVIVAL

Where wolves are not hunted or trapped, primary mortality comes from starvation, conflict with other wolves, and injury from prey animals. Reproductive rate decreases with decline in prey and increases when there is stress on the wolf population, for example with control campaigns.

SIGNS

Natal dens in burrows, at base of tree, in hollow log or other cavity. Numerous rendezvous sites (see above). Kill remnants include hair and scattered, well-chewed bones. Scats thick cords tapered at ends, about 3.2 cm (1¼ in.) in diameter, near group sites, along trails, or deposited on raised surfaces for scent marking. Frequently made scent marks, including raised-leg urination on raised objects, especially in prominent places such as trail junctions; these, as well as scratches in the dirt with diagonally opposite front and hind feet, made by alpha male and female. Impressions from rolling on back made at kill sites or to mark territory.

DOGS

TRACKS

Heel pad shows circular depressions in very clear print. ▶

◀ Claw impressions usually show (F and H).

In dry soil, furred foot often leaves indistinct prints (F and H).

FRONT

HIND

COMMON GAITS

A: Diagonal walk, direct register (common)

B: Lope (common)

C: Gallop (common)

D: Trot (occasional)

Front
Hind

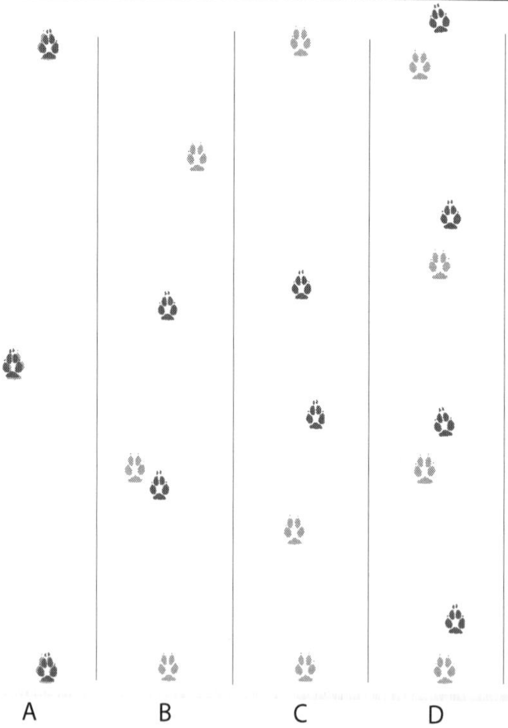

A   B   C   D

TRACK MEASUREMENTS	Average, inches	Average, cm	Usual range, inches*
Front width	1¼	3.2	¹³⁄₁₆ to 1½
Front length	1½	3.7	1³⁄₁₆ to 1⅝
Hind width	1¹⁄₁₆	2.6	⅞ to 1⁵⁄₁₆
Hind length	1⁵⁄₁₆	3.3	1⅛ to 1⅝
Trail width	2⁵⁄₁₆	5.9	1½ to 2¾
Stride	9¾	24.8	6⅞ to 12⅜

*More than 93% of my measurements fall within this range.

DOGS

A

A: Very small compared to the coyote track at left, the kit fox track can usually be confused only with a gray fox's, but the claw impressions here rule out gray fox.
B: In loose sand the pattern of the direct-registering kit fox may not show claws and may overlap in stride and trail width with the gray fox, requiring the tracker to follow the trail until a clearer impression is seen.
C and D: Clear front and hind tracks, respectively
E and F: Claw marks sometimes do not show.

FINE POINTS

The shape and tiny size of the kit fox's track leave few possibilities for confusion. The domestic dog can usually be eliminated by the fact that dogs with such small feet normally have shorter strides and a sloppier track pattern. (The closely related swift fox of the plains would have almost identical tracks though.)

However, gray-fox tracks may easily be confused with a kit fox's where they do share habitat. Gray fox and kit fox overlap in track size, in trail width, and in stride. Look first for claw impressions, which the gray fox usually lacks; if the soil is too soft to register claws, follow the trail until you get a reading, or look for the faintest of claw drags wherever you can. Kit foxes also walk up on their front toes more than gray foxes, often barely leaving a hind heel impression for that reason (see photos D and F). The front track of a kit fox is more elongated than the gray fox's round front track. Finally, read weight through track depth; a kit fox, at four and a half pounds, weighs about half what the gray fox weighs.

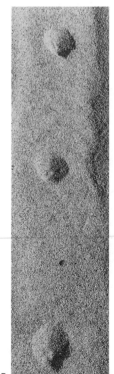

B

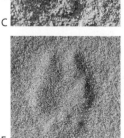

C

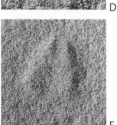

D

E

F

DOGS

The quick and agile kit fox, whose hunting excellence is automatic, really teaches the tracker about **habitat selection and use**, because this fine predator is itself so vulnerable to predation by coyotes, red foxes and bobcats. Its niche, relatively flat open space, minimizes contact with its enemies, who nevertheless account for 65% or more of the fox's mortality. Within this niche a kit fox's survival depends upon its **complex of dens**. Kit foxes are some of the only canids worldwide that den year-round. The dens are a fox's last line of defense against its predators, and a family of foxes may use ten or more dens throughout the year. One family was found to have used forty-one dens within a fifteen-month period! Active dens are chosen and refurbished from an inventory of old ones, from ground squirrel or badger diggings, or dug anew. Because kit foxes change dens on average every two to three weeks, the tracker must spend some effort discovering which dens are currently in use. A family including a mating pair and offspring generally "own" a complex of dens in a discrete area. Look for fresh diggings and tracks around entrances, and look for runs radiating out from them. Dens may have two to four entrances, but one was discovered with twenty-four entrances. From April through May you may also find active natal dens with prey remains and pup tracks at the entrances. A refurbished den may have mounds of excavated dirt with old scats in it, allowing you to study the foxes' diet.

Den exploration also leads the tracker to a glimpse of a kit fox's **social structure**. Dens are shared almost exclusively by closely related individuals, but the exact sharing may change daily. At a den entrance you may find tracks of a mated pair, of a mother and offspring, or of a father and offspring (and in late summer or early fall, of individual foxes). Try distinguishing foxes' individual tracks from one another, and get a glimpse of the local family unit.

Studying or following tracks of a four-and-a-half pound predator definitely brings the tracker into the detailed view, but the little fox also leads you to the **expanded view of habitat and weather patterns**. Local kit fox populations quite precisely follow the cycles of their prey species, principally rabbits and kangaroo rats, which in turn rise and fall with annual rainfall in their arid habitat. Rather than expand their range or change prey species, foxes generally curtail reproductive success after droughts and expand it after a year of good precipitation. As a tracker, see which cycle the local fox population is in by studying vegetation and seed supply as well as prey tracks and signs. Take the big view and also see how humans impact these little predators, which are endangered in part of their range.

In Death Valley, California, a kit fox roams the sand dunes near a popular campsite.

G

H

I

J

G: A vacant field in Bakersfield, California, is surrounded by development on three sides but provides a site for an active den of endangered San Joaquin kit foxes.

H: In a graded lot across the road, a fox feels safe enough to stop, turn to its left, and sit back on its haunches before moving on. Urban habitats provide some protection from predators such as coyotes, but diminished ability to disperse and cross-breed makes their survival there precarious.

I and J: Around entrances of an active den are found scats and prey remains, such as this kangaroo-rat leg.

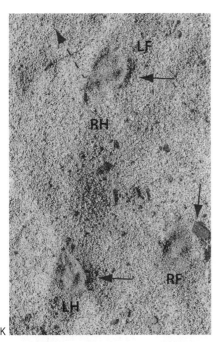

K

K: A kit fox has stopped after coming down a slope, looked sharply to the right, and then continued on in the direction of the dotted arrow. The solid arrows show plates on three tracks, which show the head turn.

L, M, N: In the open country of the desert, kit foxes use numerous gaits to travel between hunting areas or to return to a den. L shows a lope, M a gallop, and N a trot.

L

M

N

DOGS

SPECIES AND WEIGHT

Vulpes macrotis

4 subspecies in North America

1.4 to 3.0 kg
(3 to 6.5 lb.)

Male up to 20% larger than female

HABITAT Arid areas of the West, including desert, grassland, and alkali sink; prefers generally flat terrain with less than 20% cover for denning and hunting areas. Associated with saltbush, shad scale, sagebrush, and creosote bush as well as grassland and has adapted to urban and suburban areas where human development has encroached on its habitat, such as the San Joaquin Valley of California.

BREEDING Breeding usually from early December through January; female selects and cleans out natal den in January. Kit foxes tend to be monogamous, but high mortality causes numerous pair changes from year to year. Before breeding season, female may den temporarily with more than 1 male before choosing a mate. Young born in February or March, litter size averaging 4 and ranging from 2 to 5. Yearling females may breed, producing smaller litters, only in years when food resources are abundant.

DEVELOPMENT Pups raised by both parents, but male often dens nearby away from the natal den. Pup tracks may be seen around den entrance by early April or at 1 month of age. Pups weigh about 1 pound when they first emerge, gain weight rapidly, and reach weight overlapping that of some adult foxes by July or August (5 months). Rearing den may be changed once every 2 weeks on average. Pups disperse from June through October, most in July and August, but a few individuals may remain with a parent until the next spring.

SOCIAL HABITS Kit fox home ranges, usually between 5 km² and 14 km², center around a cluster of 10 or more dens used by related foxes for refuge and rest. Den use changes often and varying combinations of 2 or 3 related foxes may den together on any given day (though foxes den alone about half the time). Female ranges usually don't overlap, but males' may overlap ranges of 1 or more females. Foxes in adjacent territories are often related because pups tend to disperse to nearby areas; these "extended families" may maintain contact.

DOGS

FEEDING

Exclusively nocturnal, kit foxes hunt alone, though a mated pair may hunt in the same general area. Rodents—especially kangaroo rats and pocket mice—and rabbits make up most of diet; where these aren't available, foxes may depend upon locally abundant ground squirrels or pocket gophers. Insects often eaten. Reptiles and ground-nesting birds sometimes eaten. Kit foxes often hunt in sparsely vegetated areas, skirting the edges of shrubs or coursing through open country.

SURVIVAL

Adults and dispersing pups susceptible to predation especially by coyotes but also by red foxes and bobcats; predation typically causes 70% to 80% of mortality. Most pups die within 10 days of dispersal; adult survival rate may also be less than 45% annually in an area. A low winter rainfall drops kit fox populations drastically a year later because of decreased prey, but fox populations can rebound quickly after wet years.

SIGNS

Dens generally located in flat or gently sloping terrain with sparse shrub cover. Den entrances about 19 cm (7½ in.) wide, slightly taller than wide, usually numbering 2 to 4 but as many as 24 per den. Natal dens have fresh scats, prey remains such as rabbit and rodent feet and tails near entrances; little-used dens may be weathered and hard to find. Scats small and cylindrical, usually containing fur and insect parts, deposited along trails, near dens, and sometimes at kill sites; not deposited in latrines. Newly cleaned-out natal den may show many old scats brought up from below.

O: Kit fox den on the Carrizo Plain, California

P: Kit fox scat

TRACKS   Claws prominent
and sharp (F and H)

Chevron-shaped
depression in heel pad
(F and H) is diagnostic.

◄ H heel pad
is triangular.

FRONT   HIND

COMMON   A: Diagonal
GAITS   walk, direct
register
(common)

B: Canine
trot
(common)

C: Trot
(occasional)

D: Gallop
(occasional)

E: Slow walk
(occasional)

🐾 Front

🐾 Hind

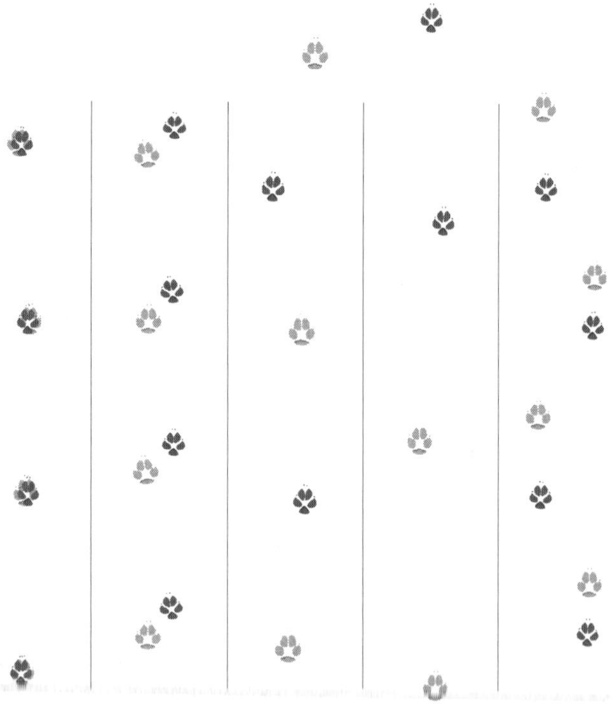

A   B   C   D   E

TRACK MEASUREMENTS	Average, inches	Average, cm	Usual range, inches*
Front width	1¾	4.4	1½ to 2¹⁄₁₆
Front length	2	5.1	1½ to 2⁵⁄₁₆
Hind width	1⁹⁄₁₆	4.0	1¼ to 1⅞
Hind length	1⅞	4.7	1⁷⁄₁₆ to 2⅝
Trail width	3⅜	8.5	2 to 5
Stride**	12⁵⁄₁₆	31.3	8¾ to 15⅛

*More than 95% of my measurements fall within this range.
**Diagonal walk

DOGS

Red-fox tracks are almost always larger than gray-fox tracks but may be confused with coyote or domestic-dog tracks. The telltale chevron-shaped depression in the heel pad—more prominent in the front than the hind—provides certainty of the red-fox ID. When track age or soil texture make the heel pad indistinct, go with other clues. The direct-register walking gait of a red fox will distinguish it from both coyote and domestic-dog trails, both of which show indirect register. The prominent claw impressions are sharp in contrast to the blunt claw marks in domestic-dog tracks. Finally, the overall shape of the hind heel pad tends to be tall and narrow, in contrast to a coyote's hind heel pad, which tends to be short and wider.

FINE POINTS

A

B

C

A: Direct-register walking pattern

B: Hind (top) and front tracks showing chevron

C: Claw marks are sharper than a domestic dog's.

DOGS

The legendary cleverness of the red fox really speaks to the **intimate knowledge of its territory**, a trait the tracker can learn from and emulate. It seems that every square foot is known for its opportunities and dangers. Begin by confirming the fox's presence, often evident from characteristic musky fox odor deposited as scent marks throughout its territory, especially at breeding time. The scent should push you to begin looking for other obvious signs. Look for natal dens, about 20 to 23 cm (8 to 9 in. in diameter), that have an apron of dirt at the entrance and emit that foxy odor. You may also find regular fox runs to hunting or foraging areas, as well as well-used day beds located aboveground even in cold weather. While these signs may be obvious, the fox also challenges you with its secrets, one of which is widespread food caching. Many dozens of vole, mouse, or rabbit parts are buried in holes that are refilled, patted down, and covered with debris; one fox was observed lightly brushing the snow over a cache with its whiskers, backing away, and covering over its own tracks! Even if you find few caches (even other foxes miss most of them), you may be able to follow a fox's trail to dug-up caches, which are usually then urinated upon to signify "no need to dig here again." Also, set up tracking boxes with a few feathers; your fox will notice these changes in its territory and may investigate cautiously, leaving some tracks to study.

Finding a natal den is a window to the red-fox **pups' development and dispersal** because examination can tell you at what stage a den was occupied. In the first four or five weeks when pups are nursed, there are few prey remains around the den and no pup tracks. In the next four or five weeks, pups will emerge, leaving playful tracks, but prey remains, if any, tend to be underground. In the last four or five weeks, the area will be littered with scats and prey remains. Remember that a fox family may change dens several times in these months. In a red fox's territory, also look for aggregations of scats and tracks, which may signify rendezvous sites used by a family after they abandon their dens but before the young disperse.

The lithe build of a red fox, more feline than canine, allows it to glide through its range, leaving perfect strings of walking or trotting tracks rich with information about the fox's alertness. As you track a fox, look for slight changes in speed and shoulder orientation, which reveal how it listens for a vole scratching in an adjacent meadow or looks for a vulnerable rabbit. You may find where a fox has turned at right angles to its trail, crouched and pounced on a mouse, or you may find a string of galloping tracks. Study the pressure releases, because even when galloping, the fox glides like a shadow.

Red-fox front track in San Pedro, California, where red and gray foxes coexist in undeveloped open space.

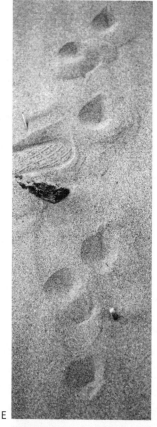

D

E

F

D: The trail of a galloping red fox may resemble a coyote's or domestic dog's, requiring the tracker to track it forward or backward to get positive ID.

E: A fox's loping trail

F: Often-seen canine trot

G: In the mountains near Storlien, Sweden, prevailing high winds eroded the snow around red-fox track compressions, leaving a line of tiny pillars. The European red fox is the same species found in North America.

G

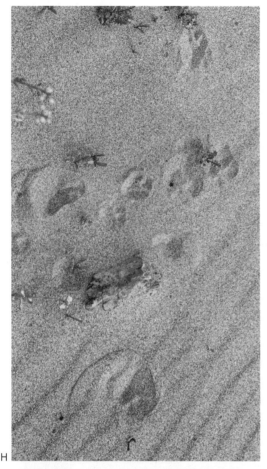

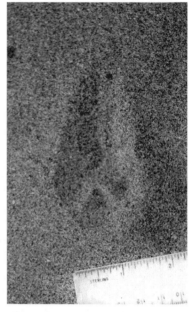

H: On California's central coast, the trail of an adult red fox crosses that of a tiny pup (center) in late February. This early sighting is possibly due to a family moving its den.

I: Detail of pup's track

J: A red fox has dug a small hole to catch a Jerusalem cricket.

RED FOX   Notes for the Tracker

SPECIES AND WEIGHT   *Vulpes vulpes*

12 subspecies in North America

4 to 5.5 kg
(8.8 to 12 lb.)

Male 15% to 25% heavier than female

HABITAT   Prefers mixture of cover (forest or brush) and open space (meadow, wetland, grassland, or cropland) that provide denning areas and hunting areas, respectively. North American range has expanded with extermination of wolves, and introductions from European lineages have occurred especially in Washington and California. Especially an animal of northern forests throughout Europe, Asia, and North America, it has adapted to agricultural and semi-urban areas.

BREEDING   Most breeding in January/February, earlier in warmer climates. Male scent marking increases; numerous dens scent-marked by pair and dug out prior to birthing. Pair travels together frequently. Gestation 52 days, litters average 5. Young of both sexes may mate in 1st year except where fox density is high, but juveniles breed later than adults.

DEVELOPMENT   Mating pair both stay near den during first few weeks of nursing. Pups weaned at 5 weeks, when they emerge from den for short periods; male and female both bring food to den, but male may bed down several hundred meters away. From age 10 weeks on, pups make forays away from den, and den area is littered with prey remains. Family may move to new den sites numerous times. After about 15 weeks family abandons dens and instead frequents a series of "rallying stations" in open areas, where their scats accumulate. In early to mid-autumn, juveniles disperse, often in fairly straight lines over 1 to 7 days. Most young foxes eventually disperse more than 8 km (5 miles), up to more than 161 km (100 miles).

SOCIAL HABITS   Breeding pairs generally maintain home ranges of 1.5 km² to 12 km², which tend to be roughly circular, while solitary foxes' home ranges tend to be larger and may be linear. Fox territories usually don't overlap and are actively marked and defended. Some female siblings may stay together as adults. Between dispersal and breeding, most foxes are solitary.

Red foxes are especially adapted to a steady diet of small rodents such as voles **FEEDING**
but also hunt larger rodents and rabbits, eat many insects and fruits seasonally,
take nesting ground birds and their eggs, and scavenge for carrion. Insectivores
killed but not always eaten. Caches many small food items in well-disguised,
15-cm-deep (6 in.) holes, to retrieve later. Hunts deliberately for staple foods of
the season but forages opportunistically also, responding to sights and sounds.
Most active in early morning, then late afternoon to midnight.

Heavy commercial trapping and hunting causes most mortality. Though coyotes **SURVIVAL**
occasionally kill them, foxes usually coexist by finding nonoverlapping niches on
the edges of coyote home ranges.

Skunk-like odor from fox scent marking, especially noticeable during breeding **SIGNS**
season. Scats usually 1.3 to 1.6 cm (½ to ⅝ in.) diameter, with tufted end especially when containing fur, and with distinctive musky odor, deposited in open
along trails and runs, often on somewhat elevated spots. Dens 20 to 23 cm (8
to 9 in.) in diameter, with prey remains and half-size pup scats especially during
latter rearing stages. Day beds usually aboveground, about 38 cm (15 in.) diameter, hair from grooming sometimes nearby, especially in spring. Kill remains
from rabbits, birds, or larger rodents, sometimes with canine punctures about
1.9 cm (¾ in.) apart. Dug-out caches, often scent-marked.

K

L

K: Along the central California coast, a red fox has scavenged a dead seabird, leaving behind
clumps of feathers with teeth marks.

L: Red fox scat

RABBITS AND HARES

HARES

TRACKS

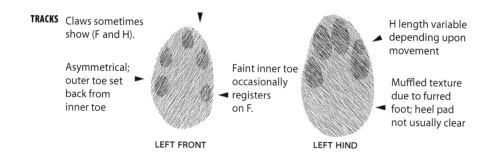

Claws sometimes show (F and H).

Asymmetrical; outer toe set back from inner toe ►

Faint inner toe occasionally ◄ registers on F.

H length variable ▲ depending upon movement

Muffled texture due to furred ◄ foot; heel pad not usually clear

LEFT FRONT

LEFT HIND

COMMON GAITS

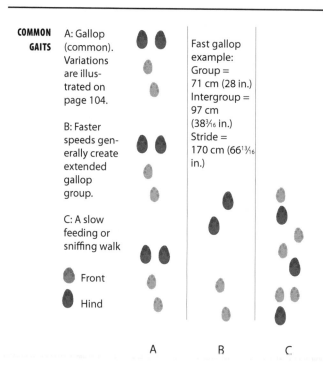

A: Gallop (common). Variations are illustrated on page 104.

B: Faster speeds generally create extended gallop group.

C: A slow feeding or sniffing walk

● Front

● Hind

Fast gallop example:
Group = 71 cm (28 in.)
Intergroup = 97 cm (38³⁄₁₆ in.)
Stride = 170 cm (66¹³⁄₁₆ in.)

A   B   C

TRACK MEASUREMENTS

	Average, inches	Average, cm	Usual range, inches*
Front width	1⁵⁄₁₆	3.3	1⅛ to 1⅝
Front length	1¹³⁄₁₆	4.7	1⁵⁄₁₆ to 2½
Hind width	1⅝	4.2	1¹⁄₁₆ to 2⅝
Hind length	2¹¹⁄₁₆	6.9	1¾ to 4½
Trail width	5¹⁄₁₆	12.8	3⁹⁄₁₆ to 8
Stride**	23¼	59.1	4½ to 42

*More than 96% of my measurements fall within this range.   **Gallop

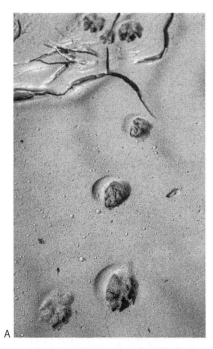

FINE POINTS

In shape, size, and number of toes, the rear track can resemble a coyote's and the front a gray fox's, especially in difficult soil. The muffled texture and the track pattern will usually help (though one of the many gallop patterns of a jackrabbit looks quite like a fox's diagonal walk, direct register). You may mistake a very young juvenile jackrabbit track for an adult cottontail track and this may happen throughout the year. Generally the front foot of a jackrabbit is more rounded at its forward edge than a cottontail's, which is tapered to a finer "point" (unless the toes are spread). Black-tailed jackrabbits also share territory with the antelope jackrabbit in Arizona. Check range maps and guides to distinguish habitat from that of the snowshoe hare and white-tailed jackrabbit, whose tracks are similar.

A: Heel area usually registers only in wet soils. The hare is galloping from top to bottom.
B: Furred foot creates muffled texture.
C: Left front showing occasionally seen inside toe
D: Right hind

When you settle down to track a jackrabbit, you may first learn something about your own patience and determination. Jackrabbits are some of the most **difficult animals to track** for their size, because, except when they are flat-out sprinting, their every footfall resembles the cushioned impact of a cat jumping upon a table. The fur-covered feet compress the soil as they absorb impact, often leaving barely perceptible imprints. This is why jackrabbit tracking is such a great teacher, and why it's necessary to find every track. Work on this for a while and you will really improve your skills.

The jackrabbit track is also a window to **amazing fluidity of motion**—beyond what almost any other animal can perform. When you watch a jackrabbit negotiate open space, you marvel at its superbly engineered body, limbs swinging pendulum-like as it moves as effortlessly as a bicycle rider. In fact, you might compare the jackrabbit to the finest racing bicycle designed—which is, however, also adapted for mountain-bike terrain! Such fluidity translates into an endless variety of gallop patterns, and as a tracker you could fill your notebook seemingly for years with subtle variations and what they say about the animal's mood, speed, and adjustment to its terrain (see page 104). Follow a jackrabbit trail, visualizing or better yet feeling its motion in every change of gait, and you have passed through a rich window indeed.

Yet another window in the jackrabbit track is the one to the **wide-open spaces it occupies**. We are accustomed to looking at dense cover to define an essential part of ideal mammal habitat, yet black-tailed jackrabbit trails and runs crisscross open terrain as if the hare had no worries in the world. Track a jackrabbit for a while in this setting and put yourself into its extraordinary awareness. Where could it not see or hear danger from a long distance? How long would it take to sprint to safety? Where is the hare most vulnerable, and how does it change its mood and behavior in these places? Also, in the cold and incessantly windy times of winter in the desert, where could it find meager shelter? Where would it rest in the burning heat of a summer day? Discovering jackrabbit beds, their orientation, and time of use, and studying the runs coming into and out of them tells you a lot about the sun and wind of the open country, how they are avoided or used to advantage at different times of the day and in different seasons. Spending a day mapping the landscape as if you were a jackrabbit gives you an entirely new appreciation of open country.

A black-tailed jackrabbit stops for a scratch in the coastal dunes of California.

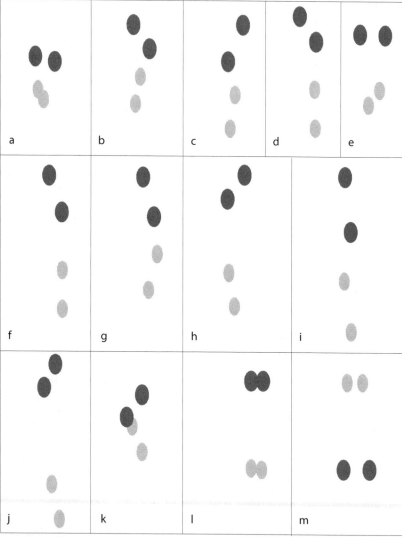

Some of the many gallop patterns created by black-tailed jackrabbits. Some of the patterns clearly show a difference in speed as suggested by the length of space between individual prints (for example figures a and k being slow hops and figures c, g, and i being faster gallops). There are also both "rotary" gallops (e.g., figures f, g, and j) and "transverse" gallops (e.g., figures c and i). Yet beyond these technical distinctions lies a tremendous versatility in fluid movement: The jackrabbit's legs sometimes move quite independently, sometimes the two front and two rear synchronize for power, sometimes the front are independent and the rear move together. There are gallops for elevation, flat-out speed, and maneuverability.

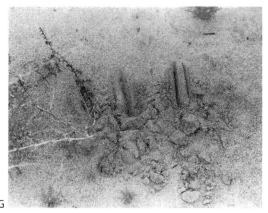

E and F: Examples of direction changes. At left a leisurely turn made possible by placement of the LF toward the new direction of travel, and a pivot off the RH. At right a quick 90-degree turn.

G: "Explode-off" pressure releases mark a jackrabbit's acceleration from a sitting position.

H: A gallop with power synchronization, i.e., two feet pushing off together

HARES

SPECIES AND WEIGHT   *Lepus californicus*

17 subspecies in North America

2.5 to 3.5 kg
(5.5 to 7.7 lb.)

Female larger than male

HABITAT   Open country, usually with dominant shrubs such as sagebrush, creosote bush, juniper, or mesquite, from below sea level to above 3,353 meters (11,000 ft.); well adapted to deserts and other arid areas. Frequently shares some of its habitat with local *Sylvilagus* (cottontail) species, but usually separate from other *Lepus* (hare) species such as snowshoe hares and white-tailed jackrabbits.

BREEDING   May mate throughout the year but usually January through August. Gestation about 40 days. Male may follow a trail for long distances with his nose to the ground to find a female. Vigorous chases and sparring during mating, one animal jumping and the other running underneath it. Litters 2 to 5, 2 to 7 litters per year depending upon latitude and length of breeding season.

DEVELOPMENT   Young can move around shortly after birth, may leave nest within 24 hours or may stay in its vicinity for several days. Body size develops more rapidly than weight. At 1 month, juvenile is at 50% adult size and tracks are cottontail size. By 2½ months, juvenile body and foot size are 90% of adult size while weight is only 50%. Weaning and dispersal at about 3 months.

SOCIAL HABITS   Two to 5 hares may be together around breeding time. Some territorial charging and sparring among females and males. Home range generally under 20 hectares (49 acres), but migrations to wintering areas (to 35 km/22 miles or more) in some habitats extend the annual home range.

FEEDING   Grasses and forbs form a large proportion of diet, especially in spring and summer. Shrubs including mesquite, catclaw, paloverde, rabbitbrush, sagebrush, and winter fat also consumed, particularly in fall and winter. Jackrabbits stand on their hind legs to reach new growth of shrubs. Active at night, dusk, and dawn; beds down during coldest, windiest, or hottest parts of the day. May move about during the day.

SURVIVAL

Hiding, stalking away from danger, and high-speed evasive runs up to 40 mph are survival strategies. Coyote is the principal predator, but other mammals and raptors prey on the jackrabbit also. Mortality in first year averages 67%, as high as 90%. Adult mortality commonly 50%.

SIGNS

Beds or "forms" may be shallow depressions, sometimes excavated to a few inches, in windbreaks or shade. Sometimes makes use of other animals' burrows. Maternal nests sometimes have fur lining. Dust baths. Well-used trails about the width of a motorcycle tire. Browse signs including gnawed bark and 45-degree cuts as high as 61 cm (24 in.) aboveground. One hare produces more than 500 pellets per day, about 9 to 13 mm (⅜ to ½ in.) in diameter.

I

J

K

I: In a piñon pine forest in California's Sierra Nevada, one jackrabbit regularly used this summer bed, excavated to reach cool soil.

J: Winter browse of mesquite bark

K: Jackrabbit scat, averaging 9 to 13 mm (⅜ to ½ in.) diameter

RABBITS

TRACKS Claws may show sometimes (F and H).

Inside toe sometimes shows in slow-moving F track.

H length varies according to speed and terrain.

Track often muffled due to furred foot; toe impressions indistinct (F and H)

No clear heel pad (F and H)

LEFT FRONT

LEFT HIND

COMMON GAITS

A: Most common gallop pattern

B: Stop-and-go hop

C: Fast gallop

D: Fast gallop

E: Gallop with front tracks paired

Front

Hind

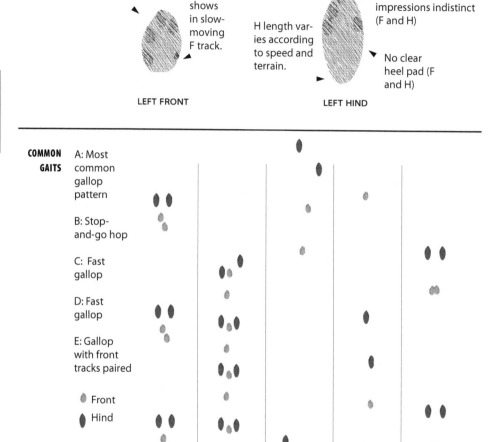

A   B   C   D   E

TRACK MEASUREMENTS

	Average, inches	Average, cm	Usual range, inches*
Front width	7/8	2.2	9/16 to 1 5/16
Front length	1 3/8	3.5	15/16 to 2 1/8
Hind width	1 1/16	2.7	11/16 to 1 1/2
Hind length	2 1/16	5.2	1 1/4 to 3 1/2
Trail width	3 1/2	8.8	2 3/8 to 5
Stride**	18 7/8	47.9	9 1/2 to 48

*More than 96% of my measurements fall within this range.   **Gallop

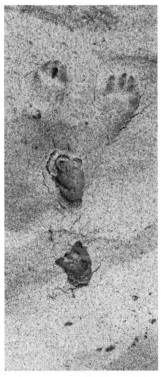

A

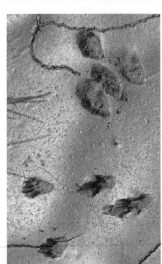

B

Because cottontail tracks almost always form a gallop pattern, they might be confused with other gallopers that have a similar trail width, such as ground squirrels or small tree squirrels. When the four toes on a hind track cannot be seen to distinguish them from the five-toed-rodent hind track, study the shape of the hind tracks: Cottontail tracks usually come to a point at the forward edge, in contrast to rodent tracks, which flatten out. Cottontail tracks may overlap in size and trail width with small jackrabbit tracks, and measurement alone cannot always distinguish them. Consider habitat, but also use your visualization skills: The cottontail's short legs create a more compressed pattern at a given speed than the jackrabbit's very long legs.

FINE POINTS

C

D

E

A: Common gallop pattern

B: Pointed front of cottontail hind tracks (top) contrasts with flatter front edge of rodent hind tracks like this ground squirrel.

C: Right front track

D: Right hind track

E: Left front track with toes spread, showing inside toe

The edges of dense brush form perfect cottontail habitat, and indeed it seems the rabbit's awareness and ability to burst to safety in a few quick zigzagging bounds create a **tethered safety zone** within which it carries on its leisurely life. Despite the cottontail's vulnerability to foxes, bobcats, coyotes, hawks, and owls, its behavior close to cover is routine and quiet, and the tracker can easily read this body language in tracks and signs— a slow hop, stop-and-listen, scratch behind the ear, a dust bath, or the playful antics of young animals. This is your chance to step beyond mere identification and study mood and behavior. Pick a set of tracks and move with it, find the rhythm of the hops and stops, and as you do so, adopt the rabbit's awareness, through which the slightest sound or sudden move- ment would trigger a run for cover. In fact, get down at rabbit-eye level and scan the brush for escape routes. You'll find little "forms," or resting places, just within the brush. If you find some sprinting tracks with their explode-off pressure releases, follow them to appreciate the cottontail's remarkable defense as well as its intimate relationship to cover.

For about eight months each year, cottontails are in the primary busi- ness of producing more of themselves, and this **breeding imperative** is another good window for the tracker. Female rabbits mate again right after giving birth, so that a new pregnancy is well under way as it nurses its young, and each female may produce three or four litters per season. Mating behavior itself is evident in tracks from vertical jumps and spar- ring, but you may also find a trail of a male cottontail following closely behind a female prior to mating. Young rabbits emerge from their nest after two or two-and-a-half weeks, weighing only about a fifth of adult size. Cottontail habitat is thus rife with tiny scats and tracks, some with a trail width just over 5 cm (2 in.) wide. Look for small tracks, distinguish- ing them from rodent tracks by shape. Look for cottontail nests that are camouflaged with leaves and grasses; the mother goes near the nest only at night to nurse.

Cottontails pick their favorite and most nutritious foods, which vary from week to week, depending upon local plant growth. This **seasonal feeding history** can be read by aging browse and scats. Get down to ground level and begin following rabbit runs to feeding areas, noticing what the cur- rent browse is and what was preferred in earlier seasons. Sometimes ends of stems are left on the ground. Runs may lead you some distance from cover, where cottontails feed communally on abundant green grasses or other green annuals. The age and abundance of scats in these open areas give you a picture of how far the rabbits venture at night, when danger is minimal.

On the edge of the Great Sand Dunes in Colorado, a cottontail's nighttime trail has persisted until the next morning.

F

G

F: In spring, rabbit runs radiate through the grasses from bedding areas to browse areas.

G: Frisky vertical jumps are common during mating season.

H: In this high-speed gallop, a cottontail is back on its heels as it lands with the hind feet (top).

H

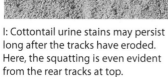

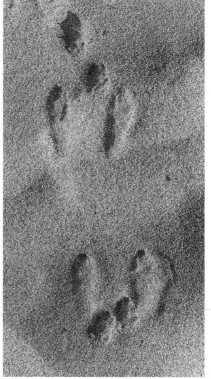

I: Cottontail urine stains may persist long after the tracks have eroded. Here, the squatting is even evident from the rear tracks at top.

J: Tiny juvenile cottontail tracks may be seen for two-thirds of the year; a trail width here of 4 cm (1¾ in.) is as small as a chipmunk's.

K: Hop-and-stop tracks abound in cottontail safe zones.

SPECIES AND WEIGHT

Sylvilagus spp.

8 species in North America

0.5 to 1.25 kg (1.2 to 2.7 lb.)

Female larger than male

HABITAT Three western species (brush rabbit, desert cottontail, and mountain cottontail) occupy different habitats from sea level to 2,286 meters (7,500 ft.), but all require cover of sagebrush, bush lupine, blackberry, wild rose, or other dense brush, in areas of coastal sage scrub, chaparral, desert, woodland, or mountain canyons. Nearby grassland or other source of green browse in spring defines ideal habitat.

BREEDING Most breeding in January through July (occasionally in Dec in temperate habitats); mountain cottontail begins breeding in February. Females breed 2 to 5 times per season and mate immediately after giving birth. Females but not males may breed in 1st year. Gestation 27 to 30 days, litters average 3 to 6. Female prepares nest of grasses, leaves, and fur. Mating may involve vertical jumps by male and female and some chasing; male hops closely behind female until mating, which lasts only seconds. Some sparring and chasing among males.

DEVELOPMENT Female watches over nest from a distance, nurses young at night. Time between nursings may exceed 30 hours. Female may chase intruders from nest area. Young leave nest after 2 weeks, weighing 0.1 to 0.2 kg (3 to 7 oz.), 10% to 20% of adult weight. Young reach adult size by 2½ months.

SOCIAL HABITS Cottontails often feed leisurely in the same area without competition, but one male sometimes chases another submissive male from feeding area. Home ranges conform to available cover, usually 3 hectares (7.4 acres) or less; males' ranges overlap more than females'. Most social interaction involves mating behavior between males and females.

FEEDING

Grasses including bromes, fescues, and poas preferred in spring, but many other green plants such as filaree, juncus, tarweed, and vetch eaten. Stems often nipped at base, then consumed basal end first. Sagebrush, wild rose, juniper, and other shrub and tree twig ends eaten. After green vegetation is gone, cottontails will eat dried seed heads of grasses and forbs, browse on shrubs, and gather cast seed heads from the ground. Feeding time peaks from 1 hour before to 3 hours after sunrise and from 2 hours before to several hours after sunset. In darkness cottontails venture farther from cover to feed. Some rabbits have been observed feeding on blackberries and climbing juniper trees to eat twig ends in summer.

SURVIVAL

Many predators including coyotes, gray foxes, bobcats, red-tailed hawks, owls, rattlesnakes, and gopher snakes depend upon cottontails as a primary food source. Cottontails flatten and freeze when danger is near, then sprint in a zig-zag pattern to elude their chasers. Most feeding occurs within 46 meters (150 ft.) of cover to allow quick escape. Acute hearing alerts cottontails to danger.

SIGNS

Scats spherical and slightly flattened, sometimes with small point on one end, up to 10 mm (⅜ in.) in diameter, deposited along trails and in browse areas. Browse cuts at 45 degrees on plants or twig ends. Branch or stem ends some-times left on ground. Dust baths. "Forms," or shallow resting places, on the edge of brush and on runs; in desert, holes dug for shade. Natal nests, sometimes excavated and sometimes enlarged from existing holes, about 15 cm (6 in.) in diameter and lined with grasses, leaves, and rabbit fur; often covered with leaf or grass camouflage. These nests sometimes under cover and sometimes in the open.

L

L: Cottontail scat

M: Cottontail browse

M

SNOWSHOE HARE   Track ID

TRACKS

Indistinct prints
due to furred feet,
esp. in winter
(F and H)

LEFT FRONT

H toes may be widely
spread or positioned
together, depending
upon substrate.

Back of H foot may not
register, depending
upon speed.

LEFT HIND

COMMON GAITS

A: Slow
gallop
(common)

B: Gallop
to stops
(common)

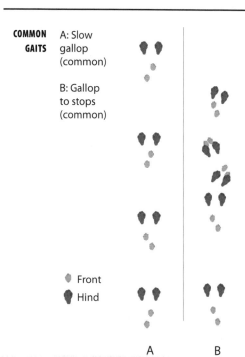

● Front
● Hind

A   B

TRACK MEASUREMENTS

	Average, inches	Average, cm	Usual range, inches*
Front width	1⁹⁄₁₆	4.0	1½ to 2⅛
Front length	2¼	5.6	1¾ to 2⅞
Hind width	2¼	5.9	1⅞ to 2¹⁵⁄₁₆
Hind length	3⅞	9.8	3 to 4¹⁵⁄₁₆
Trail width	6½	16.5	5¼ to 8
Stride**	33⅛	84.1	23 to 46¾

*More than 93% of my measurements fall within this range.   **Gallop

HARES

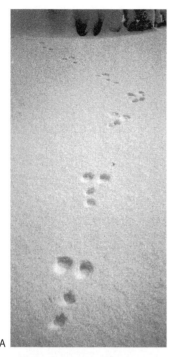

The gallop pattern with muffled prints and four toes in each track leads to the rabbit/hare group, and the size of the tracks (usually more than 5 cm/2 in. wide for a hind) allow only the snowshoe hare and jackrabbit to be considered. **Habitat** is an important clue, for snowshoe hares prefer wooded areas with adequate low cover, while **white-tailed jackrabbits**—which may be in the same general areas—prefer open habitats. (Black-tailed-jackrabbit habitat would seldom come close to that of snowshoe hares.) Between the snowshoe and the white-tail, overlap may occur in front and hind track size, trail width, and stride. While the ratio of front width to hind width is usually greater than 70% for a white-tail and usually less than that for a snowshoe, there may be overlap here too. The best strategy is to visualize the hare making the gallop pattern, because the snowshoe hare's shorter legs will create a more compressed pattern while the white-tailed jackrabbit's very long legs will often stretch out the pattern.

FINE POINTS

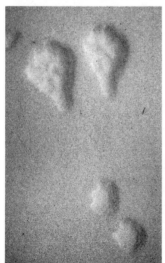

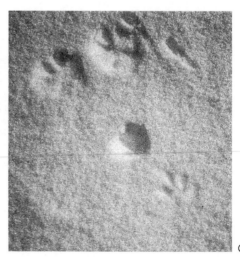

A: Gallop pattern. Snowshoe hares do venture into the open between sheltered habitat patches.

B and C: Gallop groups with front tracks below hind ones show variations in toe spread and foot registration.

An animal named after its feet must surely pique a tracker's interest, and the **snow-covered habitat** to which these feet are adapted is a good starting point to understand the snowshoe hare's biology. These hares do not range far from places with a long-lasting cover of winter snow because they are so well adapted to it: Their oversize hind feet, covered with dense fur, allow efficient travel over snow where many predators would flounder in it; the hares seem to hide easily in it; and they can subsist on the seemingly meager browse of midwinter. In this winter landscape hares do not socialize much but rather just eat and rest, two activities that leave the tracker with abundant signs to read. Look for evidence of browse such as nipped twigs and gnawed-off bark on shrubs and trees (remember that a hare often stands upright on the snow to access twigs and buds). Also look for hare beds, depressions in the snow often beneath low-hanging branches. The locations of these signs, and the trails between them, may be studied to reveal more. Hares' home ranges may compress in winter into local "refuges" of the best cover and food. Because this occurs especially when a population is low, the tracker may get a sense of local hare numbers by concentrations of signs; a higher population would spread into more open areas. If you are tracking in summer, the relationship of snow and the hare may still be read. Look at the density of underbrush about 0.9 meters (3 ft.) off the ground (or whatever height last year's snow-pack reached). The densest areas should point to heavily used hare areas. Signs of last winter's browse may also be evident there. Also, winter scats deposited on the snow will drop to the ground as the snow melts in spring.

Snow tracking a hare can also give you valuable practice in **track aging**. Because snowshoe hares move around in the middle of the night, the tracks you find the next day will often be snowed over, covered with hoarfrost, melted and refrozen, or obliterated by falling clumps of melting snow. Also, hares may wait until a soft snow surface crusts over with falling temperatures to venture out more easily, leaving only faint and variable tracks on the ice. You may need to reconstruct the patterns of temperature change, humidity, and precipitation to follow a trail.

Snowshoe hares' **summer growth period** is another good tracking window. Then, hares practice the art of camouflaged hiding; newborn hares space themselves individually a few days after birth and rendezvous with their mother to nurse only once each night for a few minutes, the rendezvous places varying. Though hares themselves are hard to find, their signs blossom with a rapidly increasing population driven by two or three litters per female per year, and with dispersal of young hares to new home ranges. Survey the habitat for current runs, browse, scats, and forms, noting that hares must travel to find each other to mate throughout the season. In mid- to late summer, young hares about half the weight of adults will be dispersing, moving to more open, less ideal habitat as the population grows.

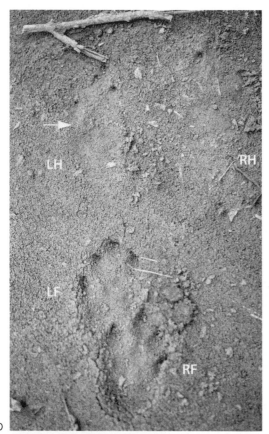

D: Reading details in a snowshoe hare's slow hop. This typical "gallop" pattern shows little forward motion in the front tracks at bottom, while the hind tracks show deliberate forward movement through the disk fissures behind the toes (arrow). However, two anomalies in the pattern must be explained. First, the right front (RF) has landed behind and somewhat on top of the left front (LF) (not beyond it as with a normal hop). This could have happened only if the hare had stopped just prior to creating this pattern. Second, the RF track, unlike the LF, shows considerable toe spread. This must have been caused by the hare balancing its entire weight momentarily on its RF track as it swung its two H feet around it and forward. The LH leg probably lagged behind the RH, causing a kick-out of soil to the right as the RF left the ground.

E: Differing browse ages show that this willow branch on the Kenai National Wildlife Refuge was browsed by a snowshoe hare earlier in the current season, as well as in the previous year.

HARES

SPECIES AND WEIGHT *Lepus americanus*

15 subspecies in North America

0.9 to 2.2 kg (2 to 4.8 lb)

Female 10% to 40% larger than male

HABITAT Coniferous and deciduous forests of the North, primarily where there is continuous winter snow cover; some hares may also occur at the southern boundaries of such habitat where winter snowpack is more variable.

Prefers habitats where new growth of conifers including fir, spruce, cedar, hemlock, and pine form dense, low understory. Also found in thickets of alder, willow, and raspberry, and in aspen forests with low conifer growth. Winter habitat, especially where local populations are low, may shrink into "refuges" of dense cover with available food.

BREEDING Two or 3 breeding periods per year, the first one beginning from late March to mid-May, depending upon location. Virtually all females age 1 year or older in a local population become pregnant. Gestation about 37 days; female breeds immediately after birthing to produce the 2nd or 3rd litter. Litters usually 3 to 6, generally smaller litters early in the season and larger ones later.

DEVELOPMENT Littermates remain together in natal hiding place in underbrush for 2 to 7 days, then disperse to individual hiding places under shrubs, under downed logs, or in dense grasses and forbs. Young gather once daily, about 1 to 2 hours after sunset and just before arrival of mother, then nurse with her for 5 to 10 minutes before returning to hiding places; rendezvous nursing location may vary slightly from night to night. Young may gradually move away from natal site for 1st 3 weeks. Weaned at about 4 weeks (year-end litters may nurse for longer period). Young are about 25% of adult weight at 18 days, 55% at 1 month, and 62% at 3 months. Dispersal occurs from about 30 to 40 days.

SOCIAL HABITS Though their home ranges tend to overlap somewhat, and though they show no dramatic territoriality, both male and female snowshoe hares space themselves, so that "activity centers" of individuals may be 30 to 500 meters (98 to 1,640 ft.) apart from one another. Recorded home ranges vary from about 3 to 15 hectares (7.4 to 37 acres), with most activity in a fraction of that area. Where local population density is large or growing, subordinate hares (such as members of a year's later litters) generally occupy more open spaces of the local habitat, which are less safe. Snowshoe hare body language observed in controlled situations, such as ear-flattening, lunges, and aggressive leaps, probably establish and reinforce a dominance hierarchy in the wild.

FEEDING

Spring and summer food consists primarily of forbs including dandelion, clover, fireweed, and many others, as well as emerging leaves of deciduous shrubs and trees. In winter twigs (esp. less than 10 mm/⅖ in. diameter), buds and bark of spruce, hemlock, fir, pine, alder, willow, and birch among others comprise the standard diet. Conifer needles and bark of trees such as aspen may be a staple locally during winter.

SURVIVAL

Snowshoe hares are preyed upon routinely by lynxes, coyotes, red foxes, bobcats, weasels, and owls; in northern areas of range, red squirrels and arctic ground squirrels feed on young hares during summer. Annual juvenile survival rates of 16% to 45% and adult survival rates of 33% to 58% are recorded, varying by area and year. Superb ability to hide by both juveniles and adults is aided by camouflaged fur, brown in summer and white in winter. In boreal forest, 10-year population cycle, in which peaks are 15% to 1,000% higher than the lows, are caused by predation and food supplies. Here, lynx, goshawk, and owl populations follow the hare cycle but lag behind it by a couple of years. In the southern part of its North American range, a hare population cycle does not exist or is muted.

SIGNS

Scats are somewhat flattened spheres, about 1 to 1.3 cm (⅜ to ½ in.) diameter, especially deposited in feeding or resting areas. Resting sites or "forms" under low branches, in thickets, or in dense vegetation; winter forms may show melted and refrozen snow from hares' body heat with hairs embedded in it. Sometimes conspicuous feeding areas, showing twigs nipped off at 45-degree angle or bark stripped off of branches or trunks. Well-used runs in snow or on low summer vegetation such as sphagnum moss. Dust baths.

F: Snowshoe hare scat

F

HARES

TRACKS

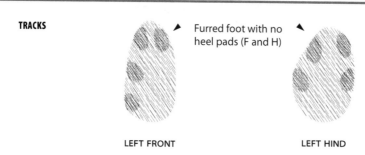

Furred foot with no heel pads (F and H)

LEFT FRONT   LEFT HIND

COMMON GAITS

A: Gallop (common)

B: Lope to slow gallop (occasional)

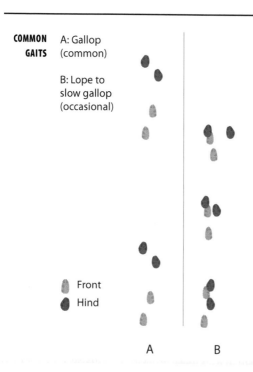

Front
Hind

A   B

TRACK MEASUREMENTS

	Average, inches	Average, cm
Front width	1¾	4.5
Front length	2½	6.4
Hind width	2⅝	6.6
Hind length	3⅜	8.6
Trail width	7⅜	18.7
Stride	37¹³⁄₁₆	96.0

A

A and B: Gallop patterns in Sequoia National Park

C: Left and right hind tracks resemble coyote tracks, except for the outer toe in each track being set back.

FINE POINTS

White-tailed-jackrabbit tracks are considerably larger than cottontail tracks but might be confused with those of **snowshoe hares** or black-tailed jackrabbits. Where their ranges overlap, snowshoe hares prefer brushy areas and white-tailed jackrabbits more open terrain; and **black-tailed jackrabbits** prefer lower elevations and white-tailed jackrabbits higher elevations. Tracks of all three species overlap somewhat in front and hind track size, trail width, and stride. However, white-tailed jackrabbits are larger than the other hares and have very long legs. In my measurements the front-width to hind-width ratio of white-tailed jackrabbits is usually 70% or more, while this ratio for a snowshoe hare is usually less than that.

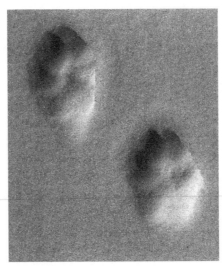

C

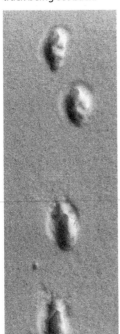

B

Finding white-tailed-jackrabbit tracks above tree line, at 4,267 meters (14,000 ft.), in the dead of winter prompts some questions about this hare's **survival adaptations**, and predictably the answers lead to some interesting winter tracking whether it be in the high mountains of the West or the plains of North Dakota. A white-tailed's winter coat is not only camouflaged for travel and resting on snow, it provides insulation equivalent to that of arctic mammals. The jackrabbit's winter metabolism is maintained easily at an air temperature of 23 °F or above, allowing it to rest simply in a depression in the snow; white-tailed jackrabbits have also been observed sitting in the open with their backs to the winter wind. Biologists have found that white-taileds actually increase their activity in the open during high winds and snowstorms; this raises their body temperature but also, we may guess, takes advantage of times when predators would prefer to bed down. The tracker may be able to follow a trail to a daytime resting spot, sometimes in a depression at the end of a snow tunnel. Also look for signs of feeding; typical winter browse consists of branches or shrubs, but you may also find digs where a jackrabbit has sought out plants beneath the snow. Another survival adaptation is the white-tailed's running ability. Heavily furred feet and long legs allow this big hare to travel easily and quickly over the snow using gallops but also lopes (a bit unusual among rabbits and hares). Follow a trail and look for gait variations caused by differing textures of snow.

The **spring and summer habits** of white-tailed jackrabbits are also illuminated by tracks and signs. During the five-month breeding season, tracks of athletic chases and leaps may be found, concentrated every six weeks or so as a local population breeds synchronously. Throughout the summer look for feeding locations where hares seek out forbs and grasses. Because one hare may deposit hundreds of pellets per day, look for concentrations of scats.

D: White-tailed jackrabbit scat

D

HARES

Lepus townsendii

2 subspecies in North America

2.5 to 4.3 kg
(5.5 to 9.5 lb.)'

Grassland and shrubland of the northern plains and open mountain areas of the West. The white-tailed jackrabbit is especially adapted to survive open habitats with cold winters and persistent winter snow cover. Year-round residency well above 3,353 meters (11,000 ft.) elevation is recorded. Where snowshoe hares share habitat, they prefer forested areas and white-tailed jackrabbits prefer more open, exposed areas.

Breeding period may last about 4½ months, beginning in late February to mid-March in the plains. Females may produce 3 or 4 litters per year, and a local population may therefore have breeding peaks about 6 weeks apart. Much chasing and leaping among males and females during breeding; several males may follow a female. Jackrabbits also travel more during this season. Gestation about 30 to 42 days, litters generally 4 to 6. Food availability affects number of litters per year.

Young born fully furred with eyes open, can move around within a few days. They may forage at 2 weeks, are weaned at 4 weeks, and are independent at 2 months, when they weigh about 3 pounds.

Generally solitary, though small groups of males have been observed. Size of home ranges has not been well recorded, but one study put it at 1 km² to 3 km².

Eats a wide variety of grasses and forbs including Indian paintbrush and clover in spring and summer. Winter diet includes shrubs such as sagebrush and rabbitbrush; woody branches as well as leaves are consumed. Active sporadically from about 1 hour after sunset to about 1 hour before sunrise.

Thick winter coat is white for camouflage except in more southern areas where winter snowpack is less permanent. Feet are thickly insulated with fur. White-tailed jackrabbits can gallop at 34 mph.

"Forms" at the base of shrubs, in grasses, or in snow. Browse signs including diggings in snow for plants. Scats are slightly flattened spheres, from 1 to 1.4 cm (⅜ to ⁹⁄₁₆ in.) in diameter.

SPECIES AND WEIGHT

HABITAT

HARES

BREEDING

DEVELOPMENT

SOCIAL HABITS

FEEDING

SURVIVAL

SIGNS

RODENTS

TRACKS

Claws often show (F and H).

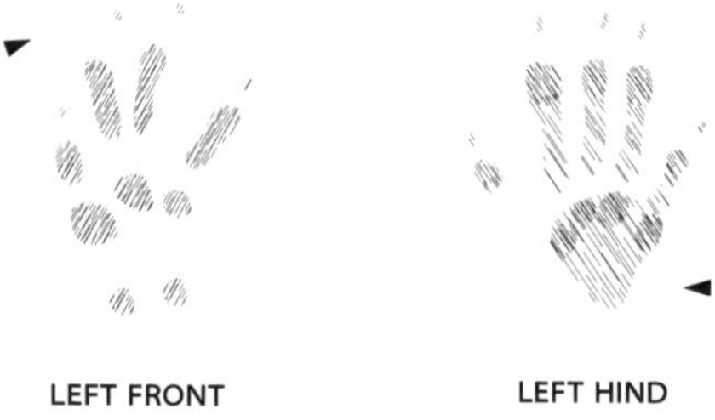

H track lacks proximal pads.

LEFT FRONT   LEFT HIND

COMMON GAITS

A and B: Gallops showing variation in F foot placement

Front

Hind

A   B

TRACK MEASUREMENTS

	Average, inches	Average, cm	Usual range, inches*
Front width	½	1.2	⅜ to ⅝
Front length	¾	1.9	⅝ to ⅞
Hind width	⅝	1.5	½ to ⅞
Hind length	1	2.5	¹¹⁄₁₆ to 1⅜
Trail width	2¼	5.8	
Stride**	13¾	34.9	

*More than 90% of my measurements fall within this range.   **Gallop

Track size, trail width, and stride overlap with chipmunk and woodrat tracks; other rodents are either bigger or smaller. Check the local habitat, because while antelope squirrels and chipmunks *may* share habitat in some areas, the former are much more adapted to hot, arid environments and the latter to forested or brushy ones. **Vs. chipmunk:** A chipmunk's gallop pattern almost always shows side-to-side placement of the front tracks, and each group of four is usually close together. The antelope squirrel often shows diagonal placement of the front feet, and the groups of four may be more elongated. **Vs. woodrat:** In clear prints look at the detail in heel-pad areas of front and hind; also follow trails because woodrats are not underground nesters. Antelope squirrel tracks may be easily studied because the squirrels are diurnal.

FINE POINTS

A: Fast-moving gallop patterns show the groups of four elongated; the front tracks may be placed side to side or diagonally.

B: Clear prints were captured at a track station dusted with diatomaceous earth.

C: The same gallop pattern, more commonly seen in dry soil

A

B

C

Unlike their cousins in other ground squirrel genera, antelope squirrels do not store fat to make it through the cold, hot, or lean times of the year. They are thus restricted to hot climates and to a constant dance with the elements called **thermoregulation** that is a good window to its behavior. Antelope squirrels usually rise after the sun can provide some initial warmth to jump-start their daily activity. After it gets hot, squirrels run at full speed, tails over their backs as sun umbrellas, between spots of shade, demonstrating the principle that more heat would be gained by a stop in the sun than by running for a few seconds. Food is often brought to shady spots such as burrow entrances or beneath shrubs to be consumed. And squirrels often seek out the cooling breeze at the top of a shrub, where they eat leaves or collect seeds. The tracker can gain a glimpse of the squirrel's strategy by studying tracks and signs. Look for full-tilt sprints between patches of shade, comparing them to more leisurely gallops made when the sun is not so high. Also look for feeding remnants in favorite shady spots.

The antelope squirrel's **seasonal choice of food** also leads to an understanding of its biology. Because these squirrels must be active throughout the dry season, they turn to insects, which are abundant and provide much moisture, as a staple after the green vegetation of spring has browned. A grasshopper may be flushed from the top of a bush, followed and pounced upon, or Jerusalem crickets may be dug up from underground hiding places. Of course, some seeds are eaten too; for example, you may find handfuls of empty pods under a mesquite tree where a squirrel has foraged. Look for diggings and food remnants where the squirrels are now foraging. Also notice well-used runs: When foraging, antelope squirrels seem to never be far from an escape burrow into which they can dive should danger threaten.

SPECIES AND WEIGHT

Ammospermophilus spp.

4 species in North America

99 to 179 g
(3.5 to 6.3 oz.)

HABITAT

Arid areas of the West, including desert shrub, piñon-juniper woodland, sparsely vegetated grassland, and dry washes. Most abundant

where soil is finely grained or loamy and where annual plant growth is sparse enough to allow rapid travel.

BREEDING

Mating December to early March depending upon species, gestation about 30 days, litter size 5 to 14, 1 litter per year.

DEVELOPMENT

Young emerge from burrow early April to mid-May, depending upon species, and begin to forage right away; they are weaned at about 65 days. At this time they weigh about 65% of adult size but hind feet are 90% of adult size.

SOCIAL HABITS

Home range about 4 to 8 hectares (10 to 20 acres); individuals usually travel less than 150 meters (492 ft.) per day. Antelope squirrels almost always den individually except when female raises young. A local dominance hierarchy prevails rather than defense of exclusive territories.

FEEDING

Prefers new green vegetation including buckwheat, filaree, phacelia, and some grasses early in season, then consumes large numbers of insects including grasshoppers, beetles, ants, and Jerusalem crickets, making up to 90% of its diet, depending upon species, in summer. Seeds of filaree, Joshua tree, ephedra, cactus, mesquite, and many other plants shelled, gathered in cheek pouches, and consumed in protected shady areas; seeds comprise up to 50% of diet seasonally for some species. Antelope squirrels also eat lizards, mice, and other vertebrates, some by catching and others as carrion. During warmer months squirrels active from half an hour after sunrise to late morning, then in late afternoon; in winter, active throughout midday.

SURVIVAL

Does not hibernate or store food. Regulates body temperature through choice of times and places to forage and by running in the sun with tail used as a sunshade. Doesn't tolerate cold well. Vulnerable to predation by badgers, coyotes, kit foxes, snakes, and diurnal raptors. Some squirrels known to live more than 4 years.

SIGNS

Numerous burrows used by each individual for sleeping, resting, or escape. These are usually old burrows of kangaroo rats or other rodents and are indistinguishable from them. Food remains, including seed husks and grasshopper and beetle parts, sometimes around burrow entrances. In foraging areas, seed pods or other plant remains.

RODENTS

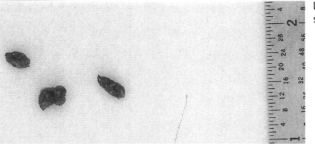

D: Antelope squirrel scat

D

RODENTS

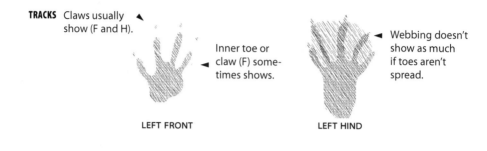

TRACKS Claws usually show (F and H).

Inner toe or claw (F) some- times shows.

Webbing doesn't show as much if toes aren't spread.

LEFT FRONT   LEFT HIND

COMMON GAITS A: Pace walk (common)

B: Diago- nal walk (common)

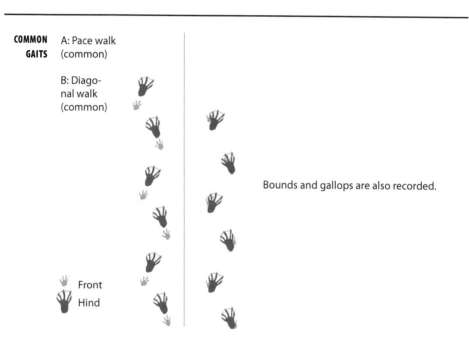

Bounds and gallops are also recorded.

Front

Hind

A   B

TRACK MEASUREMENTS

	Average, inches	Average, cm
Front width	2	5.1
Front length	2⅞	7.2
Hind width	3⁹⁄₁₆	9.1
Hind length	5¹¹⁄₁₆	14.5
Trail width	8	20.3
Stride*	8¹⁵⁄₁₆	22.7

*Pace walk

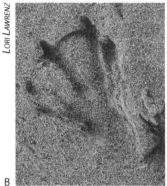

A

B

LORI LAWRENZ

Clear beaver prints are uncommon because the tail drag often covers part of the trail and because of the soggy and changeable nature of shoreline mud and sand. Hind tracks actually resemble those of a large bird more than any other mammal. Note that the hind tracks vary considerably depending upon how much the toes spread. However, the overall trail is distinctive, usually showing the tail drag over a series of partial alternating tracks 20 to 25 cm (8 to 10 in.) apart. Trails most often go straight up the shore at a right angle to the shoreline.

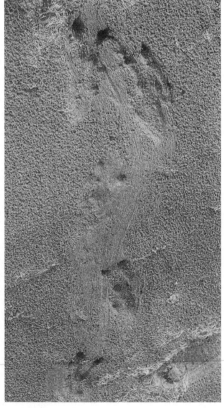

D

C

A: Left front track
B: Right hind track
C: Diagonal walk pattern
D: Common indistinct trail with tail drag

Above all, beavers teach us to be careful with preconceptions. For if we were to see, in all of those felled trees, dams, canals, lodges, and spillways, a rodent with a calculated plan, then we would merely project human traits onto an unsuspecting animal and thereby miss its remarkable essence. Yes, beavers are natural builders and modifiers, but they are **ruled by spontaneity**, not calculation. Carrying no blueprints or priority lists, beavers spend their days interacting with their landscape through a series of urges, so to speak, and in fact, almost all beaver activity is undertaken by individual animals, not pairs or groups. A feeding beaver may drop its food suddenly to caulk its dam. It may start cutting a tree, then abandon it for another project. It may cut a branch to eat, then drop it to find another kind of food. Though there are moments of focused and intense activity, a beaver's habitat is just as sprinkled with signs of random and seemingly illogical projects. Remarkably, these thousands of instinctively driven, individual acts produce impressive results—for example, a 1,219-meter-long (4,000 ft.) dam found in New Hampshire! As trackers, we should avoid seeking a logical purpose in every beaver sign, and rather step back to see the larger patterns. Start by looking at the very freshest construction signs: new mud or branches added to a dam, a very fresh tree felling, some branches dragged to the water, a muddy residue in the water from bank lodge excavation. Then, go back in time and try to see stages of beaver activity from earlier in the season, a few years ago, or decades ago. Many of today's meadows throughout America were old beaver ponds, and this bit of history is accessible to trackers who honor the impulsive beaver.

A beaver colony's **food choice** is another excellent window to behavior. Well-used trails about 30 cm (12 in.) wide may lead to favorite groves, sometimes up to 91 meters (100 yd.) from water, where trees and branches are cut and then dragged to safe feeding spots at the water's edge (or to the lodge or underwater caches). Once felled, a tree may be pruned for its branches or sectioned to provide bark. (Note that a freshly felled tree may be left for a couple of days before beavers return to clip the branches.) Some tree species may be preferred for food, others for construction. Notice the current food choices, remembering that beavers sometimes stray from favored aspen or willow to feed on introduced species or a variety of shrubs. In summer also look for browse onshore, including horsetail, grasses, and forbs that may be heavily used.

Beavers in a given colony are constantly marking their territory to ensure their food supply, so an adventurous tracker, preferably in a canoe or kayak, can get a glimpse of the **size of a local territory** by looking for scent mounds. These are scraped-up mud and debris piles generally on the edges of a territory, upon which a yellowish scent called castoreum is deposited by various members of the colony.

A beaver lodge in Alaska's Chugach State Park

E

F

E: Beavers felled these trees in the Yukon and dragged most of them down to the water. The horizontal trunk in the background is in the process of being sectioned.

F: A horizontally growing willow trunk is a beaver feeding site along the Cosumnes River in California.

G: At the Colorado River, where native trees are scarce, beavers have turned to the introduced tamarisk, a Mediterranean tree. Since the water level fluctuates widely with dam outflow upstream, many beaver projects are interrupted.

G

RODENTS

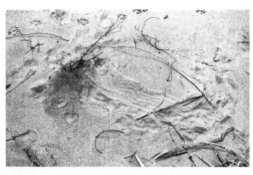

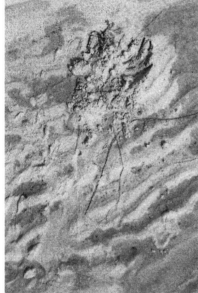

H: Along the Colorado River, beaver trails came onto shore and back into the water nine times within 59 meters (195 ft.); the arrow shows one landing.

I: Several of these spots were stained with dark orange (left) from scent marking.

J: A beaver investigates the shoreline. This spot was under shallow water when a beaver swam toward shore, dragged its chest, and then pushed off strongly with its front feet to pivot to the right and swim away without landing.

K: A well-used trail between ponds at the Cosumnes River, California

137

RODENTS

SPECIES AND WEIGHT — *Castor canadensis*

24 subspecies are described, but widespread transplantation has occurred.

16 to 32 kg
(35 to 70 lb.)

HABITAT — Lakes, rivers, streams, and ponds throughout the United States. Prefers relatively flat terrain where stands of willow, aspen, alder, or cottonwood abound but has adapted to other habitats and to introduced tree species. Requires year-round water that provides, or can be modified to provide, a safe aquatic habitat and sufficient food fairly close to water.

BREEDING — Normally in January or February between monogamous mates. Gestation about 107 days, litters usually 3 to 4 but ranging from 1 to 9; litter size probably determined by food availability. Beavers first breed at 2 to 4 years old; newly established pairs may wander for days before establishing a new territory and building a dam, lodge, or bank burrow there.

DEVELOPMENT — In early summer both parents bring cut branches with leaves into lodge to feed kits. Young first emerge from lodge around early July but travel only at night and then commonly feed on branches and other food brought to the water's edge. Kits may come out before dark by August and typically follow adult beavers or ride on their backs. By about early September, kits first go onto land to cut their own food. They grow from about 3 kg (6½ lb.) as kits to about 10 kg (22 lb.) as yearlings and 18 kg (40 lb.) as adults. Two-year-olds leave colony April to June depending upon area; most settle nearby, but dispersal of up to 238 km (148 miles) in 7 months has been recorded, as has significant overland travel by beavers who follow the scent of water. Several months of temporary living before settlement is common among dispersers.

SOCIAL HABITS — Colonies that each inhabit a section of water normally include a mated adult pair, a few yearlings, and kits of the year. All older colony members help in construction and maintenance of dams and lodges and felling of trees, but each task is usually undertaken individually by one beaver at a time (though some cooperation in moving logs is recorded). A colony's territory is continually marked with scent piles by its members. Within the colony a loose hierarchy led by the adult female and followed by the adult male and then yearlings plays out in occasional competition over food. Where neighboring colonies are dense, adults other than the mated pairs may move between territories.

FEEDING

Beavers emerge singly from their lodge beginning around dusk and feed during the night. Staple food includes bark, leaves, and twigs of willow, aspen, alder, or other common trees; small to large trees are felled and the branches are cut and taken to feeding spots, often in shallow water. After one beaver fells a tree, other members of the colony may converge to feed on it. Larger felled trees may be sectioned and the pieces rolled to the water. Especially during summer beavers feed heavily on grasses, sedges, and the blossoms, leaves, and stems of many kinds of aquatic plants; floating algae are also eaten. Where preferred trees are lacking, beavers eat bark and leaves of wild cherry, serviceberry, mountain mahogany, snowbrush, raspberry, and many other shrubs. Conifers such as white fir are also eaten. Especially in northern climates, beavers cut many branches and store them in an underwater cache near their lodge.

SURVIVAL

Vulnerable to predation by wolves, bears, wolverines, coyotes, and other predators, but legal trapping causes most mortality. Tail slapping alerts colony members of danger.

SIGNS

Conspicuous dams and lodges, built of cut branches and logs and caulked with mud and vegetation. Where stick lodges cannot be built, underground "bank lodges" with underwater entrances. Trails 38 to 51 cm (15 to 20 in.) wide, up to 91 meters (300 ft.) long, at right angles to shoreline leading to favored feeding spots. Cut and partially cut trees and branches, showing 0.6-cm-wide (¼ in.) incisor cuts and chip debris. Grazed grasses and other vegetation on land, particularly in summer. Scent-marked scrapes or piles of mud, sometimes mixed with vegetation, particularly at edges of a colony's territory. Especially in North, "plunge holes" some yards away from shore that lead through underground tunnel to water. Scats about 1.9 cm (¾ in.) wide and 2.5 cm (1 in.) long, "sawdusty," sometimes seen floating on water.

L: Beaver incisor marks
M: Freshly maintained dams show packed debris, including mud and green vegetation.

TRACKS

F and H feet often register only from the ball forward. ▶

LEFT FRONT

Slender toes; inner and outer ones in H track often spread out

◀ No proximal pads on H foot

LEFT HIND

COMMON GAITS

A: Slow gallop (common)

B: Fast gallop (common)

C: Slow gallop to bound

D: Diagonal walk (occasional)

Front
Hind

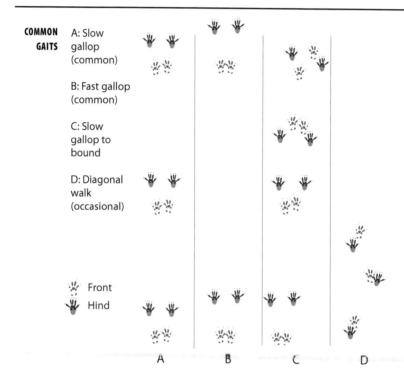

A   B   C   D

TRACK MEASUREMENTS

	Average, inches	Average, cm	Usual range, inches*
Front width	$^9\!/_{16}$	1.4	$^3\!/_8$ to $^3\!/_4$
Front length	$^{11}\!/_{16}$	1.7	$^9\!/_{16}$ to $^7\!/_8$
Hind width	$^{11}\!/_{16}$	1.8	$^1\!/_2$ to $^7\!/_8$
Hind length	$^3\!/_4$	2.0	$^9\!/_{16}$ to $1^1\!/_8$
Trail width	$2^3\!/_{16}$	5.5	$1^3\!/_4$ to $2^1\!/_2$
Stride**	$14^3\!/_8$	36.6	$6^5\!/_{16}$ to $25^7\!/_8$

*More than 95% of my measurements fall within this range.   **Gallop

RODENTS

A

The trail width of a chipmunk's typical gallop pattern, about 5 cm (2 in.), puts it in the range of a woodrat's, an antelope squirrel's, or a small ground squirrel's; other gallopers would have larger or smaller trail widths. A woodrat could be eliminated from consideration if no proximal pads register in a full hind print (see "Woodrat" pages). Antelope squirrels rarely share habitat with chipmunks, and ground squirrels usually show diagonal placement of the front tracks in a gallop, not the side-by-side placement we almost always see in the southern part of California. (Some observers, though, have recorded diagonal placement of front feet in some chipmunk species.) Most ground squirrels weigh at least 50% to 100% more than a chipmunk.

FINE POINTS

A: Common gallop pattern with front tracks placed side by side

B: Clear front (four-toed) and hind (five-toed) tracks

C: A chipmunk running on the balls of its feet tends to spread its toes and leaves no heel impressions in the hind tracks.

D: Commonly seen muffled tracks, with full hind heel showing

RODENTS

B

C

D

The cute bundle of energy called a chipmunk is so entertaining to watch, we might ask why on earth we should bother to track it. Well, we need something to do when the chipmunk has retired for its midday rest, and besides, chipmunks almost beg us to dive into the **subtle track and sign reading** required to understand them. It seems that chipmunk trails constantly go across tree limbs, through shrub branches, and over fallen logs, hitting the ground only where tracking is impossible. Here's where watching the animal, then going over to see the signs it just left, expands our tracking vocabulary exponentially. Even in pine needles, a gallop pattern with its characteristic pressure releases eventually reveals itself. The stops and starts of a chipmunk entering a foraging area, the diggings for seeds, the momentary perching on a stump to eat a nut, and the crazy pirouettes of hyperactivity all can be noticed, studied from their sign, and then put together to show something bigger about the chipmunk's habits. Put all of the signs you see into a pattern and you will likely have discovered the chipmunk's center of activity for the day, including travel routes and foraging areas. Also try to find the chipmunk's nighttime nest, which is usually some distance away from the activity center; you may have to be very aware early in the morning or at dusk, often the only times a chipmunk leaves or enters this secretive spot.

A newly emerged litter of young chipmunks offers a window to the **rapid development** critical to these species. About five weeks after birth, usually in late June to early August, young chipmunks emerge and begin exploring and playing around their nest; in many western species, the mother may soon move them to a tree nest. (They are only half the adult weight, but their feet are 80% of adult size.) In just a week they are eating solid food and begin foraging ever farther from the nest on their daily excursions until they approach adult weight by early fall. Notice additional foraging activity around a chipmunk's core area at this time. Juveniles often make long exploratory forays to new areas before hibernation.

Each chipmunk population is adapted to a different local habitat, giving the tracker a chance to study **local food choices** dictated by season and weather as well as available resources. Chipmunks are natural gatherers and storers, using their cheek pouches to carry food to scatter caches or to their underground nests. (One chipmunk had 339 lodgepole pine seeds in its cheek pouches at one time; another had 1,169 grass seeds!) Look for gathering magnets such as trees or shrubs with developing seeds or fruits. Look for evidence of digging for seeds and fungi; chipmunks are especially active diggers after a rain because they can smell underground food much better. On raised places look for food remnants such as shells or flower parts. Toward fall, notice the quality of local seed production. Ask yourself where you would find the equivalent of tens of thousands of seeds to get you through the winter and you will likely find a center of chipmunk activity.

A Jeffrey pine stump serves as a recent feeding site for a chipmunk who has left pine-nut shells.

RODENTS

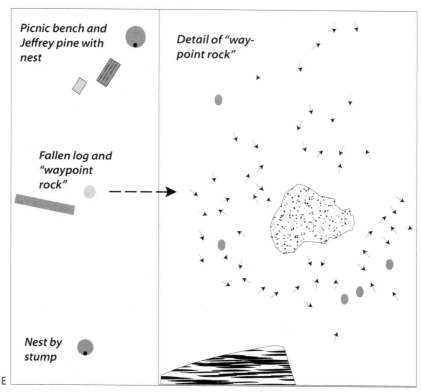

*Picnic bench and
Jeffrey pine with
nest*

*Detail of "way-
point rock"*

*Fallen log and
"waypoint
rock"*

*Nest by
stump*

E

E: Chipmunks use prominent landmarks to locate seed caches they have buried. In this chipmunk's territory, concentrated activity occurs near a rock. Each of the arrows in the detail at right shows where a set of galloping tracks in pine needles indicated a direction of travel from their pressure releases. Many of these sets are unconnected with one another and indicate many separate trips. While the chipmunk sometimes ran up onto the rock, most often it just skirted its edge between destinations. Shaded ovals indicate places where the chipmunk dug for food.

F

F: Chipmunk diggings are smaller and more delicate than those of tree squirrels. This one is about 3.2 cm (1¼ in.) wide.

G and H: The chipmunk's characteristic hyperactivity can be read in track formations and pressure releases. In G a few clear prints, in the lower right among the pine needles, lead to a sort of "pirouette" pattern common throughout this animal's feeding area. The chipmunk was observed spinning left or right, often in 360-degree turns, between bouts of rapid sniffing or light pawing of the ground. A pattern like this one was created after four to six pirouettes, after which the chipmunk ran away to another spot. In H a quick stop is evident from reverse-disk pressure releases in the hind tracks that show braking (arrows).

G

H

I: A Merriam's chipmunk has emerged from its burrow in early February, on a sunny day after a snowstorm. These temporary forays are common during the winter at 1,524 meters (5,000 ft.), where snow does not accumulate for more than a few days.

I

SPECIES AND WEIGHT   *Tamias* and *Neotamias* spp.

21 species in North America

28 to 120 g (1 to 4 oz.)

Female usually slightly larger than male

HABITAT   Western species occupy montane coniferous forests (fir, pine, cedar, and spruce), piñon-juniper woodland, oak woodland, chaparral (especially manzanita), and coastal forests of redwood, fir, and madrone; habitats range from sea level to 3,700 meters (11,000 ft.). Eastern US species inhabits deciduous forests and hardwood stands within boreal forest. Many species prefer rocky areas, the edges of open meadows, or brushy understory that provide secure nesting places. Sagebrush desert and alpine tundra are habitats for one species.

BREEDING   Breeding follows emergence from annual hibernation, lasts about 1 month in a given area, usually April and May (earlier in arid southern habitats, later at high elevations). Female in estrus may "chip" repeatedly, then males may congregate, with much chasing, and follow a female prior to one copulating with her. Pair bonding does not occur. Gestation 32 to 36 days, depending upon species, litters usually 3 to 6, born in underground nest. Eastern US species may have 2 breeding periods, February through April and June and July.

DEVELOPMENT   Young emerge from nest about 5 weeks after birth, usually late June to early August, depending upon location and year. At this age, young are half or less of adult weight, but feet are 80% of adult size. Rapid growth occurs for about 3 weeks as young play and explore. In numerous western species the mother commonly moves her litter from the underground natal burrow to a tree nest shortly after their emergence. Young are almost adult weight, and feet are adult size, by 4 to 6 weeks after emergence. Juveniles may use crevices or cavities as temporary dens as they disperse.

SOCIAL HABITS   Home ranges about 0.8 to 2 hectares (2 to 5 acres), often overlapping, but individual chipmunks' "activity centers," where most foraging occurs, are spaced apart and enforced by occasional chases of intruders. Underground or tree nest may be at edge or in center of home range. During raising of young, female chases away intruders from an area 30 to 50 meters (98 to 164 ft.) around the den. Home ranges fairly stable from one year to next, but most juveniles disperse. Alarm calls differ in character for different chipmunk species in the same area, but these calls apparently are not used for spacing. In eastern chipmunk, home ranges are reportedly smaller and there are more displays of territoriality than in western species.

FEEDING

Seeds, especially of pines, oaks, junipers, and hardwoods, comprise a major part of the diet, are collected in cheek pouches, and stored in scattered buried caches during summer and in overwintering nests in the fall. Seeds from shrubs (including manzanita and ceanothus), forbs, and grasses are important in some areas. Flowers, roots, caterpillars, and arthropods supplement the diet, and fungi, especially underground, are eaten in large amounts, especially when seed crops are low. Green vegetation may be eaten when other foods are scarce. Most chipmunks are active for several hours after dawn, and in late afternoon. Buried seed caches are found through random searches, memory, and olfaction.

SURVIVAL

Chipmunks are vulnerable to predation by weasels, martens, bobcats, red-tailed hawks, goshawks, and northern harriers among others; mortality is higher for males because of their wide-ranging behavior during breeding season. Alarm calls alert other chipmunks and include "chucks," "chips," "trilling," and, while a chipmunk is running away, "chippering." Most species hibernate for about 5 months per year, but in parts of their range, 1 or 2 species do not hibernate.

SIGNS

Underground nests have an inconspicuous entrance about 5 cm (2 in.) in diameter, without an apron of dirt; they are often located at base of shrub or rock. At least 12 western species are known to use tree nests in summer, in woodpecker holes or on branches of trees, especially under dense aggregates of twigs and foliage called witches'-broom. These nests are usually composed of dried grasses and are about 30 cm (1 ft.) in diameter. Some summer nests are temporarily used crevices or holes. Scats are about 0.6 cm (¼ in.) long, tubular, usually unconnected, sometimes found at feeding spots. Numerous diggings for buried seeds or fungi. Feeding "perches" on stumps, logs, or rocks with seed or flower remnants.

J

J: Chipmunk scat

RODENTS

FOX SQUIRREL Track ID

TRACKS

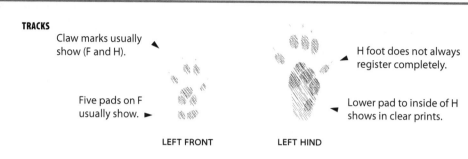

Claw marks usually show (F and H).

Five pads on F usually show. ▶

H foot does not always register completely.

Lower pad to inside of H shows in clear prints.

LEFT FRONT   LEFT HIND

COMMON GAITS

A: Gallop (common)

B: Diagonal walk (occasional)

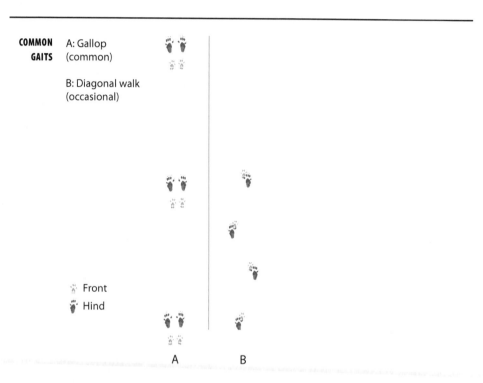

Front

Hind

A   B

TRACK MEASUREMENTS

	Usual range, inches	Usual range, cm
Front width	1 to 1⅜	2.5 to 3.5
Front length	1¼ to 1⅞	3.2 to 4.8
Hind width	1³⁄₁₆ to 1¾	3.0 to 4.4
Hind length	1⅛ to 2	2.9 to 5.1
Trail width	3⅞ to 4½	9.8 to 11.4
Stride*	6 to 30	15.2 to 76.2

*Gallop

A: Common gallop pattern
B and C: Left front and left hind tracks, respectively

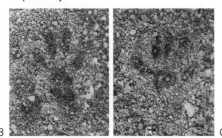

B

C

Fox squirrel trails almost always show a gallop pattern, usually with the front tracks positioned side by side, not diagonally. The four (front) and five (hind) tracks resemble other rodents'; they are usually smaller than a woodchuck's and are in the range of gray squirrels' for track size, trail width, and stride. In the eastern United States, fox squirrels are generally larger than gray squirrels, but in the West, where fox squirrels have been introduced, fox squirrels may be smaller than gray squirrels. Distinguishing the two from tracks is challenging; note that fox squirrels commonly venture considerably farther from the tree canopy than gray squirrels. **Vs. ground squirrels:** Ground-squirrel trail widths are usually smaller than fox squirrels', and ground-squirrel tracks lack the back heel pad that fox and gray squirrels have.

FINE POINTS

RODENTS

DOUG GAULKE

DOUG GAULKE

D and E: Left front and left hind feet, respectively

D

E

149

RODENTS

In a rodent personality test, the fox squirrel would score high on the extroversion and independence scales, because it is so comfortable living on woodland edges and venturing into open space where gray squirrels would fear to go. This **"edge affinity"** is a major part of its biology, affecting choices about food, nesting sites, and travel routes. Not only does this make interesting study for us trackers, it has also made fox squirrels quite accessible. The conversion of dense forests to agricultural and recreational land has allowed the fox squirrel to thrive throughout much of the Midwest and East, and also in urban and suburban areas of the West where it has been introduced. College campuses, city parks, golf courses, and the wooded edges of farmland are perfect habitat for this squirrel, which plays out its natural biology there in very interesting ways. Start by noticing travel routes in the open; one squirrel carrying a corncob was tracked half a mile from a field to its forest refuge. Also look for diggings as far as a hundred yards from the forest edge—perhaps out on the fairway or in a grassy area across the parking lot from a city park.

If you're tracking fox squirrels in modified habitat, study food choice adaptations. A fox squirrel may make seasonal routes from nesting areas to an orange grove, where it leaves behind peels from the eviscerated fruit. Or it may feast on eucalyptus seeds, palm fruits, or the cones of ornamental pines. Discovering fox squirrel nests is another fascinating exercise, especially where trees are not native and landscapes are manicured. Ask yourself where sheltered locations and building materials might be; you will likely be led to some surprises, such as a nest at the top of a palm tree or constructed entirely from eucalyptus bark. If your habitat is relatively unaltered, there may be both gray and fox squirrels present; this is your chance to settle down for a few hours observing differences in habitat use. While food choices of the two species are very similar, biologists have noticed differences in nest locations and materials, and in the amount of ground activity, as well as slightly different activity times. Because the variations are local, you need to learn directly from the squirrels.

The fox squirrel's **social behavior** offers some interesting observation possibilities. Squirrels communicate a lot using their tails, and during breeding season a male's approach to a female is often accompanied by a slow-moving, circular or front-to-back tail wag that is responded to by the female with, shall we say, open paws. On the other hand, a male approaching with a vigorous tail wag often precipitates a chase. A male following a female, sniffing the ground where she has been, is also a common sight. Like gray squirrels, fox squirrels scent-mark during breeding time as well as to mark where they have been. Observe the squirrels and also look for chewed areas on branches or tree trunks where squirrels have left scent from oral glands. In city parkland notice how fox squirrels space themselves according to regular food sources and nesting sites by scent marking and occasional chases.

F

G

H

F: In an Arcadia, California, city park, introduced fox squirrels have little nest-building material because of the manicured vegetation. A nest is instead located in the dead fronds at the top of a tall palm tree.

G: A tracking station dusted with powdered clay recorded interesting sideward motion of the left hind foot. As the squirrel exited to the right, this foot was the last to move, leaving plates both from the side of the foot and from the bottom heel pad.

H: A well-used route up a tree is marked with claw marks.

I: At the onset of the breeding season, a fox squirrel was observed chewing on the bark of a regularly used tree to scent-mark (arrow). The mark is minutes old.

I

FOX SQUIRREL   Notes for the Tracker

SPECIES AND WEIGHT   *Sciurus niger*

10 subspecies in North America

0.7 to 1.2 kg
(1.5 to 2.6 lb.)

*Fox squirrels have also been intro-
duced into limited areas of Washington, Idaho, California, and New
Mexico.*

HABITAT   Wooded areas of the eastern United States, including deciduous forests and, especially in the Southeast, pine and mixed pine forests. Prefers woodland with open areas, and frequents forest edges adjacent to open space. Well adapted, therefore, to sparse woods adjacent to agricultural and suburban areas, and to urban parklands. Introduced into urban and suburban areas of the West.

BREEDING   Breeding usually January and February or June and July; some females may breed twice annually. Males approach estrous females and the pair communicates through tail displays. Chases, "passing over," and "identification kisses" may follow. Play behavior or grooming may follow copulation. Gestation about 45 days, litters usually 2 or 3. Natal den either in a tree cavity or well-constructed leaf nest. Fox squirrels may breed first usually at 10 to 14 months.

DEVELOPMENT   Young, born naked and blind, are weaned at 8 to 12 weeks, become self-sufficient at 3 to 4 months (mid-June to mid-July for young born from winter breeding). Adult weight achieved at about 16 months.

SOCIAL HABITS   Nonterritorial, but spacing is aided by scent marking with cheek or oral glands. Some chases, especially among males. Amicable behavior including mutual grooming, oral-nasal contact, and play wrestling. Home ranges of 0.4 to 7.4 hectares (1 to 18 acres) recorded. Some nest-sharing of 2 to 5 adults observed, but fox squirrels are more solitary than gray squirrels.

FEEDING   Seeds or nuts of trees including oak, hickory, beech, walnut, Osage orange, mulberry, and pine constitute much of diet, supplemented seasonally with fungi and with flowers and buds of trees such as elm. Near altered habitat, fruits from cultivated or ornamental plants seasonally important, such as corn, wheat, apples, oranges, and eucalyptus. Nuts cached in shallow ground depressions, especially in cooler months; caches covered with loose debris. Some foods retrieved from under snow and recached in tree crevices. High level of moisture in soil allows easier retrieval of cached nuts by scent. Diurnal with activity peaks often in early morning and early afternoon.

SURVIVAL Hawks, owls, snakes, and mammalian predators take some fox squirrels. Squirrel hunting is allowed in many states.

SIGNS Dens in cavities in trees such as beech and oak, with circular entrance about 7.6 to 10.2 cm (3 to 4 in.) in diameter, sometimes with evidence of gnawing around it where tree's new growth begins to fill in. Also, nests built of sticks and leaves, positioned at branch junctions or high in trees such as oaks and pines; these nests often have inconspicuous entrance at one end. Leaf nests commonly used in winter as much as, or even more than, cavity dens. Lighter summer nests may be present in the vicinity of a more permanent den. Feeding signs including nut remnants and diggings. Scent-marking blemishes on branches or on tree trunks. Scats are pellets, about 0.5 cm (³⁄₁₆ in.) in diameter.

J

J: Fox squirrel scat

K: Remnants of a chewed fruit at the base of a palm tree in an urban park

K

RODENTS

GRAY SQUIRREL Track ID

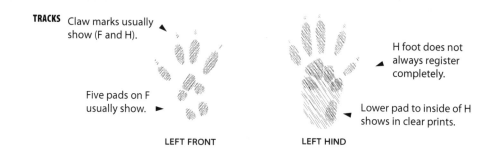

TRACKS

Claw marks usually show (F and H).

Five pads on F usually show. ►

LEFT FRONT

H foot does not always register completely.

Lower pad to inside of H shows in clear prints.

LEFT HIND

RODENTS

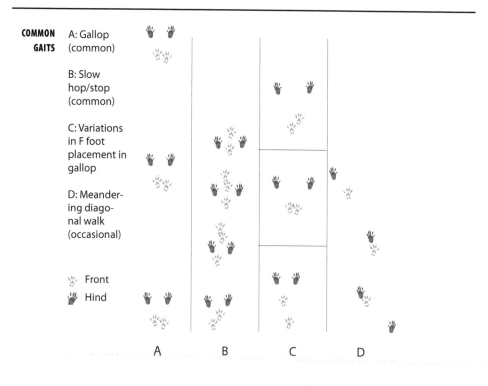

COMMON GAITS

A: Gallop (common)

B: Slow hop/stop (common)

C: Variations in F foot placement in gallop

D: Meandering diagonal walk (occasional)

Front
Hind

A   B   C   D

TRACK MEASUREMENTS

	Average, inches	Average, cm	Usual range, inches*
Front width	1⅛	2.8	7⁄16 to 1½
Front length	1⁹⁄₁₆	3.9	15⁄16 to 2
Hind width	1⁵⁄₁₆	3.4	⅞ to 1¾
Hind length	1¹¹⁄₁₆	4.4	1 to 2½
Trail width	4⁵⁄₁₆	11.0	3½ to 6¼
Stride**	19⅝	49.9	9 to 37⅛

*More than 95% of my measurements fall within this range.   **Gallop

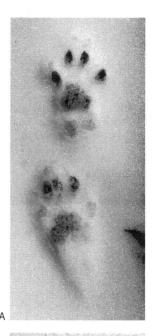

The gallop pattern and the four (front) and five (hind) toe count puts you in the rodent family, and measuring trail width eliminates all but a few possibilities. **Ground squirrels** may weigh the same as small gray squirrels, but their trail widths are almost always less than 8.9 cm (3½ in.) while gray squirrels' are usually at least that. If the hind track registers fully, look for the rear heel pad to the inside of the track, which the ground squirrel lacks. The **Douglas's (red) squirrel** tracks may overlap the gray squirrel's in track size and trail width, but usually the Douglas's front track pairs in a gallop are right next to each other, while the gray's front pairs are usually somewhat staggered and variable. The Douglas's squirrel also lacks the hind heel pad mentioned above. (Douglas's squirrel also weighs half as much as the gray.) The **fox squirrel**, introduced in some urban areas of the West, is about the same size as the gray squirrel and its tracks are very similar.

A

RODENTS

C

D

A: Front (top) and hind tracks in snow

B: Common high-speed gallop

C: The tassel-eared squirrel of the Grand Canyon area tends to place its front feet next to each other.

D: The western gray squirrel often places its front tracks diagonally. In this photo the hind feet do not register completely.

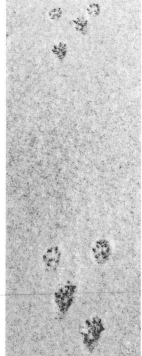

B

A gray squirrel's **three-dimensional habitat use** not only rescues the tunnel-visioned tracker from fixation on the ground, it is the very best entry point to the squirrel's biology. Squirrels depend upon the tree canopy for safe travel, nesting, and resting, but they also need terra firma—for caching and retrieving nuts throughout the year, for other foraging, and for travel between foraging areas. Squirrels, in fact, spend about half their daylight hours on the ground. Our principal task as trackers, then, is to ask, where do the squirrels come to the ground, and what do they do when they get there? We can begin by finding regular aboveground travel routes (in trees, along fallen logs or fences, even across telephone wires).

 Observing squirrels themselves, especially in early morning or late afternoon, is a good starting point. Listen and look for squirrels, follow them with your eyes; look for travel origins like conspicuous leaf nests, destinations like favorite feeding trees, and logical routes down to the ground. Decide where you'd travel as a squirrel, and confirm your judgment by setting up tracking boxes where they would come to the ground. Signs and tracks on the ground tell us why a squirrel uses some ground areas and not others. Pay attention to sunlight and shadows, for squirrels often choose dappled shade, where they are best camouflaged, to bury and retrieve food. When you find squirrel tracks in open areas, notice where they originate and end, and read the regularity of the trail. Squirrels moving on the ground from forest to open areas usually stop and hesitate more often than they do when returning to safety.

Seasonal food preferences can be read with great precision by a dedicated tracker, but the key is aging the feeding signs to discover what activity is current within hours or days. In late winter and early spring, look for cache-retrieval digs. In June squirrels in the pine forest begin to harvest developing pine cones, "working" certain individual trees for several days. Use your wide-angle vision to scan the forest for dropping debris, and survey a squirrel's habitat for fresh cone remnants. In the fall, when acorns are gathered and buried, look for areas where squirrels have made dozens of trips per day between an oak tree and a preferred caching area. Note that squirrels often dig two or three "dummy" holes for every real one, to confuse potential cache robbers, and they methodically disguise their caches—a good test for a tracker's awareness!

 Following the energetic barking of squirrels can lead to an understanding of the gray squirrel's **social hierarchy**. Dominant squirrels bark, foot-thump, and chase rival squirrels. In the mating season, between January and March, you may find an entourage of three or more male squirrels following a female in estrus, the dominant male leading the way and periodically chasing rivals away. After mating, the female may be found carrying nest material to a tree nest. Sometimes long twigs or shredded material drop to the ground under a nest.

A gray squirrel's favorite feeding spot is revealed by numerous cores and bracts of Jeffrey pine cones; gray squirrels usually "work" certain individual trees for a few days to extract the developing seeds from green cones.

Habitat use by several generations of western gray squirrels in Frazier Park, California. Squirrels almost always preferred aboveground routes, using a rail fence, trees, and the house roof, and traveled on the ground only in certain food-caching and foraging areas. Ground travel away from trees was limited to a few regular routes between the habitat shown here and other foraging areas. Most foraging was done in the shade, and nest trees were never approached from the ground. Certain trees were magnets for food gathering: the two Jeffrey pines with their maturing green cones in June, piñon pines in August, and canyon oaks in October. Throughout the year cached food was dug up, and in drought years piñon and Jeffrey pine bark was eaten. Nest material was gathered from a straw bale archery target and from hammock rope gnawed off and fluffed up. Two Jeffrey pines and the roof were "social areas" where squirrels chased one another.

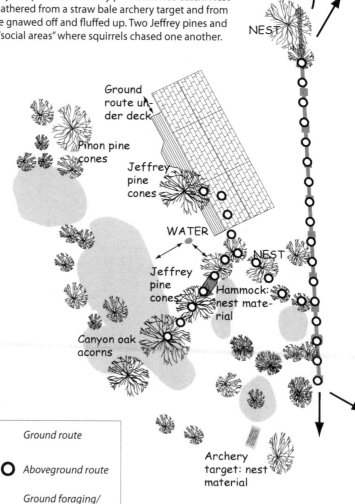

Pinon pine cones

NEST

Ground route under deck

Pinon pine cones

Jeffrey pine cones

WATER

Jeffrey pine cones

NEST

Hammock: nest material

Canyon oak acorns

Archery target: nest material

→ Ground route

O O O Aboveground route

Ground foraging/ caching area

E: Leaf nests, or dreys, become conspicuous when deciduous trees, like this oak in the Kern River Preserve, California, drop their leaves.

F: Nesting material is shredded from this hammock as a squirrel would do from bark.

G: Gray squirrels often choose logs as routes, even though they may be only a few inches off the ground.

SPECIES AND WEIGHT

Sciurus spp.*

5 species in
North America

520 g to 1.0 kg
(1.1 to 2.2 lb.)

Eastern gray squirrel smaller
than western gray squirrel

HABITAT   Forested areas from sea level to
2,438 meters (8,000 ft.) where oaks,
pine trees, madrone, California bay,
hickory, chestnut, or other trees producing large seeds afford adequate food and
nest sites. Prefers forests with larger-diameter trees and favors canopies that
allow arboreal travel.

BREEDING   Most mating between December and February (Feb to Mar for tassel-eared
squirrel), but some late spring and summer mating common, especially for eastern gray squirrel. Females have 1 litter (usually 2 to 4 offspring) per year, and
may breed in 1st year where food is abundant. Several males congregate near
an estrous female's nest in early morning and follow her throughout the day.
Dominant male initiates many chases of subordinate males, and female often
repels suitors until she is ready to breed. Dominant males breed most, but often
a female breaks away from her following entourage and mates with a subordinate male. Gestation about 44 days, young born in a tree cavity where available
or in a leaf nest high in a tree.

DEVELOPMENT   Female may move nestlings to a new leaf nest shortly after birth. Young may
take short trips from nest at 4 to 5 weeks, weaned at 8 to 9 weeks (usually mid-
Apr to June), and independent at 4 to 5 months (usually July through Aug).
Much overlap between juvenile and adult weights in a local population, because
adult squirrel weight decreases in summer prior to fall nut crop.

SOCIAL HABITS   Gray squirrels are generally solitary except when young travel near mother for a
while after leaving nest, and during breeding season. Nevertheless, dominance
hierarchy exists in a local population, expressed occasionally during feeding
competition and often during breeding season, through tail wagging, foot
thumping, barking, and chasing. Some males show wounds on tail, flanks, or

*Western and eastern gray squirrels (*S. griseus* and *S. carolinensis*), tassel-eared squirrel (*S. aberti*), Arizona
squirrel (*S. arizonensis*), and red-bellied squirrel (*S. aureogaster*)

neck from breeding combat. Subordinate squirrels show submissive body language when approaching common food source. Home ranges usually 0.4 to 7 hectares (0.8 to 18 acres); males' ranges overlap, females' generally do not. Two squirrels sometimes share a nest for sleeping; eastern gray squirrels often congregate in larger numbers in tree cavities in winter.

FEEDING

High-energy nuts from oaks, pines, walnuts, hickories, or California bay, and nuts from developing pine cones, make up vast majority of diet seasonally. Nuts buried in fall in individual "scatter caches" are retrieved throughout winter and spring, using excellent spatial memory as well as scent. Fungi, especially underground species associated with tree roots, comprise up to 85% of diet in some areas during summer; inner bark of pine trees also may contribute more than 50% of diet when higher-energy foods are scarce. Tree buds, developing male pine flowers, mistletoe berries, wildflower leaves and seeds, and even carrion supplement the diet. Squirrels are active from dawn to sunset, usually with rest periods during midday, and often spend half their time on the ground foraging or caching food. Foods usually consumed from a tree perch; individual trees are heavily foraged at peak production time.

SURVIVAL

Principal predators are hawks, especially goshawks, but some squirrels are caught by mammals also. Principal natural mortality, especially for juveniles, is starvation from low food production in some years. Squirrels are legally hunted in many states, and road kills contribute to mortality. While squirrels routinely take advantage of water sources, they seem to survive droughts.

SIGNS

Conspicuous leaf nests, 36 to 48 cm (14 to 19 in.) in diameter, with 15-cm-diameter (6 in.) inner nest filled with shredded bark or grasses; located high up in large-diameter oaks, pines, or other trees. Nests built by females for raising young but subsequently used and maintained by other squirrels also. (Winter nests in tree cavities where these are available.) Marking spots along travel routes, consisting of gnawed bark and branches rubbed with scent, especially by adult males. Abundant feeding signs including pine cone debris, clipped pine branches, acorn and other seed husks, and conspicuous diggings in soil, often concentrated around favorite trees. Scats resemble small deer pellets, usually 0.3 to 0.6 cm (⅛ to ¼ in.) long, deposited in groups on elevated surfaces.

H: A gray squirrel has stripped a developing Jeffrey pine cone, leaving bracts, seed remnants, and the core of the cone.

H

RODENTS

161

TRACKS

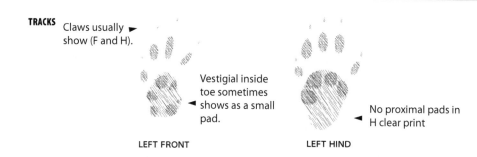

Claws usually ▶ show (F and H).

Vestigial inside toe sometimes ◀ shows as a small pad.

No proximal pads in ◀ H clear print

LEFT FRONT

LEFT HIND

COMMON GAITS

A: Gallop (common)

B: Slow gallop (occasional)

C: Diagonal walk (occasional)

D: Pace walk (occasional)

⠿ Front
⠿ Hind

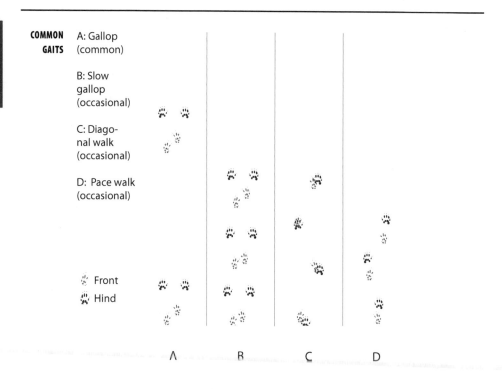

A   B   C   D

TRACK MEASUREMENTS

	Average, inches	Average, cm	Usual range, inches*
Front width	$^{11}/_{16}$	1.7	$^{3}/_{8}$ to 1
Front length	$^{7}/_{8}$	2.3	$^{3}/_{8}$ to $1^{1}/_{4}$
Hind width	$^{7}/_{8}$	2.2	$^{5}/_{8}$ to $1^{1}/_{2}$
Hind length	$1^{1}/_{8}$	2.9	$^{5}/_{8}$ to $1^{3}/_{4}$
Trail width	$2^{3}/_{4}$	7.1	2 to $3^{1}/_{2}$
Stride**	$16^{1}/_{4}$	41.3	$4^{1}/_{4}$ to 33

*More than 97% of my measurements fall within this range.   **Gallop

Ground-squirrel tracks must be distinguished from those of other medium-size rodents in your habitat. **Gray-squirrel** tracks are usually larger, commonly showing a trail width of at least 8.9 cm (3½ in.). Also, a ground-squirrel hind track lacks the proximal pad that tree squirrels show. **Chipmunk** tracks are usually smaller; chipmunk trails also almost always show side-by-side placement of the front tracks in a gallop, as opposed to the diagonal placement of ground-squirrel front tracks. **Antelope squirrel** tracks are also usually smaller. **Woodrats** may overlap in weight with some ground squirrels; look for the knobs at the back of the hind heel pad, which ground squirrels lack. Because there are twenty ground-squirrel species in North America and they vary in weight, it's best to know the size of your local species and to catalog the two or three other medium-size rodents whose tracks may be confused with the ground squirrel's.

FINE POINTS

RODENTS

A: Common gallop pattern
B: The left front track showing vestigial fifth toe at bottom right
C: The right hind track
D: Gallop patterns in dry soil often look scuffed due to high speed; this photo also shows a light drag from the squirrel's bushy tail.

RODENTS

Ground squirrels may appear to be self-absorbed in their daily activities of feeding, grooming, sunning, and running about. But try stalking up on a colony for a closer view and you will notice the **hyperawareness** that is the very key to their lives. At least one squirrel always seems to be on the alert, scanning its surroundings in a three-point posture (two back legs and the tail) called a "picket." At the slightest sign of danger, an alarm call may go out, sending every squirrel diving down into their burrows. Ground squirrels are known to distinguish real threats from harmless intruders; for example, a raven carrying food in its beak is reacted to less than a raven with an empty beak. Ground squirrels know their territory well, and Beechey ground squirrels even patrol their ranges for snakes to protect their young (who, unlike adults, are not immune to rattlesnake venom). Many tracks and signs illuminate the squirrels' vigilance. Try to find lookout posts on fences, rocks, or burrow mounds that show constant use. Because of their vulnerability in open space, ground squirrels seem to have only two gears in their transmissions: hurry and stop. As you study tracks, notice the characteristic disk behind the toes of most hind tracks, showing high speed; also look for stop-and-start groups out in the open. Notice the location of squirrel burrows and runs and how the choice of open habitat maximizes their awareness skills.

The **annual rhythm of a ground squirrel's life**, built around food availability, is another good window. Use tracks and signs to lead you to the point in the cycle the local population is in. Male squirrels emerge from their annual dormancy first (Jan to Apr, depending on the area) and establish their territories. Two or three weeks later, females emerge, and they mate soon after. At this time look for signs of fresh digging as burrows are refurbished. Females may dig less conspicuous natal burrows and chase other squirrels away from their area. Also at this time look for early feeding signs; ground squirrels commonly forage right around their burrows first, clipping all of the vegetation away, and gradually move outward. Two months after mating, the young squirrels emerge and spend their first week within a few feet of the burrow entrance. If you observe a natal den with the young outside, study tracks outside the burrow during the squirrels' midday nap. Young squirrels gradually move away from the burrow in their daily foraging and after a few weeks begin to establish their own burrows; at this time look for expanded trail networks, as well as fresh diggings on the outskirts of a mother's territory. From this time until they go into estivation or hibernation, ground squirrels "binge feed" to gain weight (one adolescent female doubled her weight in eight days!). If your local population is in this period of its cycle, follow tracks and runs to find primary food sources. Ground squirrels may climb high in trees to feed on acorns, Joshua tree seeds, or elderberries, for example.

After a brush fire scoured this grassland on the Santa Rosa Plateau in Southern California, a previously hidden Beechey-ground-squirrel run became apparent.

E

F

G

E: Diagonal walk pattern, moving from right to left
F: While this pace walk (right to left) resembles a skunk's trail, the shape of the front and hind tracks, as well as the absence of long claw impressions, makes this a ground squirrel.
G: A ground squirrel scent mark

H: The burrows of many ground-squirrel species, including the Beechey ground squirrel in Southern California, show large aprons of earth outside their entrances (but entrances in dense underbrush may be less conspicuous). Other species may show no dirt aprons. Burrows may be plugged from within during hot weather, especially among desert species.

I: Networks of well-used runs lead between entrances, as well as to feeding areas. This squirrel colony is on the outskirts of Bakersfield, California.

RODENTS

SPECIES AND WEIGHT *Xerospermophilis, Ictido-mys, Callospemophilis, Otospermophilus, Polioc-itellus,* and *Urocitellus* spp.

20 species in North America

100 to 950 g (3.5 to 33.5 oz.)

Male larger than female

HABITAT From sea level to 3,566 meters (11,700 ft.) in many habitats including grassland, shrubland, mountain meadows, deserts, sagebrush, chaparral, rocky canyons, roadsides, open woodland, yellow-pine forests, and agricultural areas. All species depend upon soil that can be dug for underground nests, and most prefer open space with high visibility around or near burrows.

BREEDING Breeding shortly after females emerge from annual dormancy, e.g., February in lowlands to May at highest elevations. Much territorial chasing of males by other males, and females by other females, before and during mating season. Copulation takes place in burrows after females seek out nearby males' dens. Gestation about 30 days, litters usually about 5 to 6. Female may dig new natal den or refurbish unused den rather than use most conspicuous burrow; natal den entrance sometimes plugged from within for a time and may lack conspicuous dirt apron outside.

DEVELOPMENT Young emerge from burrow about 1 month after birth (Apr 1 to early May at low elevations, to June or July at highest ones), spend their first week or so within 4.6 meters (15 ft.) of their burrow, then gradually move farther away in daily foraging. Much play and chasing among young squirrels. About 1 month after emergence (depending upon species), young begin to dig or renovate their own burrows, and there are many new prominent trails and diggings. At emergence, young are about 30% of adult weight, but their feet are already more than 80% of adult size. Weight gain is rapid and young are adult size by beginning of dormancy (Aug to Nov depending upon species). Some young, especially females, settle close to their mother's burrow.

SOCIAL HABITS Males are especially territorial and dominant during breeding season; females are territorial and dominant during pregnancy and rearing of young. Chases and fights define territory. Degree of sociability (burrow sharing and interaction) varies by species. Home ranges 0.03 to 1.9 hectares (0.07 to 4.7 acres), males' and females' equivalent. Most squirrels commonly travel less than 150 meters (492 ft.) from burrow, some to 300+ meters to feeding source or to explore dispersal area. Considerable fidelity of individual squirrels to their burrow and home range from year to year.

FEEDING

Diet consists primarily of seasonally abundant new grasses, forbs, roots, and seeds near burrow system, including bromes, fescues, filaree, miner's lettuce, turkey mullein, buckwheat, ceanothus, acorns, elderberries, and many other plants. Insects such as grasshoppers and caterpillars make up small but steady part of diet in some areas; underground fungi important in some areas. Foraging begins near burrow entrance and widens out. Most foraging from dawn to around 10 a.m., then again in late afternoon. Some ground-squirrel species transport food such as acorns to burrow, using cheek pouches, then periodically bring food to surface to eat aboveground. From summer to annual dormancy, ground squirrels may more than double their weight.

SURVIVAL

Annual dormancy (estivation or hibernation) corresponds with food scarcity and temperature and lasts from 4 to 7 months, depending upon climate, elevation, and species (for example Aug to Jan along Northern California coast, and Nov to Apr at 1,829 meters/6,000 ft. in the Sierra Nevada). Ground squirrels vulnerable to many raptors, mammalian predators, and snakes. Superb overhead and wide-angle vision, combined with alert calls and shared vigilance in the more social species, contribute to survival. Beechey ground squirrels seek out and harass snakes to protect young; adults in some populations are immune to rattlesnake venom.

SIGNS

Usually conspicuous burrows, some with multiple entrances 5 to 13 cm (2 to 5 in.) in diameter, showing new excavation, especially after annual dormancy and when young disperse. Runs between burrow entrances and to feeding areas. Scat 0.5 to 0.6 cm (³⁄₁₆ to ¼ in.) in diameter, mostly deposited in underground latrines, but small groups of pellets also deposited aboveground in scent marking associated with scratches and shallow digs. Scent-marking dust baths, showing rub of cheek, then rollover onto back; also belly-dragging dust bath. Evidence of collection of grasses, pine needles, or bark as nest material by adults and dispersing juveniles throughout year but especially by pregnant females.

J: Beechey ground squirrel scat

J

RODENTS

KANGAROO RAT   Track ID

RODENTS

TRACKS

F tracks are very small, often indistinct due to furred foot. ◄

Back of H foot sometimes doesn't register at higher speeds. ►

Some species have 5 toes on H, some 4. ◄

◄ Many H tracks are indistinct because of furred foot.

LEFT FRONT   LEFT HIND

COMMON GAITS

A: Bound, full foot impressions

B: Bound on balls of feet with slight overlap

C: Slow hop, no tail drag

D: Slow hop, tail drag

E: Fast bound, slight tail drag

• Front

Hind

A   B   C   D   E

TRACK MEASUREMENTS

	Average, inches	Average, cm
Front width	⁵⁄₁₆	0.8
Front length	³⁄₈	0.9
Hind width	⁷⁄₁₆	1.2
Hind length	¹¹⁄₁₆	1.7
Trail width	1½	3.8
Stride	3⅜ to 27+	8.6 to 68.6+

The averages at left apply to common, medium-size species such as *Dipodomys merriami*. Large species such as *D. deserti* would show front tracks ½ in. wide by ¾ in. long, hind tracks ¾+ inch wide by 1⅜ in. long, and a larger trail width.

170

FINE POINTS

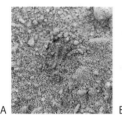

A

B

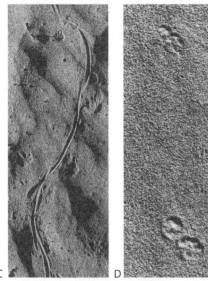

C

D

When you find snowshoe-shaped hind tracks or patterns of paired hind tracks bounding without any front tracks, kangaroo rat track ID is simple. Though the sweeping tail impression is common, note that the tail may or may not drag either at slow or high speeds. **Pocket mice and jumping mice** also often show tail drags, but their track patterns usually show both front and hind tracks registering in a gallop. Kangaroo rat tracks are often muffled because of a furred foot, unlike most other rodents. Most kangaroo-rat hind tracks show four toes; even though many species actually have five toes, the fifth toe is often not seen.

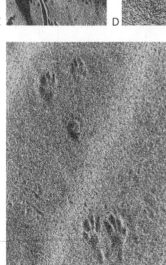

E

F

A: Left front track
B: Left hind track
C: Commonly seen bound with tail drag
D: Bound without tail drag, on balls of feet
E and F: Clarity of tracks varies with species and soil.

A kangaroo rat's territory is decorated with artistic tail sweeps and paired hopping tracks, but the tracker who merely identifies these things without probing more deeply misses an opportunity to understand an extraordinary survival adaptation based on this rodent's **bipedal locomotion**. From a standstill, a k-rat can dive 0.6 meter (2 ft.) into a burrow with one leap; it can zigzag at high speed with 61-cm (24 in.) hops, using its long tufted tail as an airborne rudder to keep its balance; and it can even twist the body in midair by whipping its tail around, so as to land heading in another direction. But the k-rat can show us even more. It can bound quickly and directly to a new feeding area, either back on its heels or up on its toes, and the hind feet can land in unison or in a one-two sequence. While it hops slowly on hind feet, tail dragging behind, the front feet are freed up to sift the soil for seeds entirely by feel. In a "scouting hop," the k-rat may roll forward on little two-footed hops with its whiskers touching the ground. K-rats can gallop, quadrupedally of course, and some have even been seen walking with alternating steps of the hind feet. As a tracker, move beyond mere identification of these tracks and discover how your kangaroo rat is really moving. Is it hopping quadrupedally or bipedally? How is the tail being used and what is the k-rat's posture? Look for evasive trails or sudden escapes; it's probable that k-rats, with built-in "sound chambers" in their skulls, can actually hear an owl flying.

Tracks and signs also illuminate the kangaroo rat's **foraging behavior**. An animal may spend only an hour or less a day foraging within perhaps 10 to 40 meters (33 to 131 ft.) of its burrow—giving the tracker a concentrated space to examine its foraging strategy at a given time. Follow a trail and then look for diggings where seeds are gleaned from the soil and then stuffed into cheek pouches. Seasonally the k-rat also harvests intact seed heads from grasses or other vegetation; look for remnants of stalks, or husks from seeds (the smaller species will husk seeds before jamming them into their cheek pouches). When its cheeks are full, the k-rat will hop back to its burrow to store the seeds, or make shallow, covered caches in soil nearby. One observer discovered dozens of little caches after a rain had sprouted the seeds in little clumps around a k-rat's burrow!

Though kangaroo rats live singly in their burrows, they do communicate to one another, especially at breeding time. You can get a glimpse of their **social interaction** by looking for dust baths, little elongated depressions where k-rats regularly clean their fur and deposit scent. During breeding time male k-rats scent-mark this way more often, and several males may congregate around a female's burrow. At this time males will chase one another and occasionally fight, wrestling on the ground. If it's breeding season and you find a direct k-rat trail longer than 100 meters (328 ft.), it may signify that a male or female has taken up residence in a distant burrow to be close to potential mates who are not closely related to it.

The trail of a slow-hopping kangaroo rat is crossed by a bobcat in the East Mojave Desert of California.

G: Following a heavily used kangaroo rat run from a burrow toward the top of this picture leads to . . .

H: . . . a seed-collecting area beneath a desert shrub.

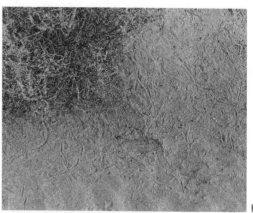

G

H

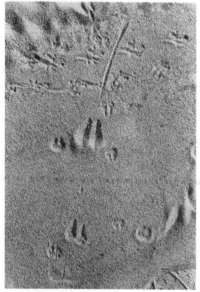

I

J

I: On the Carrizo Plain in central California, two k-rat species are evident from trail width and track size.

J: In Death Valley, California, these five-toed hind tracks probably belong to a chisel-toothed kangaroo rat.

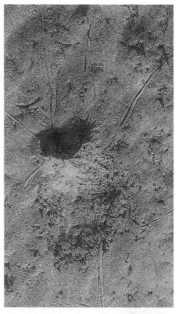

K

L

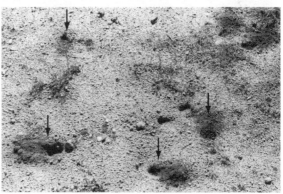

N

K: In the southern Sierras, excavations from a k-rat burrow reveal stored piñon pine nuts.

L: A dug-up seed cache

M: A kangaroo rat dust bath

N: K-rat foraging diggings in California's Antelope Valley

KANGAROO RAT   Notes for the Tracker

RODENTS

SPECIES AND WEIGHT   *Dipodomys* spp.

16 species in
North America

Most species
45 to 80 g
(1.6 to 2.8 oz.),
larger species
to 195 g (6.9 oz.)

HABITAT   Generally arid areas of the West.
Habitat varies by species and
includes coastal sage scrub, coastal
plains, chaparral, grassland, sagebrush,
piñon-juniper woodland, desert creosote,
desert shad scale, and desert dunes. Usually requires open space for foraging.
Two or even 3 species may be present in an area.

BREEDING   Breeding peak between January and April, depending upon species; some species
may breed again in late summer. Sparring and chasing among males in many
species; several males may be attracted to female's burrow at time of estrus.
Some males and females may travel 100+ meters (more than 328 ft.) from home
burrow to reside near potential mates during breeding time; female usually
mates with male in nearby burrow. Mating pair does mutual circling before
copulation; males especially increase sand bathing at breeding time. Gestation
29 to 34 days, litters average about 3.

DEVELOPMENT   Young leave burrow at 4 to 6 weeks depending upon species; weight is about 60%
of adult weight but foot size is 80% to 95% of maximum. Most young disperse
nearby to burrows 25 to 60 meters (82 to 197 ft.) away from natal burrow, but
some individuals travel 200+ meters.

SOCIAL HABITS   Each kangaroo rat lives singly in burrow except when female raises young.
Female home ranges exclusive; males' overlap females' and, in most species,
other males'. Rats may change burrows frequently as some are vacated. Home
areas range from 0.02 to 1.6 hectares; most rats travel no more than 100 meters
(328 ft.) from their birthplace during their lives. Some species display more
aggressive territorial behavior than others. Largest species (*D. deserti*, *D. ingens*,
and *D. spectabilis*) use foot drumming for communication.

Seeds from grasses, forbs, trees, and shrubs collected from under shrubs and in open areas by digging and sifting soil with forefeet. Seeds are stuffed into cheek pouches and then stored in burrow or in many shallow "surface caches" scattered around it. Seed choices vary by season and by species size, and include grasses, creosote bush, lupine, piñon pine, buckwheat, filaree, ceanothus, rabbitbrush, mesquite, and juniper among many others. Some species gather whole seed heads; these may be stored whole or hulled before caching, depending upon kangaroo rat species. In spring, green vegetation including grasses and leaves gathered and eaten, generally not stored. Insects sometimes eaten. *D. microps* specializes in eating saltbush leaves.

FEEDING

Exceptional hearing, good eyesight in dim light, and a good sense of smell warn kangaroo rats of danger. Bipedal hopping allows evasive moves, using the long tail to help change direction; a kangaroo rat can dive into a burrow in an instant or cover 5.2 meters (17 ft.) in 1 second. These adaptations allow foraging in open spaces more safely than other rodents. Because it collects and caches food for later consumption, its foraging is limited to 15 minutes to 2 hours per day. Burrows have escape tunnels ending inches from the surface. Foot thumping warns potential predators, and some species kick sand at snakes.

SURVIVAL

RODENTS

Burrows with multiple entrances, 4.4 to 10 cm (1¾ to 4 in.) wide depending upon species, usually with apron of excavated dirt outside. Some species often show no dirt mound. Some species occasionally plug up entrances from inside. Conspicuous runs among burrows and to feeding areas. Numerous foraging digs. Remains of grass or forb stalks cut for seed heads. Elongated dust baths, cupped in center, near burrows. Scats about 0.3 cm (⅛ in.) diameter, elongated with pointed or rounded ends, in feeding areas or windblown into surface depressions. Seed caches in soil a few inches deep, inconspicuous.

SIGNS

P

O

O: Kangaroo rat burrow

P: Close-up of scat

MARMOT/WOODCHUCK Track ID

TRACKS

3 palm pads
and 2 heel
pads ►

LEFT FRONT

LEFT HIND

► H track does not
always register
completely.

RODENTS

COMMON GAITS

A: Pace
(common)

B: Diagonal
walk to lope

C: Gallop
(common)

D: Bound to
lope

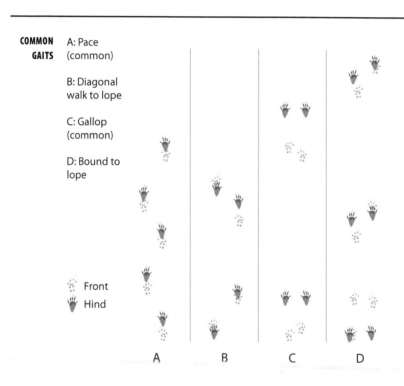

Front
Hind

A   B   C   D

TRACK MEASUREMENTS

	Usual range, inches	Usual range, cm
Front width	1⅜ to 1⅞	3.5 to 4.8
Front length	1⅝ to 2¹⁄₁₆	4.1 to 5.2
Hind width	1½ to 2	3.8 to 5.1
Hind length	1⅝ to 2¾	4.1 to 7.0
Trail width	5¼ to 6⅜	13.3 to 16.2
Stride*	3½ to 10	8.9 to 25.4

*Diagonal walk

This large rodent's common walking pattern, either a diagonal walk or a pace (overstep) walk, should withstand confusion with other rodent walkers' patterns (beaver, muskrat, or porcupine) by track size and shape. When galloping, a marmot/woodchuck's pattern falls in the range of a tree squirrel's, both in trail width and in track size. Look at habitat and the origin or destination of the trail, marmots anchoring their movements with obvious burrows. Also, a tree squirrel's toes are more slender and make "cleaner" impressions from toe and palm pads.

FINE POINTS

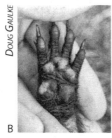

A: Alternating walk pattern of a woodchuck

B and C: Woodchuck left front and left hind foot, respectively

D and E: Woodchuck left front and right hind track, respectively

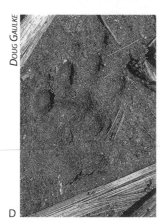

To understand the biology of marmots or woodchucks, we must start with **hibernation**, a phenomenon—the animals will show us—a bit more complex than just digging a hole and sleeping. During their five- to eight-month winter rest, marmots must retain enough body heat, and thereby fat, to emerge in the spring, mate, and begin carrying young before the best food is available. A hole not deep or well-insulated enough, or not protected from predators or floods, means trouble, and competition for viable hibernation burrows may relegate subdominant individuals to marginal and possibly fatal dwellings. Marmot species prefer somewhat concealed locations, in underbrush or among rocks, for hibernation burrows; underground roots or rocks there also deter predators. While the entrances to these burrows are plugged up during the winter, you can identify active ones in the spring in several ways. Look for tunnels in the snow emerging from hibernation burrows; also look for aprons of excavated plugs, often with scats and nesting material, outside their entrances. If you find one of these, come back in May to early July—whenever the young first emerge in your area—to find activity around the burrow entrance. During the summer marmots often move their centers of activity to summer burrows closer to feeding areas.

The summer agenda of a marmot contains two items: eating and being careful about eating. **Alert behavior** is actually a good tracking window because marmots organize their home-range use around it. Between a burrow and a feeding area, there are numerous "safety stops" near the entrances of temporary burrows or on rocks or logs. Runs between them are often very well used. Where you see galloping-marmot tracks, look at the terrain to see if you have found a vulnerable marmot-crossing area; where you see leisurely gaits, notice what features might provide safety. In summer marmots often prefer open areas with little brush so that potential predators such as coyotes can't ambush them. One marmot study found that subdominant marmots, living in burrows near shrubs, sustained most of the colony's predation.

While their social structure varies by species and area, all marmots are, shall we say, **territorially aware**, and this can be studied for its local manifestations. A first step might be to map all of the local burrows, runs, feeding areas, and lookout sites, determining by track and scats which are most active. At feeding areas marmots may tolerate just members of their immediate family or an extended family of several generations. You can observe marmots during morning and late afternoon feeding times for friendly or agonistic interactions. Male and female marmots also scent-mark with cheek rubs near burrow entrances to define burrow use, especially in the presence of other marmots; principal burrows can have a distinctive smell. In the West a male may have a "harem" of several females with young; he will patrol his territory daily along a regular route to each burrow.

F: In the Klamath National Wildlife Refuge, a rock formation supporting one or more dens and numerous lookouts for yellow-bellied marmots shows a large apron of bedding material and scats pushed out from winter hibernation.

G: A nearby safe area in the flats adjacent to a feeding area has at least twenty different scat piles of different ages.

F

G

SPECIES AND WEIGHT   *Marmota* spp.

5 species in North America

1.6 to 7 kg
(3.5 to 15.4 lb.)

Male larger than female

HABITAT   Preferred habitat includes meadows or fields with abundant forbs and grasses for feeding, and adjacent forest edges, rock outcrops, or talus slopes for digging hibernation burrows. Woodchucks *(M. monax)* of the East commonly feed in agricultural fields. Marmots of the West occur in basin lands or at higher elevations.

BREEDING   Breeding usually occurs during the first 2 weeks after emergence from hibernation (Feb and Mar for woodchucks, Apr and May for western marmots). Woodchuck males may travel widely seeking receptive females. In many populations of western marmots, a dominant male breeds with several females in his "harem." In the East some woodchucks breed as yearlings and 2-year-olds, while in the West most marmots usually breed first at 3 years of age. Gestation about 30 days, litters usually 3 to 6.

DEVELOPMENT   Young emerge from natal burrow when nearly weaned, about 4 weeks after birth (usually May among woodchucks, to June or early July among higher-elevation western species). Young approach one-half adult weight by fall. Many woodchuck juveniles begin dispersing in midsummer, with considerable wandering, and may dig shallow dens with single entrances. However, in most western marmot populations, young remain with their mother, hibernating with her through the 1st and often 2nd winter.

SOCIAL HABITS   *Marmota* species vary in their social structures, and there may also be differences based on a local population's food resources and hibernation-burrow availability. All marmots and woodchucks can display dominance/submissiveness toward other individuals through body language (such as tail position), scent marking, and chases. Woodchucks are generally solitary animals, the home ranges of reproductive females overlapping only slightly. Yellow-bellied marmots throughout the West tend to form larger female-kin colonies, sharing food resource areas; a dominant male often associates with several female groups.

RODENTS

Species in the Pacific Northwest tend to form groups in which a male associates with one breeding and several nonbreeding females. Home ranges usually 0.2 to 3 hectares (0.5 to 7.4 acres); noncolonial males' ranges are sometimes larger.

FEEDING

Primarily herbivorous, marmots and woodchucks prefer sedges, grasses, and especially forbs including vetch, clover, plantain, native mustards, lupine, and dandelions among many others. Leaves of shrubs such as blackberry, rose, and serviceberry eaten. Woodchucks also may climb deciduous trees seasonally for their leaves, and commonly consume cultivated crops where available.

SURVIVAL

Hibernation lasts from 4½ to 8 months, depending upon species and habitat (e.g., Nov through Feb for woodchucks, Sept through Apr for yellow-bellied marmots). Quality of hibernating burrow affects survival; some western populations suffer significant overwinter mortality, especially of young. Predation, especially of juveniles and yearlings, by coyotes, badgers, golden eagles, black bears, and martens. When moving to forage areas, woodchucks and marmots often stop momentarily at safe locations or scan for danger from rock outcrops. Western species prefer open forage areas to minimize predators' ambush opportunities, and their alarm calls, especially single or multiple whistles, alert other marmots of danger. Pitch and duration of calls probably signal high or low danger. Marmots may live up to 6 or 8 years.

SIGNS

Conspicuous burrows with entrance holes usually 13 to 25 cm (5 to 10 in.) in diameter, often with freshly excavated earth outside (especially the case among woodchucks). Hibernation burrows commonly dug among tree roots or rock outcrops, while additional summer-use burrows may be more in the open and closer to forage sites. Burrows, especially the former, often have multiple entrances. Among western species, snow tunnels leading from hibernation burrows after spring emergence. Scats variable (pellets, cords, or amorphous piles), often deposited in latrines at lookouts. Well-used runs between burrows and forage areas.

RODENTS

H

H: Marmot scat

RODENTS

TRACKS

These tracks are of the deer mouse, *Peromyscus maniculatus,* the most widespread mouse species in North America.

LEFT FRONT    LEFT HIND

FINE POINTS

The many species of mice in North America have four toes on their front feet and five on the hind; track patterns are almost always gallops, with trail widths usually from 2.9 to 4.1 cm (1⅛ to 1⅝ in.). You can explore for travel routes, feeding sources, and nests without first knowing the species (see "Track Windows"), but if you want to go further with ID, you should first obtain a list of small rodent species in the specific habitat where you track. Fortunately, there are likely to be only about one vole and two to four mouse species in a given area. By drawing and measuring tracks—using track stations with finely sifted soil or flour—you can begin to sort out local species. Notice differences in size and position of toes,

Gallop pattern of a *Peromyscus* mouse

and in shape and position of heel pads. From a mammal field guide, chart the relative weights of your local mouse species; they may vary considerably, and trail widths are roughly proportional. Mark Elbroch's *Mammal Tracks & Sign* (see Recommended Reading on p. 380) has good photos and drawings comparing mouse species.

TRACK MEASUREMENTS

Mouse track size examples (inches)*

	Front width x length	Hind width x length	Trail width
Deer mouse	³⁄₁₆ x ⅜	⅜ x ⁷⁄₁₆	1⅜
Grasshopper mouse	³⁄₁₆ x ⁵⁄₁₆	⁵⁄₁₆ x ⁷⁄₁₆	1⅜
Harvest mouse	¼ x ¼	½ x ⅝	1¼
Pocket mouse	⅜ x ⁷⁄₁₆	⅜ x ¹¹⁄₁₆	1½

*Examples, not averages; jumping mice (*Zapus* spp.) and introduced house mouse (*Mus musculus*) not included here.

A: Most of this mouse activity on California's central coast occurred in one night because the wind scours the sand dunes each afternoon.

B: This deer-mouse nest was revealed under a lumber pile beneath a deck in Frazier Park, California. The exterior is made of numerous dried yucca leaves, which the mouse retrieved from a soaking trough 0.6 meter (2 ft.) away; many of the leaves had to be teased apart and fluffed. The soft interior was made from lint, gathered from a clothes-dryer vent 12 meters (40 ft.) away; pieces of cotton string of unknown origin; and Osage orange shavings gathered under a bow-making workbench 42 ft. away.

C: An acorn-storage and feeding site inside an old running shoe in a garage

The tracker of mice is a humble person—or will soon become one. This is because these mammals, so small and short-lived, know far more about their microhabitat than we will ever know. Their daily routines of foraging, breeding, raising young, and spacing themselves within their niche seem simple, but there is much complexity in a local area. Some mice are generalist feeders, and some are specialists. Some (the pocket mice) are seed gatherers and storers, while others (the *Peromyscus* mice) tend to forage and eat in the field. Some (the harvest and *Peromyscus* mice) spend a lot of time foraging in bushes and trees, while others (grasshopper and pocket mice) stay on the ground. Some (harvest mice and *Peromyscus* mice) nest aboveground, while others (pocket mice and grasshopper mice) nest in underground burrows. Some mouse species are dominant over others and therefore dictate local spatial use and foraging choices.

A good starting place into this complex world is any **well-used mouse trail**. Many of these skirt the edges of fallen logs, shrubs, or rocks and are pockmarked from little foot impressions. Others are on top of fallen logs or other raised surfaces that are quieter and safer for a mouse to run across; dusting one of these places with finely sifted soil before nightfall will surely yield tracks by morning. Following a trail in one direction may lead you to nesting areas, either in a burrow or in an aboveground nest. If you find a nest, carefully examine it and then leave it be. The materials used in a nest can lead you to a mouse's gathering area.

The other end of a trail will likely be a **food-gathering area**. Remember that virtually every seed, fruit, flower, fungus, and insect in the microhabitat is potential food for some mouse, wherever it is and however it must be gathered. Look for evidence of foraging, such as remnants of shells or seeds, or little digs in the sand. A mouse's teeth marks can be found on nuts, mushrooms, or a piece of bone. Mouse scats can often be found at a feeding site. Pay attention to the food that is most available in the season, and look for regular mouse runs between these areas and likely nesting spots. In grassy areas harvest mice especially take advantage of vole runs, often making many trips per night. You can prepare a thin, narrow board or piece of cardboard, dusted with flour or powdered clay, to get tracks there.

RODENTS

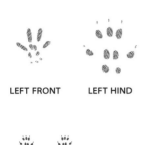

LEFT FRONT   **LEFT HIND**

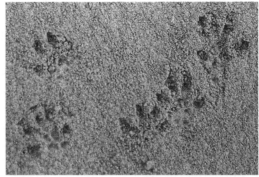

The tracks pictured here were caught on a powdered clay surface in a meadow at 1,524 meters (5,000 ft.) elevation. They belong to one of the *Peromyscus* mice.

Nearly every habitat in the lower forty-eight states has one of the sixteen *Peromyscus* species (sometimes called white-footed mice); many habitats have both the deer mouse (*P. maniculatus*), which seems to thrive everywhere, and one or more other species that may be adapted to specific habitats. These mice eat seeds, fruits of shrubs, fungi, green vegetation, and arthropods. Breeding occurs throughout much of the year but is not prolific: Litters commonly number two per year of two to five each. Many *Peromyscus* species are excellent climbers. Nests may be in rock crevices, under logs, underground in other rodents' abandoned burrows, and sometimes in woodrat nests. One was even found in a tree 24 meters (80 ft.) aboveground.

RODENTS

HARVEST MICE   (*Reithrodontomys* Genus)

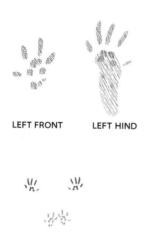

LEFT FRONT   LEFT HIND

North of San Francisco Bay, the tracks of an endangered salt-marsh harvest mouse were captured during field research.

RODENTS

The five species of harvest mouse throughout North America are abundant in grasslands and marshes but are also found in sagebrush scrub, grassy areas of deserts, pine-oak forests, and on the edges of riparian areas. Their globular nests, 7.6 to 13 cm (3 to 5 in.) in diameter, are usually aboveground among grasses, under logs, or in branches of shrubs; nests have a side entrance about 1 cm (⅜ in.) wide. Primarily, harvest mice eat flowers and seeds (gleaning these from the ground or harvesting them from stems) but will also eat leaves, insects, and larvae. Harvest mice frequently use vole (*Microtus*) runways.

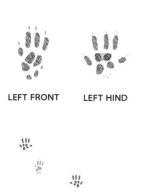

LEFT FRONT   LEFT HIND

A southern grasshopper mouse, here released onto a tracking board, was live-trapped in a research project in Kern County, California.

The three North American species of grasshopper mice all inhabit arid or semiarid habitats, especially grassland, desert, and scrubland. Their primary diet consists of beetles, scorpions, grasshoppers, and arthropods, but they are also known to kill and eat mice and other small vertebrates. Seeds make up a small percentage of their food. Their home ranges are relatively large (up to 3 hectares/7.4 acres) and are marked through dust bathing and through periodic high-pitched "howls" audible to humans and lasting about one second. Grasshopper mice are known to dig their own burrows where they nest; they also dig holes to store excess food.

RODENTS

POCKET MICE   (*Chaetodipus* and *Perognathus* Genus)

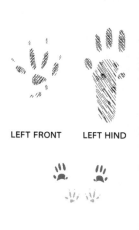

LEFT FRONT   LEFT HIND

The pocket mouse whose tracks are pictured here is the California pocket mouse, *Chaetodipus californicus*.

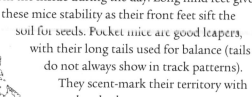

Many habitats of the West, including deserts, prairies, scrubland, chaparral, and piñon-juniper woodland, support one of the twenty species of pocket mice, which are generally adapted to arid environments and which go into torpor during winter months. Pocket mice gather large numbers of seeds in their cheek pouches and then store them in caches or in their burrows. These are usually extensive underground systems with entrance holes about 2.5 cm (1 in.) in diameter, often plugged with soil from the inside during the day. Long hind feet give these mice stability as their front feet sift the soil for seeds. Pocket mice are good leapers, with their long tails used for balance (tails do not always show in track patterns). They scent-mark their territory with dust baths.

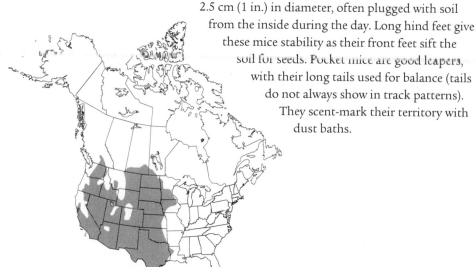

You can study local mouse ecology by recording tracks on fine substrate, then photographing them using a ruler in the image. An easy track medium to use is flour dusted on a board or on a regular mouse run such as a boulder or log, but it has the disadvantage of not holding detail for very long. Better is field chalk used for marking sports fields. In the field we have used diatomaceous earth that is spread in a thin layer on hard-packed ground, and then smoothed with a paint roller covered with a section of PVC pipe. Some biologists have used powdered graphite in solution with alcohol and mineral oil that is sprayed onto a surface. My favorite medium is powdered artist's clay, sifted onto the rough side of a piece of hardboard. Some of these methods are illustrated here. Track stations may be baited with a few nuts or seeds; ideally the boards should be large enough to capture the mouse's regular track pattern and allow measuring trail width as well as individual tracks.

A

A: A track tunnel dusted with powdered artist's clay is placed unbaited on a mouse run.

B

B: Mouse tracks on a track station dusted with diatomaceous earth.

C

C: A salt-marsh harvest mouse was released onto 4' x 4' hardboard dusted with powdered artist's clay in order to capture a regular track pattern. Notice the tail drags.

MUSKRAT Track ID

TRACKS

A small inside toe may occasionally show in very clear print.

LEFT FRONT

Slender toes (F and H) ►

Prominent claw impressions sometimes show as extentions of the toes (F and H).

LEFT HIND

COMMON GAITS

A: Diagonal walk (common)

B: Pace walk (common)

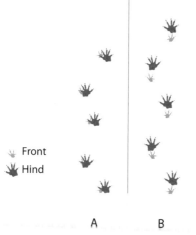

Front

Hind

Bounds, lopes, and gallops are also recorded.

A   B

TRACK MEASUREMENTS

	Usual range, inches	Usual range, cm
Front width	1 to 1½	2.5 to 3.8
Front length	1¹⁄₁₆ to 1½	2.7 to 3.8
Hind width	1³⁄₁₆ to 2	3.0 to 5.1
Hind length	1⅜ to 2	3.5 to 5.1
Trail width	3½ to 3⅞	8.9 to 9.8
Stride*	3 to 5	7.6 to 12.7

*Diagonal walk

The common diagonal walk or pace walk pattern of the muskrat helps in identification, because the other rodents that might commonly produce these patterns are generally either smaller or larger. The introduced Norway rat's tracks and trail width are usually smaller, and a woodchuck's or marmot's are usually larger. A galloping muskrat's trail might give roughly the same measurements as a tree squirrel's, but the latter's palm pads are clearer and more prominent. Muskrats sometimes drag their tails, especially in snow, which also aids identification.

FINE POINTS

A

B

C

A: Common diagonal walk pattern

B and C: Right front and right hind feet, respectively

D: Right hind track at bottom left, and right front track

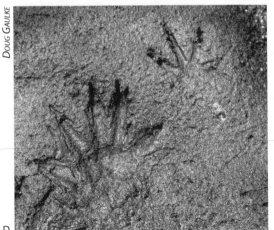

D

Muskrats' **adaptation to water** will not only impress any hydrophile but will also teach us trackers how to read the quality of a local watery habitat and its impact on animal behavior. Muskrats can cruise underwater at nearly 2 mph using only their back feet and tail for propulsion. They can dive for 15 or more minutes at a time, surface without a ripple, and dive again. Membranes that close behind the teeth allow muskrats to chew off underwater food, like cattail roots, and carry it away to dwellings or feeding stations with underwater entrances. In fact, a long foraging session, including cycles of exploration, harvesting, transport, and feeding, commonly occurs without the animal ever being seen above water. Prime muskrat habitat therefore not only includes such food that can be gathered easily and safely but also fairly shallow water 76 cm (30 in. or less) where summer lodges can be constructed of cattails, bulrushes, and other plants without being vulnerable to waves and high winds. In these areas look for lodges 0.9 to 1.2 meters (3 to 4 ft.) high that mark a muskrat family's home range; also look for feeding stations within a short underwater swim from a lodge. Remnants of eaten plants may be found on feeding stations or floating in the water. If your habitat has too much or too little water seasonally, ask yourself how a muskrat might adapt. In a spring flood that would take out lodges and bank burrows, explore higher ground, looking for temporary muskrat shelters and food sources. In a late-year drought, muskrats may concentrate activity where there is water, or they may travel overland to find wet places. A severe freeze may close off muskrat water routes, driving animals to other areas. In all these cases, look for tracks on land that lead to alternative food, such as the bark of trees or shrubs, or roots that are dug up.

Dependency upon good habitat has engendered in the muskrat a **very strong territoriality** that is another good tracking window. A female may tolerate the presence of her young-of-the-year in her home range as she raises additional litters, but these juveniles must find their own sleeping places away from the natal chamber. During the summer and early fall, look for lodges and floating vegetation riddled with holes, and tunnels excavated by these house hunters. In late fall muskrats begin to construct durable winter shelters, so look for new lodge construction or bank excavations by juvenile muskrats on the edges of a home range. Some animals may also travel overland to find a place to settle at this time. In spring muskrats travel more widely and try to establish breeding territories. Look for muskrat tracks crossing between bodies of water; muskrats are more vulnerable to coyotes and mink at this time. During this season many fights between muskrats occur, with larger animals usually winning; scuffles on land, showing tracks, fur, and blood, have been recorded near bank burrows. Subdominant muskrats may retreat to marginal habitat, so don't forget to look for tracks and signs even in places like drainage ditches. Also look for territorial marking by scats and scent-marked piles on elevated places near dwellings.

RODENTS

RODENTS

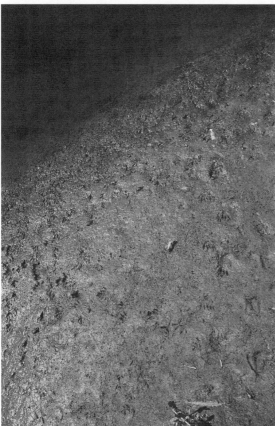

E: Muskrat lodge in the Klamath National Wildlife Refuge, Oregon

F: In late May a muskrat makes an exploratory foray on the shore of an agricultural drainage ditch far from ideal muskrat habitat. The muskrat walked about 3 meters (10 ft.) onto shore and immediately returned to the water.

MUSKRAT

SPECIES AND WEIGHT *Ondatra zibethicus*

16 subspecies in North America

0.7 to 1.8 kg (1.5 to 4 lb.)

HABITAT Lakes, rivers, ponds, and marshes throughout most of North America, where aquatic vegetation provides food and where shelters can be constructed from plant materials or dug out in banks. Core muskrat areas usually have shallow water (usually 25 to 76 cm/10 to 30 in. deep) with abundant plant materials such as cattail and bulrush. Marginal habitats such as drainage ditches or temporarily wet upland areas may be used by dispersing individuals and by others when their primary habitat floods. Highest density occurs in areas with the most stable water levels. Muskrats have been introduced into some areas of North America.

BREEDING Breeding usually begins in late March; fights during establishment of breeding territories leave many males and females wounded, and scuffles sometimes occur on land near burrows. Copulation takes place in the water, gestation 25 to 30 days; females in many areas have 2 to 3 litters per year, with birthing peaks about a month apart beginning in late April to early May. (Muskrats in the southern United States may breed year-round.) Litters average 6 to 7.

DEVELOPMENT Though young can swim well, dive, and hide in water at 3 weeks, they remain in the natal nest at least until they are weaned at 4 weeks. Young remain in the vicinity of the nest through the summer, often sharing feeding stations with other subadults. Away from the primary nest, young begin to dig numerous holes, tunnels, and resting chambers into existing lodges and rafts of vegetation. By mid- to late fall, as young approach adult weight, they disperse to edges of mother's home range and begin to renovate or construct winter burrows or lodges.

SOCIAL HABITS A home range centers around one well-maintained lodge or burrow where a female muskrat raises her litters in the spring and summer; this area is used by related animals and also includes feeding stations and temporary resting spots. Most muskrats venture no farther than 30 or 60 meters (100 or 200 ft.) from their central site as they forage. In winter, especially where temperatures are low,

RODENTS

groups from 2 to 6 commonly share a dwelling. In late winter to early spring, a local population is in flux as many females and especially males travel farther to establish territories. Fighting during this period usually favors the largest animals.

FEEDING

Aquatic vegetation preferred, especially tubers and root stalks of cattail and bulrush, also stem bases and shoots of these and other plants, including water lily, arrowhead, and sedges. Food often brought inside feeding houses or dwelling houses to eat and to cache; many remnants of feeding on selective plant parts remain at these sites or float in the water. Where preferred plants are unavailable, for example from flooding, muskrats may gather food onshore, sometimes digging for roots there or eating bark from trees or shrubs. Muskrats may eat some crustaceans and fish.

SURVIVAL

Muskrats are vulnerable to predators including mink and coyotes, especially in the early-spring dispersal period. The ability to dive for many minutes at a time and to surface and hide quietly near water's surface make muskrats relatively inconspicuous. Change in habitat from flooding, drought, and heavy freezing causes a local population to fluctuate. Muskrats are heavily trapped for their fur.

SIGNS

Conical dwellings constructed of plants such as cattail and bulrush, sometimes with mud added, usually 0.6 to 1.2 meters (2 to 4 ft.) high. Houses have a nest chamber, tunnels, and 2 or more plunge holes leading directly into water, but entrances above water may also occur. Burrows in banks, with underwater entrances, also common; some have entrances aboveground also. Feeding stations on floating logs or debris, with feeding remnants present; also small feeding houses constructed of floating vegetation up to 0.5 meter (1½ ft.) high with an underwater entrance. Scats about 20 mm (¾ in.) long, sometimes deposited on exposed surfaces near dwelling; scent-marking piles of vegetation and mud. In winter, piles of vegetation called "push-ups" around plunge holes in ice.

RODENTS

G

G: Muskrat scat

TRACKS

Claw marks sharp and prominent (F)

H track slightly smaller than F, shorter claws

LEFT FRONT   LEFT HIND

COMMON GAITS

A: Trot (common)

 Front
 Hind

Walks, with the hind foot falling behind or partially on top of the front on each side, are also recorded.

A

TRACK MEASUREMENTS

	Average, inches	Average, cm
Front width	7/16	1.1
Front length	15/16	2.4
Hind width	3/8	1.0
Hind length	7/8	2.1
Trail width	2 3/8	6.0
Stride*	3 15/16	10.0

*Trot

RODENTS

198

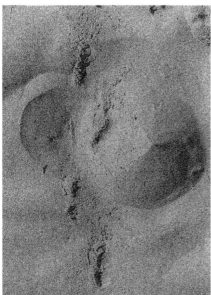

A

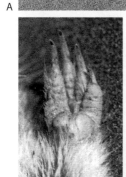

B

C

D

In clear prints pocket gophers show five toes on both the front and hind tracks, unlike most other rodents, which show four and five. The front claws, adapted for a life of digging, are long and very prominent, extending farther away from the toes than any other rodent's. Clear prints are, however, rare because of how seldom gophers venture aboveground. The typical track pattern is a fast walk or trot, as shown in the diagram on the opposite page and in photos A and D here. Gallops have not been recorded to my knowledge, so together the track pattern, long claw marks, and size of the tracks should allow a positive ID. Note that pocket gophers are entirely different from the "gophers" or woodchucks of the Midwest and East, which are about eighteen times larger (see "Marmot").

FINE POINTS

RODENTS

A: Trotting pattern crossing a human footprint

B: A Botta's pocket gopher left front foot

C: A left hind foot

D: Detail from a trotting pattern, left front track at bottom and left hind track at top

199

Trackers share an affinity for dirt with the pocket gopher, who spends most of its life moving within it and bringing it to the surface. While gopher tracks are fairly rare to find, their **mounds of dirt** are seemingly everywhere, and this digging can be read to illuminate the behavior of this fantastically well-adapted animal. In a day, a gopher may move five to eighteen pounds of soil, using its claws and its teeth to excavate. (That's a lot of dirt for a 0.1 kg/one-third-pound animal, equivalent to a medium-size man moving one to four tons!) Gophers dig to reach roots that they eat and to make underground chambers for sleeping, birthing, rearing young, storing food, and defecating. A lot of fresh digging within a relatively small area may mean that a gopher has taken over a new area and is renovating or expanding a tunnel system. This takes place especially in late summer or fall, when the young disperse. Alternatively, a lot of digging in the spring may indicate that a gopher is eating much new plant growth to prepare for breeding and raising young. In areas where it snows, look for cords of dirt that gophers push up into snow tunnels and that later settle to the ground when the snow melts. Old nesting material and scats may be found in some of these.

Aboveground travel is a good window to a gopher's life because it is done for such limited reasons. A juvenile will travel on the surface to disperse from its mother's tunnel system. Each system is occupied by an individual gopher and is unconnected to any other. A gopher looking for a new home senses where vacant tunnels are, because a vacant system is usually reoccupied within minutes or hours. Gophers also travel aboveground to find mates. Whatever the purpose, gophers almost always leave running tracks aboveground because they are so vulnerable. Finally, new spring plant growth often lures a gopher to graze aboveground. It will pop out of its burrow, cautiously move a few steps to munch a plant, then run backward into its burrow, looking like it was attached to a bungee cord. Look for backward-running tracks and evidence of browse all around a burrow entrance.

Gophers are enormously important as a **food source for predators**. Coyotes, rattlesnakes, gopher snakes, badgers, weasels, and owls all depend upon gophers as a staple food. You may be able to watch a coyote or heron poised over current digging activity, waiting for the gopher to pop up. In an active gopher area, look for predator tracks. Look for gopher skulls and incisors in scats and owl pellets. These signs are more prevalent in seasons when gophers venture aboveground. Pocket gophers also contribute significantly to the local ecosystem by moving tons of soil to the surface, increasing plant germination and decreasing erosion.

E: A gopher has pushed soil from its winter digging into a snow tunnel, leaving a solid core that rests on the ground after the snow melted. Part of a tunnel just at ground level is also exposed.

F: Currently used tunnels are plugged from inside for safety.

G: Gophers usually push soil out in one direction, in contrast to moles, which push soil straight up to form volcano-shaped mounds. This location shows the gopher's fresh excavation as well as soil of three different ages from previous diggings.

RODENTS

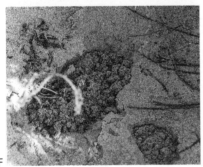

Thomomys, *Geomys*, and *Cratogeomys* spp.

18 species in North America

Usually 46 to 300 g (1.6 to 11 oz.)

SPECIES AND WEIGHT

PORCUPINE Track ID

TRACKS

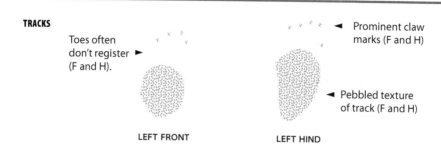

Toes often don't register ► (F and H).

◄ Prominent claw marks (F and H)

◄ Pebbled texture of track (F and H)

LEFT FRONT

LEFT HIND

COMMON GAITS

A and B: Pace-walk patterns showing different degrees of H overstepping F

C: Tail drag prominent in deep snow

D: Diagonal walk pattern

● Front
● Hind

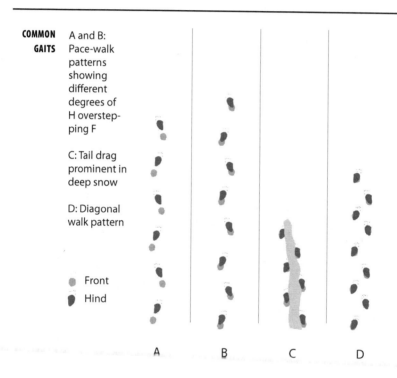

A   B   C   D

TRACK MEASUREMENTS

	Average, inches	Average, cm	Usual range, inches*
Front width	1⁷⁄₁₆	3.7	1¼ to 1⅞
Front length	1¹⁵⁄₁₆	5.0	1½ to 2¾
Hind width	1¹⁵⁄₁₆	4.9	1⁵⁄₁₆ to 2½
Hind length	2¹³⁄₁₆	7.2	2¼ to 3½
Trail width	5⅜	13.6	3¾ to 7
Stride**	7⁷⁄₁₆	18.9	5¼ to 10

*More than 95% of my measurements fall within this range.   **Pace walk

Clear porcupine tracks are distinguished by their prominent claw impressions in both front and hind tracks, by the inward pitch of the tracks, and by the "pebbled" texture of the heel-pad area. (Note that even with clear prints, the toes may frequently not register.) A trail with indistinct tracks, such as in snow or on hard-packed soil, may be identified by the claw marks along with a tail drag (though this is sometimes faint and must be looked for). No other mammal except the badger might show a pigeon-toed trail with similar-size tracks, stride, and trail width, but, of course, the badger would show no tail drag, and toe/heel-pad impressions differ considerably.

FINE POINTS

RODENTS

A: Pace-walk pattern, with hind slightly overstepping
B: Same pattern in snow, with tail drag
C: Left hind track showing drag of hairs on underside of tail
D: Old left front track
E. Old left hind track
F: Pinching of the hind track for traction can make a track appear segmented.

Porcupine trails that snake cleanly through the forest, uncluttered with stops or direction changes, suggest a **knowledge of the land** that both indigenous people and modern biologists have noticed. The Koyukon people of central Alaska ascribe a deep understanding of the land to the porcupine, one elder saying that "the whole of Alaska is . . . inside the palm of a porcupine's hand." In the early 1900s a psychologist documented through laboratory maze tests that porcupines have an outstanding and durable spatial memory. Much of their knowledge is passed on maternally. Baby porcupines follow their mothers, learning the locations of hiding places, feeding trees, and the routes between them. Then, the young females (who tend to be the dispersers) go out and learn a new territory and pass that knowledge on to *their* young. We trackers can learn about porcupines by asking, "what is so important to remember" for an animal that should have no worries, fortified as it is with 30,000 quills? One answer is shelter, for whatever predation does occur on porcupines is almost always in the open. Juveniles, especially, need rock crevices or hollows on the ground to protect them until they can climb up to dense foliage to hide. And all porcupines have a better chance of survival where winters are harsh if they have secure dens. Walk through porcupine habitat looking for dens and hiding places, identified by abundant scats at their entrances. Dens are often used year after year by individual animals.

Another answer to the question above is food. Porcupines select specific trees or plants to forage on, choosing ones with the most protein and least acid at any given time if they can. Porcupines often have certain favorite trees to which they return, and individual animals in the same area may feed on different species. For the tracker, the local **food choices** make a good window to porcupine behavior, and there should be abundant clues to interpret. Look for naked patches on trees where bark has been eaten, aging them to discover short- or long-term use of certain trees. Porcupines sometimes eat a small "test patch" of bark, then reject that tree for a better alternative. Beneath trees or shrubs, look for "niptwigs," branches that porcupines have clipped off while foraging, and notice whether porcupines are currently choosing the bark, leaves, or buds in their selective feeding. When new forbs appear in spring and summer, remember to check porcupine foraging on the ground or even in shallow water where aquatic plants are eaten. Solitary feeders, porcupines space themselves by scent, leaving urine at the base of their feeding trees and along trails. Porcupines are always sniffing the air to detect the presence of other porcupines and to find the best food as well. Look for occasional stop-and-sniff-the-air tracks, which can be read through pressure releases.

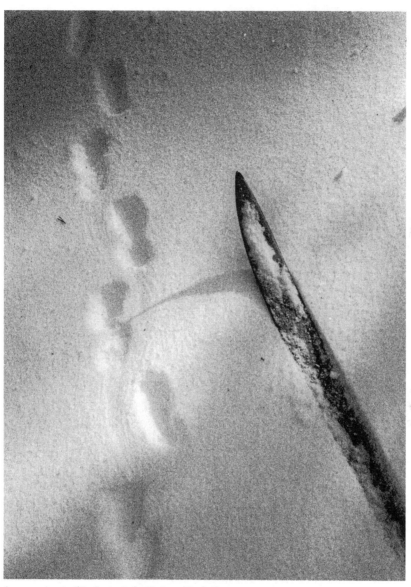

A porcupine trail in Crater Lake National Park, Oregon

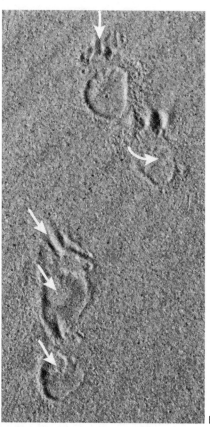

G

H

G and H: Reading how terrain is reflected in a porcupine trail. In contrast to most porcupine trails, which vary little in foot placement, the trail in G stands out. The right hind track consistently falls to the inside of the right front, and both the left front and left hind tracks show considerable motion. When detail is examined (photo H), it is noticed that the left tracks show diagonal movement in the claws and in disks pushed by the heel pads (arrows). These are caused when the right hind leg swings to the inside in a hybrid gait that is closer to a pace walk than a diagonal walk. Meanwhile, the claws on the right tracks push straight back. There is also a plate and a ridge on the lower right of the right front heel pad, indicating that weight has shifted to the back when the right front touches the ground. While these details (and others evident in the photos) could suggest an injury or deformity in the right hip (porcupines sometimes do fall from trees), the only explanation that satisfies all of them is that the porcupine is walking on a slope, which in fact it is. The slope is uphill to the left, in the direction of the dotted line in G.

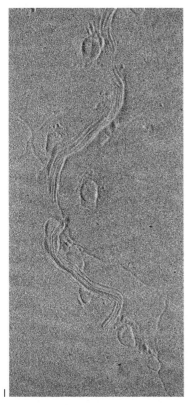

I: A porcupine's tail does not always drag passively behind. It can be lifted from time to time or used for balance.

J: Reading a hesitation and turn in a weathered porcupine trail. After identifying which are front and hind, left and right tracks, role-playing reveals the probable sequence of leg movement. Then pressure releases, evident even in these old tracks, confirm the reading. At the moment of hesitation, the labeled RH, LF, and RF feet are touching the ground, and all three bear weight in the pivot to the right. In the photo detailing the RF track, there is pressure at the back left of the heel from the pivot. Because the claws barely touch in contrast with other tracks in the sequence, the porcupine probably has its head raised, possibly to sniff, as the hesitation occurs.

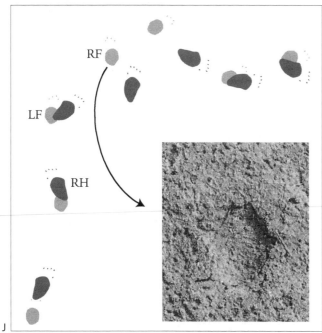

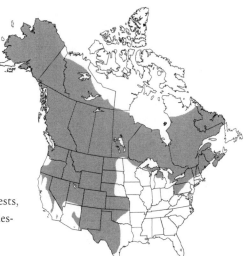

SPECIES AND WEIGHT

Erethizon dorsatum

7 subspecies in North America

3.5 to 18 kg (8 to 40 lb.)

Male larger than female

HABITAT Coniferous and deciduous forests, tundra, and riparian areas of deserts, chaparral, and plains.

BREEDING Breeding season lasts about 1 month, usually between mid-September and November, depending upon the area. Males sexually mature in fall of 2nd year. Males travel widely, seeking out females by scent at dens and at bases of feeding trees. Breeding male guards female from other males for 1 to 3 days. Fights among males may produce injuries including quill impalements; loosened and extracted quills from fights may be found on the ground. Largest males tend to be dominant breeders. Gestation about 210 days, births in May to July, depending upon area. Litters almost always 1.

DEVELOPMENT Young weigh about 1 pound at birth, grow to about 1.6 kg (3.5 lb.) by end of 1st summer. Quills are functional in first day. Young stay near mother for first 6 weeks, often rest hidden at base of mother's feeding tree or in nearby hiding spot while she feeds. Throughout mid- to late summer, young travel with mother but feed and rest in trees lower than mother to remain hidden in foliage. Over summer, mother-young spacing gradually increases; young are able to defend themselves fully. Juveniles may be active more than adults during summer foraging. Nursing ends after 4 months. In fall young females tend to disperse while males remain near natal territory. Dispersals of 2.4 to 31 km (½ to 19 miles) have been recorded.

SOCIAL HABITS Female home ranges generally exclusive from one another and fairly constant; males' ranges may overlap each others' and some females'. Home ranges of 5 to 65 hectares (12.4 to 161 acres) have been recorded; winter ranges may shrink dramatically when snows are deep. Porcupines usually feed alone. Denning is also usually solitary, but some adult male-female pairs, or a mother and juvenile, may den together occasionally. Outside of breeding season, females may fight for territoriality, leaving scattered quills.

RODENTS

Inner bark, twigs, buds, and leaves of trees and shrubs are staple food, includ- **FEEDING**
ing hemlock, spruce, fir, pine, larch, maple, aspen, willow, elderberry, cedar, elm,
locust, and linden, among many others. However, in a given area each porcupine
is commonly a selective feeder, concentrating on 1 or 2 species at a certain time,
and then feeding on either their buds, leaves, or bark, depending upon season.
In the desert porcupines are known to eat ocotillo bark as well as shrubs. Where
available, acorns are picked from branches in fall, shelled, and consumed. In all
areas, spring and summer forbs and even grasses are eaten on the ground. Pond
lilies are consumed for sodium content, and porcupines seek out salt sources,
eating bones and even mud.

Quills provide both passive and active defense; a powerful tail slap can embed **SURVIVAL**
quills entirely beneath an attacker's skin. They are barbed and lubricated to
allow penetration, but are also coated with a natural antibiotic, possibly to protect porcupines themselves from infection after fights or falls. Only mountain
lions and fishers are efficient porcupine predators. Nevertheless, porcupines use
warning coloration of black and white quills, emission of a strong odor, warning chatter, climbing trees, and concealment to avoid danger. Younger animals
spend less time in the open than adults. Falls from trees cause numerous deaths
and injuries; starvation and human causes also contribute to mortality. Infant
mortality is very low, and porcupines may commonly live 5 or 10 years.

Scats about 1 cm (⅜ in.) diameter, 1.9 to 2.5 cm (¾ to 1 in.) long, sometimes **SIGNS**
curved, numerous at den entrances or under feeding trees; scats yellowish,
red, or black, depending upon food. Feeding trees show large patches of bark
removed by incisors; in larger trees outer bark pieces, removed before consumption of inner bark, may be found on ground. Small test patches of removed
bark may also be found. Branch ends or "niptwigs," clipped off and the leaves
or buds eaten, sometimes numerous at base of feeding trees. Preferred dens are
rock crevices, but hollows at base of trees, fallen logs, and other natural cavities
also used. Porcupines may rest in trees during summer; some even do so all winter, using conifers with
densest foliage. Urine
deposits are common
along porcupine trails
and especially at the base
of feeding trees and at
den entrances. Feeding
and resting trees may
be different species at a
given time.

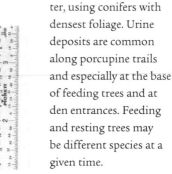

K

K: Porcupine scat

209

RED SQUIRREL Track ID

TRACKS

F and H tracks sometimes don't register entirely on solid ground. ▶

LEFT FRONT

◀ No proximal pad on H foot

LEFT HIND

COMMON GAITS

A: Gallop (common)

B: Gallop changing to diagonal F foot placement (occasional)

C: Slow hop (occasional)

D: Bound in snow with drag-out and drag-in marks (common)

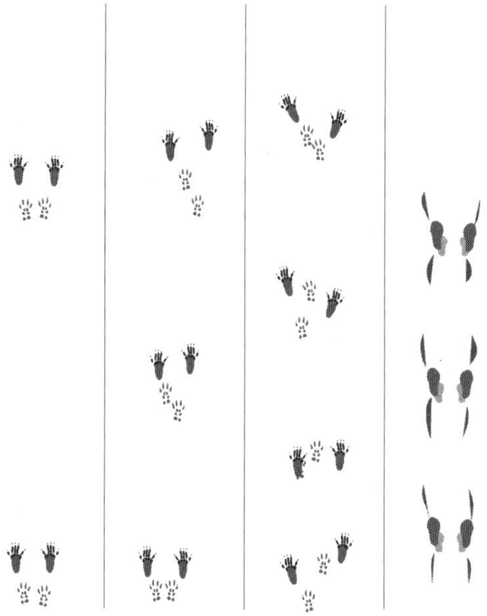

 Front

 Hind

A   B   C   D

TRACK MEASUREMENTS

	Average, inches	Average, cm	Usual range, inches*
Front width	¾	1.9	⁹⁄₁₆ to 1¹⁄₁₆
Front length	1¹⁄₁₆	2.7	¾ to 1⅜
Hind width	1¹⁄₁₆	2.7	¾ to 1¼
Hind length	1⅜	3.6	1 to 1⅞
Trail width	3⅝	9.3	2¼ to 4½
Stride**	20¹¹⁄₁₆	52.5	12 to 34½

*More than 94% of my measurements fall within this range.   **Gallop

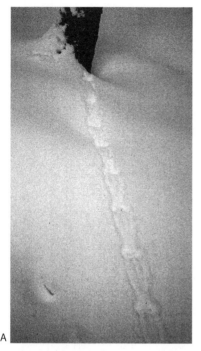

A

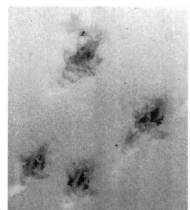

B

C

Among forest rodents that typically gallop, red squirrels (including the western Douglas's squirrel and the eastern/northern pine squirrel) fall in size between the larger gray squirrel and the smaller flying squirrel and chipmunk. All of these typically create gallop patterns with the front tracks positioned next to one another, rather than diagonally placed (as with ground squirrels). The track size and trail width help, but be careful since there may be some overlap. **Vs. gray squirrel:** Small gray squirrel tracks may overlap in trail width and even track size. Look for the absence of a lower heel pad in the red-squirrel track, and remember that gray squirrels weigh at least two to three times more than red squirrels. **Vs. flying squirrel:** Flying squirrels have a fused heel pad on the hind track and usually weigh about one-third to one-half less than the red squirrel.

FINE POINTS

RODENTS

D

A: Common gallop pattern in snow, showing foot drags
B: Gallop group, front tracks at bottom and hind tracks at top
C: Detail of right front
D: Left hind (bottom) and left front tracks

RODENTS

All red-squirrel trails, so to speak, lead to the essence of its biology, which is **food harvesting, caching, and retrieval**. Because they do not put on fat for the winter nor hibernate, pine and Douglas's squirrels must rely on stores of food—especially fir, spruce, and pine cones in the North and West, and nuts in the deciduous forests of the East. Hinting at the seriousness of a squirrel's harvesting, one Douglas's squirrel was observed cutting down 537 giant sequoia cones in half an hour; all but 15 of them had been moved from where they had fallen to hidden cache sites within three days! We can track a squirrel's harvesting in late summer and fall first by noticing which of the local tree species (and individual trees) are producing cones or nuts; red squirrels follow the ripening resources week by week. Look for newly cut cones or nuts that have fallen to the ground. (To get to the cones, squirrels often must nip off twigs and needles that also drop.) Next, look for caching sites and runs to and from them. Red squirrels habitually cache food in moist and shady spots because fir and spruce cones are thus kept from opening and scattering their seeds. By the middle of fall one squirrel may have cached thousands of cones, some of them in scattered groups of a few each, and some in groups of up to 500 or more. In winter and early spring, we can then track cache retrieval. Because squirrels remain in their territories then, most trails in snow will be to and from caches. Look also for feeding sites indicated by cone remnants or nut shells. During the period up to the next harvest (May through Aug), red squirrels may feed on tree buds and male flowers, and they may harvest fungi that they hang out to dry.

Territoriality of red squirrels is another good tracking window. Individual squirrels maintain territories primarily by vocalizing to one another, using "rattles" or chattering calls to announce periodically where they are, and using screeches to challenge an intruder. Meanwhile, nonresident squirrels may respond with "appeasement" calls—all of this to minimize energy-robbing chases (which do nevertheless take place). Neighboring squirrels apparently know their boundaries quite precisely, but a tracker must work a little to discover where they might be. First, look for middens—piles of feeding debris used over years that indicate a principal location in one squirrel's territory. (A single squirrel may have several smaller middens also.) Next, look for potential nesting sites, remembering that preferred places are in closed or semiclosed forest canopy with abundant arboreal escape routes, with shade and with ground moisture allowing long-term food storage. A main nest is often located away from the principal midden. Natural land features often serve as territorial boundaries. Sit, watch, and listen for squirrels to discover more about local territories, which in the West are often only 0.25 to 0.8 hectares (like a circle 56 to 100 meters/184 to 329 ft. across). In fall juvenile squirrels make forays into areas adjacent to their natal territories, looking for spots to settle. At this time, there are increased squirrel interactions. Once spaced, territories remain stable until the next spring's mating season.

E: Gait variations: A gallop pattern moving downslope at right shows huge leaps, while the upslope trail at left shows a bound, initially with hind tracks falling on top of front ones, then eventually behind them.

F: In Sequoia National Park, California, Douglas's squirrel runs radiate to and from a cache under a fallen log; remnants of a recently eaten cone appear at a feeding spot.

G: A red squirrel midden of spruce cones on the Kenai Peninsula, Alaska

RODENTS

E

F

G

RED SQUIRREL   Notes for the Tracker

SPECIES AND WEIGHT   *Tamiasciurus douglasii,* *T. hudsonicus,* and *T. fremonti*

28 subspecies in North America

140 to 312 g (5 to 11 oz.)

HABITAT   Coniferous forests of the West, Midwest, and Northeast, especially in spruce and fir, and in dense pine forests such as lodgepole and jack pine; also in mixed conifer and hardwood forests of the Midwest and East; sea level to 3,350 meters (11,000 ft.). Prefers forest canopy, allowing easy arboreal travel and abundant food sources such as conifer cones that can be cached. Marginal habitats on the edges of these may be used temporarily by dispersers.

BREEDING   Most breeding March to May, with earlier or later extensions based on weather and food availability. Some populations, especially in eastern United States, have a second breeding peak June to September, and some females may breed twice in a year if conditions warrant. Females relax their territoriality near estrous period; males congregate in estrous females' territories. Chases of females by males, with territorial vocalizations common. Gestation about 33 days, litters 2 to 7. Litter size and percentage of breeding females decrease with short food supply.

DEVELOPMENT   Young emerge from nest at about 7 weeks, weaned at 8 weeks. Mother does not bring food to them. Young begin to wander in mother's territory for several weeks, learning to gather and feed. By late summer to fall juveniles settle into their own territories, either on the edge of, adjacent to, or somewhat distant from their natal territory, having explored and responded to neighboring squirrels' territorial signals. There are apparently no gender patterns in dispersal.

SOCIAL HABITS   Red squirrels maintain exclusive, usually contiguous territories based on food sources and food caches. (In deciduous forests of the eastern United States, territoriality is somewhat less rigidly expressed.) A resident announces its territorial presence through frequent "rattle" calls; intruders are challenged with screech calls and/or chases. Territoriality is expressed especially in the spring, when males roam looking for estrous females and when yearlings seek out vacant territories, and in the fall when juveniles disperse. Home ranges usually 0.25 to 2 hectares (0.6 to 4.9 acres), generally inversely proportional to an area's stable food supply. Some winter den sharing has occasionally been recorded.

FEEDING

Staple foods are fir, spruce, sequoia, or pine seeds, eaten directly from cones on trees or from cones cached in ground middens. (In eastern deciduous forests, nuts of oak, hickory, and beech are eaten and cached.) In late summer and fall, cones are cut from trees in great numbers, and then gradually moved from the ground surface to middens. Summer foods, which are eaten and not cached, include developing tree buds and male flowers, and fruits from shrubs such as wild rose and raspberries. Fungi harvested in late summer to fall, put out to dry on branches or in tree crevices. Bark of conifer trees also eaten, especially in winter. Red squirrels are usually active from just before dawn to just after sunset, usually with a midday break.

RODENTS

SURVIVAL

Predation on squirrels especially by accipiters (especially goshawks), red-tailed hawks, coyotes, weasels, and martens. Loud alarm calls when potential predators are sensed. Significant mortality of young before emergence from nest, then again while young establish new territories. Young squirrels overwintering in territories without prior food stores have low survival rate.

SIGNS

Globular nests in trees made of grasses or other fine materials, about 30.5 cm (1 ft.) in diameter, either placed against trunk or several feet away on branches. Nests also in tree cavities or sometimes underground, under tree roots, for example. One squirrel's territory commonly has numerous backup nests. Middens of debris from eating cones; often large (to many feet across and 46 cm/18 in. deep) from years of use. Cone-storage sites in caches of a few cones to hundreds, buried in moist soil or hidden in hollow logs or cavities; cones often stored in or near middens. Other feeding signs include fallen twigs and conifer needles from cone harvesting, nipped branches, and fungi collected and set out to dry. Bark gnawings showing fine tooth marks. Scats sausage-shaped, about 0.3 to 0.5 cm (⅛ to ³⁄₁₆ in.) in diameter.

VOLE Track ID

TRACKS

▲ Notice relatively long toes.

The rear parts of tracks (F and H) often do not register. ►

◄ Single proximal pad on H foot

LEFT FRONT　　　**LEFT HIND**

COMMON GAITS

A: Walk (common)

B: Trot (common)

C: Bound (common in snow)

Front

Hind

A　　　B　　　C

TRACK MEASUREMENTS

	Example, inches	Example, cm
Front width	$7/16$	1.1
Front length	$3/8$	1.0
Hind width	$9/16$	1.4
Hind length	$9/16$	1.4
Trail width	$1\,5/8$	4.1
Stride	$2\,1/2$	6.4

Track size examples here refer to *Microtus californicus,* a medium to large vole in its genus. Stride length refers to a trot.

RODENTS

There are seventeen species of the *Microtus* genus (described here) as well as ten species among the genera *Arborimus, Myodes, Lemmiscus*, and *Phenacomys*. Voles generally fast-walk or trot, rather than gallop as mice do, but especially in snow, voles may bound or gallop. The drag of its small tail may occasionally be seen in snow, as illustrated in figure C on the opposite page, but most often vole trails show no tail drag. In clear prints the relatively long toes and the position and number of heel pads can be used in addition to the gait to distinguish vole tracks from those of mice.

FINE POINTS

A: Trotting pattern

B: Bound pattern

C: Group of clear prints in a tracking box, from L to R left front, left hind (superimposed over a F), right front, right hind

A

B

C

If you get down on your belly in just about any meadow, you'll eventually come face-to-face with a vole of the genus *Microtus,* and thence be led into a **microhabitat of tunnels and runs** that begs to be explored. A vole run, identified by pruned vegetation, scats, and constant use, should lead from a hidden nest (above or below ground) to food sources. Look for clipped grasses and forbs that are often carried back to the nest for storage and consumption. Look for nests and food caches sometimes aboveground after the snow melts. Voles travel both by night and day, and their runs serve as highways for many other animals. Dust a well-used run with fine soil, or set up tracking stations to determine the voles' trail mates. Harvest mice are heavy users of vole runs, but you may also find evidence of snakes, lizards, birds, rabbits, and deer mice.

The **prolific reproduction** of the many *Microtus* species leads the tracker right to the vole's importance in the local ecology. A female vole may produce four to eleven litters per year, and some of these offspring also breed, providing a staple food supply for predators including owls, weasels, coyotes, foxes, and snakes. Check the edges of prime vole habitat for well-used predator runs, and look for regurgitated owl pellets beneath nearby trees. Wait quietly near such a meadow at dusk or dawn to watch a fox or coyote hunt there. Egrets and herons also feed on voles during the day. You may be able to read expanding and crashing vole populations by studying vole-run use. In a high-density period, there may be hundreds of voles per hectare, with each vole family making many short-range trips daily. In a low-density period, there may be only a few voles per hectare.

Some *Microtus* species, as well as many voles in the genuses listed below, have adapted to quite different habitats including conifer forests, stream edges, marshes, and sagebrush, and exhibit quite different biology. Make a list of vole species close to you and begin to study their biology as well as their tracks.

SPECIES AND WEIGHT   *Microtus, Lemmiscus, Phenacomys, Myodes, Synaptomys,* and *Arborimus* spp.

29 species in North America

15 to 83 g
(0.5 to 3 oz.)

RODENTS

D

D and E: Vole tunnels in grasses

F: Vole scats from a runway

G: Clipped grasses and scats in an open area among vole tunnels

E

F

G

TRACKS

Claws some-
times do not
show (F and
H).

LEFT FRONT

Diagonally
positioned
proximal pads
(H) ◄

H track does not
always register
completely.

LEFT HIND

**COMMON
GAITS**

A: Gallop
(common)

B: Diagonal
walk
(occasional)

C: Trot
(occasional)

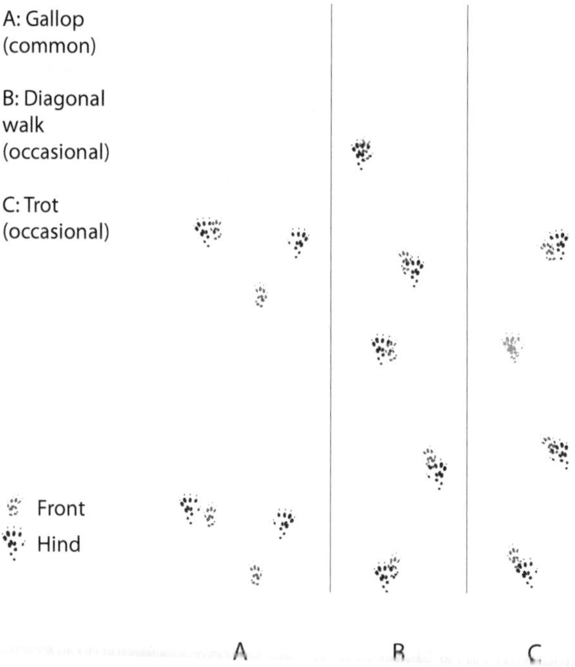

Front

Hind

A   B   C

**TRACK
MEASUREMENTS**

	Average, inches	Average, cm	Usual range, inches*
Front width	½	1.3	⁷⁄₁₆ to ⅝
Front length	⁹⁄₁₆	1.4	⁷⁄₁₆ to ¾
Hind width	⅝	1.6	½ to ¾
Hind length	¾	1.9	½ to 1¹⁄₁₆
Trail width	2¼	5.7	1¾ to 2⁹⁄₁₆
Stride**	9¼	23.5	5⁷⁄₁₆ to 12½

*More than 90% of my measurements fall within this range.   **Gallop

If you have a gallop pattern, begin with the trail width, because there are usually only one or two other mammals in a given habitat that would show a similar measurement. **Chipmunks** usually show side-to-side placement of the front tracks in a gallop, not the diagonal placement of a woodrat. Woodrats also weigh more (more than twice as much) than most chipmunks. In the desert **antelope squirrels** are about the same size as small woodrats, and elsewhere small **ground squirrels** may also overlap in track size, trail width, and stride. Both of these also may create a gallop pattern like the woodrat's, with diagonally placed front feet. The telling detail is the clear hind track; the two diagonally placed proximal pads are lacking in all three mammals mentioned above.

RODENTS

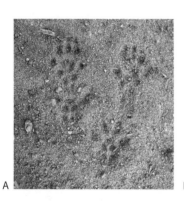

A

B

C

A: Gallop pattern

B and C: Left front and left hind, respectively

D: Right hind (top) and right front (bottom)

D

E

E: Comparing front tracks of a woodrat (left arrow) and Beechey ground squirrel (right arrow) shows that the woodrat is a much lighter animal.

F: Diagonal walk pattern

F

Many a beginning tracking student has been magically transformed after first recognizing that pile of sticks in the forest as a woodrat nest. After that realization, awareness expands and nature begins to speak with its many voices, for the ordinary has become rich. Woodrat nests are the products of a compulsive gatherer and builder. (In captivity, one woodrat carried 359 sticks and other materials to his construction site in one night!) Woodrats are always constructing new nests, reclaiming dilapidated ones, and adding materials to occupied ones. This **building imperative** is a good window to the woodrat's biology. Each house is occupied by a single woodrat, but since an individual rarely lives more than a year or two, building work is really an investment in the future. Commonly, around half of the houses in an area may be temporarily vacant, but their upkeep is vital for newborn woodrats, who would expose themselves to undue danger if they had to undertake a seven-day construction project as soon as they dispersed. As trackers, we learn a lot by examining the local woodrat real estate. To determine which houses are occupied, look for newly clipped building materials added to the top of the nest; notice whether entrances have been kept free, and look for fresh scats. You can prepare tracking boxes around a nest, thereby also finding mice, shrews, and other animals sharing the nest. Old houses torn apart can be examined for their internal nest and food-storage chambers. (Do not tear apart a nest that's intact.) Also look for "starter homes" that may consist of only a few sticks propped up against a tree or log. After surveying a neighborhood, you realize that the old saying about location is also true for a woodrat. Ask yourself why the biggest, most enduring nests are where they are, and you've not only begun to understand the woodrat, you can predict where they will be.

Travel routes that radiate out from nests are another good track window because they reveal **home-range use**. About 9 cm (3½ in.) wide, they lead primarily from a house to a foraging area, or from one foraging area to another, and are so well used that, in the desert, they appear like dirt bike trails. Often runs take advantage of cover, and woodrats are known to keep them free of new debris so that they can move to safety quickly. When you examine these routes, think vertically because woodrats are exceptional climbers, and remember that a woodrat's range may be as small as the tree surrounding its nest or as big as an acre. The determining factor is primarily food, which is your cue to look for signs. Survey surrounding shrubs and trees for freshly cut twigs that form a staple food. Individual woodrats, even when living in houses next to one another, may have separate foraging areas. Away from their house, woodrats often find nooks in a foraging area, protected on three sides and above, in which to feed; in these places look for food remnants such as twigs with bark and leaves removed. You may also find runs between nests; both males and females are known to visit others' houses, and newly dispersed juveniles do a lot of exploring for future housing.

A woodrat nest under a juniper in the High Desert Preserve in California is constructed primarily of juniper twigs and pieces of lichen.

G: Symbols show woodrat nest locations at the base of Frazier Mountain, California, elevation 1,631 meters (5,350 ft.). All nests are at the base of scrub oak, canyon oak, or ceanothus trees. Three nests (white symbols) in open locations had been torn apart by predators. The concentration of nests in dense brush to the left includes at least one small "starter" nest.

H and I: Two years after a woodrat nest (H) was photographed, it was dug apart by a predator (I). The natural hollow visible here contained the sleeping chamber and food-storage area.

J: The padded foot allows climbing on cacti and other challenging surfaces.

K: Woodrats will chew around each tuft of thorns on a prickly pear cactus, drop the tuft to the ground, and then eat the flesh. Fruits are also eaten.

L: In a poor acorn year, woodrats resorted to eating inner bark during the fall (arrow).

M: Fresh cuts on this birch-leaf mountain mahogany indicate that a nearby nest is being supplied with food.

WOODRAT Notes for the Tracker

SPECIES AND WEIGHT *Neotoma* spp.

13 species in North America

100 to 585 g (3.5 to 20.5 oz.), most species 130 to 385 g (4.6 to 13.4 oz.)

Male usually larger than female

HABITAT Coastal scrub, chaparral, deciduous and coniferous forests, brushlands, streamside thickets, desert, juniper, and oak woodland, from sea level to 3,962 meters (13,000 ft.). Found primarily where relatively dense undercover provides nest sites or where cactus stands, rock outcrops, or talus provides shelter.

BREEDING Breeding seasons vary by species and area, for example, November through May in desert, February through September along coast, April through August in high mountains. Females may produce 1 to 3 litters per year depending upon area, each litter with 2 to 4 young. Gestation 27 to 37 days, depending upon species. Apparent competition among males for breeding, evidenced by territorial scent marking.

DEVELOPMENT Young attached to mother's nipples for first 15 days even when she needs to move about. Weaning at 9 to 10 weeks; young continue growing throughout their 1st year but foot is adult size by 40 days. Young disperse temporarily to unused nests, females generally staying closer to their mother's home and males dispersing farther. Subadults in some species are known to make numerous exploratory trips from their temporary nests before establishing a permanent home or building a new nest.

SOCIAL HABITS Each nest is occupied by a single woodrat except when a female is raising young. About 50% to 60% of nests in an area may be unoccupied, only used by dispersing young or to escape danger when necessary. Woodrat home ranges usually 0.02 to 2.6 hectares (0.05 to 6.4 acres), sometimes overlapping (especially males' over females'). Both males and females are known to visit others' nests.

FEEDING Leaves, twigs, blossoms, and fruits from trees and shrubs including oak, willow, blackberry, rose, snowberry, creosote bush, cedar, juniper, and many chaparral plants make up majority of diet. Branch ends are clipped and either eaten in the field or brought back to the nest to eat or store. Developing flowers or catkins are also preferred seasonally. Desert woodrats rely on cactus flesh and fruit as well as leaves and bark from local trees or shrubs. Seasonally, seeds such as acorns, maple seeds, and mesquite pods are collected and stored in the nest. Many dozens of fresh twigs, and up to 9 kg (20 lb.) of acorns, for example, have been found in single nests. Food eaten in the field is often consumed in a spot sheltered from predation from the sides and above.

SURVIVAL

High mortality from predation by owls, foxes, coyotes, bobcats, badgers, weasels, and other predators leave many woodrat nests temporarily vacant. An individual woodrat is unlikely to live more than 1 or 2 years. Nests are vulnerable to fires and floods.

SIGNS

Conspicuous houses, up to 1.8 meters (6 ft.) in diameter and 6 ft. high, usually built at the base of trees or shrubs where there is cover; houses constructed of sticks, bark, or other locally abundant materials, often adorned with miscellaneous items such as tin cans, coyote scat, or spent shotgun shells. A small percentage of nests are in trees. Houses feature a few to many entrances at ground level or above, and inside chambers for sleeping, food storage, and defecation. In desert and high mountains, nests are often cavities in rocks protected by masses of sticks or other materials, without the elaborate inside chambers of stick houses. Other desert nests are highly fortified with cactus segments. Scats sausage-shaped, usually 0.5 cm (³⁄₁₆ in.) in diameter and about 1 cm (⅜ in.) long, accumulated in latrines or on eating perches near nest. In some species heavy aggregations of dried white urine, added to by streaks of new yellowish urine, at latrines. Well-used runs about 8.9 cm (3½ in.) wide, radiating from nests to food-gathering areas or other nests. Feeding signs include small green branches clipped at 45-degree angle from trees or shrubs around nest or in food-gathering areas.

N: Woodrat scat

RODENTS

WEASELS AND SKUNKS

WEASELS

TRACKS

F claws prominent, curved toward inside of foot ▶

H smaller than F, claws less prominent

Second pad sometimes shows on F. ▶

Arc-shaped heel pads, H narrower than F

LEFT FRONT LEFT HIND

COMMON GAITS

A: Diagonal walk, indirect register (common)

B: Slow walk, which may be seen when the badger hunts (occasional)

C: Lope (occasional)

D: Trot (occasional)

 Front

Hind

A B C D

TRACK MEASUREMENTS

	Average, inches	Average, cm	Usual range, inches*
Front width	2	5.2	1⁷⁄₁₆ to 2¾
Front length	2⅛	5.3	1¾ to 2⅝
Hind width	1⅝	4.1	1¼ to 2⅜
Hind length	1¹⁵⁄₁₆	4.9	1½ to 2¼
Trail width	4⅛	10.5	1½ to 6
Stride**	9⁵⁄₁₆	23.7	7 to 14½

*More than 96% of my measurements fall within this range. **Diagonal walk

A badger's very pigeon-toed diagonal walk pattern is usually a giveaway, even when clear prints are not showing. Note that the hind track usually pitches inward more than the front. At first glance clear prints may sometimes resemble a **coyote**'s if the small inner toe isn't seen. Look for the claw marks way ahead of the toes and positioned to the inside of the foot as well as the severe hind pitch. The five-toed **raccoon** track, especially walking on the ball of its foot, may resemble a badger's but without the long claws and with toes more uniformly shaped than the badger's. The raccoon also rarely creates a diagonal walk pattern. A **porcupine**'s trail may sometimes show a waddling diagonal walk pattern with visible pitch, but its heel pad is entirely different; it has shorter claws and normally shows a significant tail-drag mark.

FINE POINTS

A: Typical pigeon-toed diagonal walk pattern (each double print pitched inward)

B: Indirect registering double prints

C: Left front track

D: Left hind track

Tracking a badger for a long distance absorbs you completely into the **energy of a restless hunter**. Rather than follow regular trails, a badger explores its hunting territory with a wound-up energy propelling it, tank-like, over hillocks and through thickets, making abrupt turns and circling back over its trail. An hour or two of "becoming the animal" may make your head spin, but the payoff is a rich understanding of the badger's spirit. As you follow the badger, pay attention to sudden gait changes such as slow walks, stops, and starts, which indicate increased alertness. Pick one of these spots and read the exact sequence of foot placement (prominent claw drags sometimes show you how each foot exited as the animal made a turn). Also read pressure releases here, perhaps picking up head position and direction as the badger sniffs and listens. Such an investment can bring you quite precisely into a moment of a badger's life. Often a badger makes a beeline from one hunting area to another. In difficult soil you can sometimes key in on the prominent claw impressions to follow it.

Another window to tracking the badger is its **hunting strategy**. The badger usually depends upon a core prey species such as ground squirrels, gophers, or kangaroo rats but may catch a variety of other prey, including ground-nesting birds and reptiles, as it hunts opportunistically. Either way, it digs for its prey, often quite furiously, and indeed one was observed even digging through an asphalt road. The badger may enlarge an entrance to a burrow or may dig straight into the ground toward the nest of its prey, sometimes after plugging up alternative entrances to corner it. Or it might dig shallow depressions exploring for sleeping lizards, snakes, or even insect larvae. The badger also often revisits its old diggings to catch animals using these depressions as convenient hiding places. Notice the kind and type of its diggings to get an idea of its hunting technique at this time and place. Also check for nearby coyote tracks: Coyotes sometimes follow a badger or even entice it along in a hunting partnership if the terrain and prey distribution warrant.

Seasonal denning habits may give you another insight into interpreting badger signs. In summer a single badger may excavate a new sleeping den virtually every night, while in fall and winter it may reuse old dens often, even retreating to a single one for weeks. In the spring the female's natal den is much deeper than an overnight den and will show twice the apron of excavated soil. Relate the number and freshness of the dens to the season and gain some insight into your badger's use of its home range.

A badger trail in the East Mojave Desert of California

E

F

G

E: A badger skids to a stop investigating the top of a previous dig.

F: A badger, moving from bottom to top, looks right, then left in a typical stuttering pattern.

G: Entering from bottom left, a badger completes a curious loop.

H

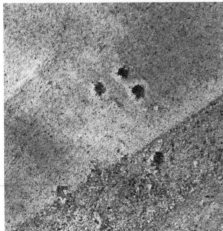

H: Claw impressions in a badger's trail stand out even when the foot doesn't otherwise register prominently (arrows in top photo). The position of the claws indicate the particular track, for example, a right hind in the bottom photo.

I: A female badger with two young has burrowed entirely under a two-lane road, dislodging large chunks of asphalt as she emerged.

SPECIES
AND
WEIGHT

Taxidea taxus

4 subspecies in
North America

4 to 12 kg (9 to 26 lb.)

Male 20% larger than
female

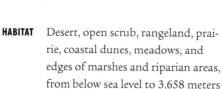

HABITAT   Desert, open scrub, rangeland, prairie, coastal dunes, meadows, and
edges of marshes and riparian areas,
from below sea level to 3,658 meters
(12,000 ft.) where ground-dwelling prey are
locally abundant. Prefers light sandy or gravelly soil but will occupy heavy clay
soils. Forests and areas with dense vegetation avoided.

WEASELS

BREEDING   Mating usually between June and August. Some females, but no males, breed in
their 1st year. After delayed implantation, a litter of 1 to 5 (average 3) are born
between February and early April.

DEVELOPMENT   Female raises young alone, sometimes using numerous dens in addition to the
natal den. Young emerge after 6 weeks and may bask in sun near den. Female
hunts with young until May or June, sometimes providing food after weaning.
Young usually disperse between May and July, often crossing marginal habitat.
Longest observed dispersal was 110 km (68 miles). Male solitary except during
breeding season, female solitary except during breeding and rearing seasons.
Fighting not uncommon during breeding season.

SOCIAL HABITS   An area's prey density generally determines home-range size; females' ranges
have been documented from 0.2 km² to 15 km² and males' from 0.5 km² to 35
km². Females' home ranges usually do not overlap much with each other, while
males' overlap with each other's and several females'. Ranges compress substantially in winter, especially in colder climates. Badgers are usually nocturnal,
but there is more daytime activity, especially among juveniles, in June through
August. In summer new dens may be dug almost daily; in autumn and winter
dens are often reused. Unrelated badgers sometimes, but rarely, occupy the same
den at the same time.

Core diet is usually burrowing rodents such as ground squirrels, prairie dogs, pocket gophers, and kangaroo rats, supplemented by ground-dwelling mammals (rabbits, mice, voles, chipmunks, shrews), ground-nesting birds, snakes, lizards, toads, and insect larvae. Digs out prey, in spring focusing on newly born rodents; revisits old diggings to catch prey using them for temporary shelter. Sometimes plugs up alternative entrances before digging for trapped prey; sometimes ambushes prey from underground. Travels and hunts with coyotes where terrain and prey distribution make it mutually advantageous.

SURVIVAL

No natural enemies; human-caused mortality from road kills, trapping, poisoning, and habitat destruction has resulted in the badger being designated a California Species of Special Concern.

SIGNS

Sleeping burrows 20 to 30 cm (8 to 12 in.) wide with large apron of excavated dirt. Old burrows sometimes appropriated and enlarged by coyotes and foxes. Natal burrows 1.2 to 2.1 meters (4 to 7 ft.) deep, with twice the excavated dirt, mixed with badger hair, and many tracks coming in and out. Scat usually buried in burrows or at base of diggings, rarely found exposed. Numerous exploratory diggings, some of them shallow.

WEASELS

J: Active badger den

K: Fresh badger digging

FISHER Track ID

TRACKS

Proximal pad sometimes shows (F only). ►

Inner toe smaller (F and H) ◄

◄ No proximal pad on H foot

LEFT FRONT   LEFT HIND

COMMON GAITS

A: Bound (common)

B: Lope (common)

C: Gallop (common)

D: Walk (esp. in deeper snow)

Front

Hind

A   B   C   D

TRACK MEASUREMENTS

	Usual range, inches	Usual range, cm
Front width	2 to 3¼	5.1 to 8.3
Front length	2⅛ to 3⅞	5.4 to 9.8
Hind width	2 to 3½	5.1 to 8.9
Hind length	2⅛ to 3	5.4 to 7.6
Trail width	3 to 5½	7.6 to 14.0
Stride*	7 to 14	17.8 to 35.6

*Diagonal walk

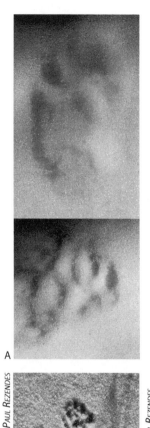

A

B

C

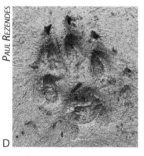

D

A fisher's track measurements put it in the range of three other mammals with five toes on the front and hind feet, namely raccoons, martens, and river otters. A raccoon's elongated toes and common pace-walking pattern should easily distinguish its tracks from a fisher's. **Vs. marten:** Track widths greater than about 7 cm (2¾ in.) very probably belong to a fisher, but a smaller female fisher's and male marten's tracks overlap in size. Fisher tracks tend to have less hair in winter than martens', therefore showing a more distinct palm-pad area. Also, a fisher's inner toe tends to register more often. Fishers walk rather than bound in deep snow, while martens rarely do, and a walking stride of 25 cm (10 in.) or more should indicate fisher. Fishers usually weigh at least twice as much as martens. **Vs. river otter:** Fisher tracks lack webbing, and their inner toe is smaller than the others, in contrast to the hind inner toe of the river otter, which is larger.

A: Right front (top) and left hind (bottom) tracks

B: Detail of lope, from bottom to top F-H-F-H

C: Left front track

D: Left hind track

239

A fisher's **track patterns**, though familiar to those who track its relatives the mink, marten, and weasel, can lead us to some interesting observations about a mammal's size and its consequent relation to habitat. For while fisher tracks can overlap in size with martens', the fisher is heavier and stockier, on average at least twice the weight of a typical marten. That's why you see diagonal walking patterns among fishers when snow is deep or when snow is thinly crusted and collapsible. And that's why fishers may avoid deep-snow areas entirely, or else follow only packed hare trails in these places, when snow is soft. At these times notice how your fisher changes its habitat use because its hunting requirements remain the same. Of course, like other mustelids, fishers also bound and lope. Look at location and speed of these trails: Though fishers are much less vulnerable to predation than martens or weasels, they nevertheless avoid open spaces as much as possible, skirting them or dashing across them quickly between patches where they change their speed and gait to hunt. Perhaps this avoidance is an evolutionary holdover from its ancestors.

Adaptive to its local prey, a fisher's **hunting style** is another good tracking window. Following memory, a fisher may set out on a direct line to investigate each known porcupine den in its range, zoning in to active ones by scent. When a porcupine is caught or driven into the open, a fisher repeatedly circles to attack its face, and trackers have found these stories in tracks—including the final act, a porcupine skin with quills left behind. Or, a fisher may set out on a multi-kilometer grid search for a favorite food, the snowshoe hare, sniffing out every likely nook until a hare is flushed and caught. On the way a fisher may surprise a foraging squirrel on the ground, or dig where it hears a mouse. The key for the tracker here is noticing habitat patches, i.e., concentrated hunting areas where a fisher may spend several days before moving on to another patch. Remember to look for evidence of scent marking along every fisher trail.

SPECIES AND WEIGHT	*Pekania pennanti*
	2.0 to 5.5 kg (4.4 to 12.1 lb.)
	Males about twice the weight of females

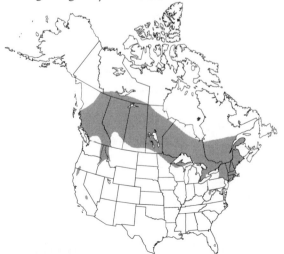

Forest areas of the Northeast, upper Midwest, Rockies, and West, especially in stands of conifers or mixed deciduous/conifer trees with high canopy cover. Avoids open areas for hunting and dispersal and selects higher cover areas seasonally for resting spots. Generally, but not always, prefers habitats containing snowshoe hares or porcupines.

HABITAT

Breeding usually March through April, about 10 days after a female has given birth; increase in scent marking and irregular trails then. Mating described as "prolonged and vigorous." Delayed implantation until following January or February, gestation about 30 days, litters usually 2 to 3. Natal nests high in tree hollows.

BREEDING

Young nursed in den for about 8 weeks; female may use up to 3 rearing dens. Female and kits may travel together to age 4 or 5 months (until July or Aug), when kits approach adult weight. In fall young become solitary and usually establish home range by late winter.

DEVELOPMENT

Solitary except for breeding and kit rearing. Home ranges 8 km² to 49 km², males' larger than females'. Ranges typically overlap those of opposite sex but not of same sex.

SOCIAL HABITS

Where abundant, snowshoe hares or porcupines make up a large portion of diet; hares flushed from hiding, and porcupines attacked on ground or in trees with bites to face. Otherwise carrion (e.g., deer), birds, squirrels, and small mammals (including mice, voles, and shrews) are important diet items regionally and seasonally. Fungi may be eaten commonly, and some fruits supplement the diet. In California's southern Sierras, lizards, pocket gophers, and ground squirrels are eaten.

FEEDING

Predation of fishers by raptors or other carnivores is rare. Some states and Canadian provinces allow trapping, which takes a high proportion of juveniles and adult males. Habitat destruction, for example, clear-cutting that eliminates areas of cover, hinders population expansion in the West.

SURVIVAL

Scats often folded cords, tapered at ends, sometimes overlapping in size with mink scats. Resting sites in tree cavities (especially deciduous trees); in tree nests such as squirrels' nests, large birds' nests, or dense clumps of branches; or in burrows such as woodchuck holes. Many resting sites not heavily reused. Scent posts marked with urine, scat, or glandular secretions on raised areas such as stumps or logs.

SIGNS

WEASELS

TRACKS

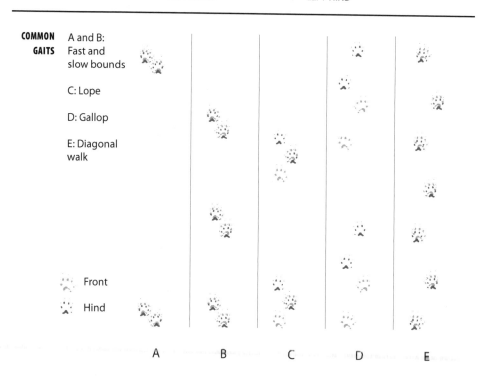

Proximal heel pad sometimes shows in F foot. ►

Furred foot, especially in winter, muffles toe and heel pads (F and H).

◄ Inside toe faint (esp. H)

LEFT FRONT   **LEFT HIND**

WEASELS

COMMON GAITS

A and B: Fast and slow bounds

C: Lope

D: Gallop

E: Diagonal walk

Front

Hind

A   B   C   D   E

TRACK MEASUREMENTS

	Average, inches	Average, cm	Usual range, inches*
Front width	1¾	4.4	1⅜ to 2
Front length	1¾	4.5	1⅜ to 2
Hind width	1⁹⁄₁₆	4.0	1⅝ to 1¾
Hind length	1⅝	4.1	1⅜ to 2
Trail width	3¹¹⁄₁₆	9.4	2¾ to 4½
Stride**	22⅞	58.0	10 to 33½

*More than 96% of my measurements fall within this range.   **Bound

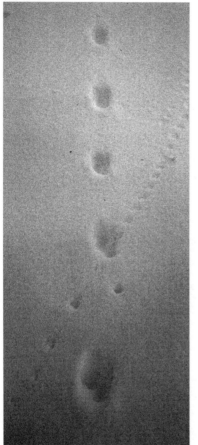

Typical marten trails, usually bounding or loping, put the tracks in the weasel family category and might be confused with those of mink or fisher, as there could be an overlap in track size (long-tailed weasels being too small in trail width and track size). **Vs. mink:** Marten tracks lack webbing between the toes; habitat away from water and tree-climbing behavior would also suggest marten. **Vs. fisher:** A large male marten's tracks may overlap in size with a small female fisher's, but remember that even then, the fisher is likely to weigh twice as much and make deeper track impressions. Also, a marten's heel pad (especially in winter when it is covered with fur) appears smaller than a fisher's. In deep snow fishers walk more often and leave a body trough not left by martens.

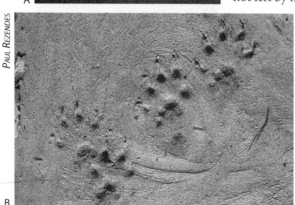

A: Common bound pattern, moving from top to bottom

B: Clear prints, from left to right LF-LH-RF-RH

C: Loping pattern, F-H-F-H from bottom to top

Following a marten trail over the snow, sharing every stutter and stop and turn, is a spellbinding experience equivalent only to the marten's own **spontaneous, completely absorbed drive to hunt**. When the temperature is very cold and the marten would lose precious heat, it hunts. When the snow is soft and makes the going difficult, it hunts. Showing no methodical visits of previous feeding sites, a marten trail is a passionate in-the-moment search, whose inborn nature is suggested by biologists who noted that marten released from live traps began to hunt immediately, rather than run away to safety. The questions prompted by a marten's trail—"What is this animal thinking?" and "How is it perceiving?"—may be revealed by reading the tracks, even when snow consistency obscures the pressure releases. Look for subtle changes of speed, hesitations, or lead changes from one side to the other that may be caused by head turns. If your marten stops, picture whether it remains on all fours or stands up on its hind feet; where is it looking, listening, or sniffing? Marten often stop to investigate fresh trails of potential prey like red squirrels or snowshoe hares and indeed may follow them for long distances. While a marten likely smells the freshness of a trail, we trackers can use track-aging skills in snow to understand why some trails are followed and others bypassed. Much of a marten's winter hunting takes place under the snowpack where voles are active or a red squirrel rests near its cache of cones. As does the marten, look for downed logs and tree trunks that provide access under the snow, trying to read why a marten selects some and not other tunnels to use.

A marten's **summer foraging** must be read in other ways, because the forest floor holds few clear prints and tracking is more challenging then. Marten may wait in ambush outside a ground-squirrel nest, they may try to dig out a burrowing squirrel or chipmunk, they may enlarge a red squirrel's tree den or raid a bird's nest. They may hunt for voles on the ground and may also climb trees or rocks near meadow edges to attain a good vantage point for listening and watching, whence they can pounce onto potential prey. Look for hunting signs, but also, in spring and summer look for potential marten den sites in rocks or logs, which may have latrines and prey remains nearby showing what's in the marten's current diet.

A marten's **habitat dependency** is another good tracking window. Marten survive harsh winters by choosing dens beneath the snowpack that are best insulated, especially cavities in fallen logs and root clumps characteristic of old-growth forests. The colder the winter, the more these dens are used. Marten also require good hunting areas, either in forest areas with much understory vegetation or along meadow edges. For safety, marten rarely cross large open spaces greater than 50 meters (164 ft.) and choose canopied travel routes—limiting their habitat and their ability to disperse. Logging and development that remove old-growth trees and forest management practices that result in islands of forest separated by open space do not provide good habitat for marten and, some would say, destroy the health of the forest as well.

A marten lopes across open space in Sequoia National Park.

WEASELS

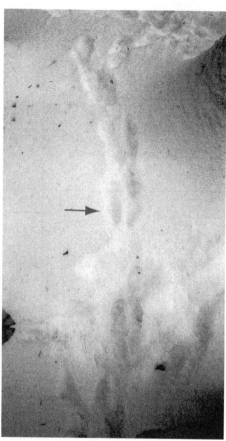

D

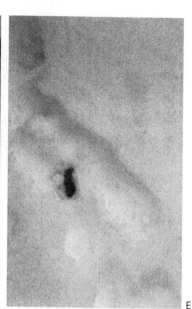

E

D: At the middle of this image, a marten has bounded to a stop and raised up on its hind feet, leaving elongated hind tracks (arrow). It continued for two more bounds before stopping again and then turning off to the right.

E: After a snowstorm in Sequoia National Park, a marten, moving toward the bottom of this photo, has squatted to defecate.

F: This bound, with hind tracks partly covering the front tracks, is unusual for the placement of the hind tracks slightly to the right of the front ones; the pitch of the front tracks to the left also confirms that this marten has its shoulders angled to the left.

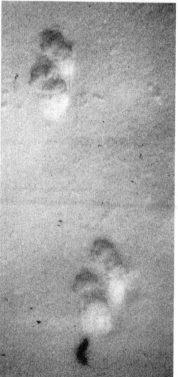

F

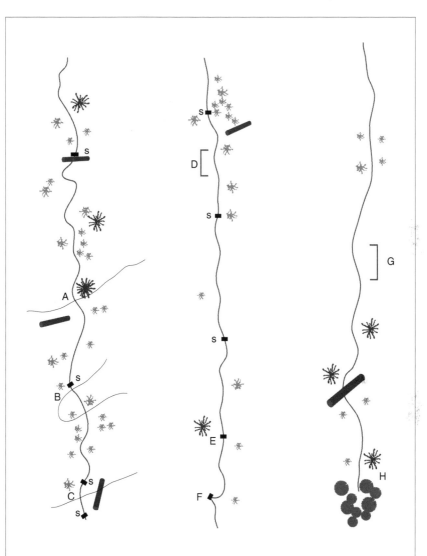

A marten's bounding trail in snow at Sequoia National Park, California, begins at the top left and moves downward in sequence through these three trail segments. Key: s = stops. A = Crosses another pine-marten trail. B and C = Crosses Douglas's squirrel trails. D = Changes lead from right to left for four bounds, then changes back. E = Stops, squats, and urinates. F = Stops, turns to the right, and looks. G = Changes lead from right to left for seven bounds, then changes back. H = Trail lost inside tight grove of sequoias, where marten probably climbed into the trees.

WEASELS

WEASELS

SPECIES AND WEIGHT
Martes americana

8 subspecies in North America

280 to 1,250 g (10 oz. to 2.8 lb.)

Male up to 65% larger than female

HABITAT Spruce, fir, and lodgepole pine forests, and some mixed conifer forests of the North and West. Prefers old-growth forest areas, where snags and fallen logs provide denning sites and access to hunting beneath the snow in winter. Marten prefer to travel where there is substantial forest canopy and rarely cross large open spaces. Riparian areas, and meadow edges within these forests, are preferred hunting areas.

BREEDING Breeding usually July to August; breeding pair may travel together for several days. Gestation 7 to 9 months including delayed implantation. Births usually March to April, litters average about 3. Natal den often near ground level, under logs or rocks, or in snags; may show latrine and prey remains nearby.

DEVELOPMENT Young weaned at about 6 weeks, emerge from den thereafter. Female continues to raise kits, often using numerous other "maternal dens" in rocks, snags, logs, or red-squirrel middens. Various combinations of a mated pair and their offspring have been observed traveling together from fall until the next spring. Juvenile dispersal of up to 40 km (25 miles) has been recorded; some may breed in their 2nd year.

SOCIAL HABITS Home ranges usually 3 km² to 10 km²; some male ranges to 27.5 km² recorded. Marten space themselves apart from one another through scent marking and sometimes vocalizations. Some females show fidelity to home range from year to year; others may establish entirely new territories if the food supply dictates.

FEEDING In most habitats marten's staple food throughout the year consists of voles of the genera *Myodes* and *Microtus,* hunted in forest debris and along meadow edges, respectively. In certain areas and years, snowshoe hares are also important prey. Seasonally, marten also feed on pine squirrels, Douglas's squirrels, ground squirrels, chipmunks, birds, berries such as huckleberry and wild rose, and insects (especially social ones like yellow jackets). Carrion is consumed opportunistically and may cause a marten to remain in one area for a few days. Marten hunt by ambush or by digging prey from their hiding places. In winter marten course through their territory often looking for logs or tree trunks that are access points to areas underneath the snow where they can hunt; marten may also follow a prey's tracks for a long distance. Prey is often taken to a protected spot or to a den to be consumed; especially larger prey may be cached and later retrieved. Though they hunt primarily on the ground, marten are known to use trees, logs, and rocks as vantage points from which they can pounce on prey they detect.

SURVIVAL

Marten depend upon large-scale woody debris on a forest floor for insulated resting sites in winter; these areas also support abundant prey. Hence, loss of old-growth forest habitat has shrunk marten range in recent years. Marten are vulnerable to predation from owls, eagles, and sometimes fishers, among other mammalian predators. Travel routes take advantage of cover for safety.

SIGNS

Scats are twisted cords about 0.6 to 1 cm (¼ to ⅜ in.) in diameter, with pungent musky odor; seeds may occur in them as well as animal fur. Scats deposited along trails, on raised surfaces, and in latrines near dens. Summer resting places in rock piles, under logs, in tree or snag cavities, or in dense branches or mistletoe clumps in conifers. Winter resting sites generally at ground level; in coldest weather, cavities in woody debris are preferred. Red-squirrel middens are used extensively for dens in some areas. Prey remains and scats near dens. Runs found to and from resting spots; snowshoe hare runs may be used when snow is deep and soft.

WEASELS

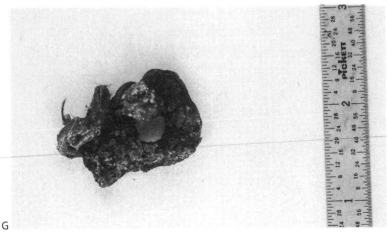

G

G: Marten scat

TRACKS

Proximal pad in F track visible in clear, complete print ►

Webbing between toes faintly visible (F and H) ►

Inside toe sometimes faint (F and H) ◄

LEFT FRONT   LEFT HIND

COMMON GAITS

A: Bound (common)

B: Lope (common)

C: Diagonal walk (common)

D: Gallop (occasional)

(D is smaller scale)

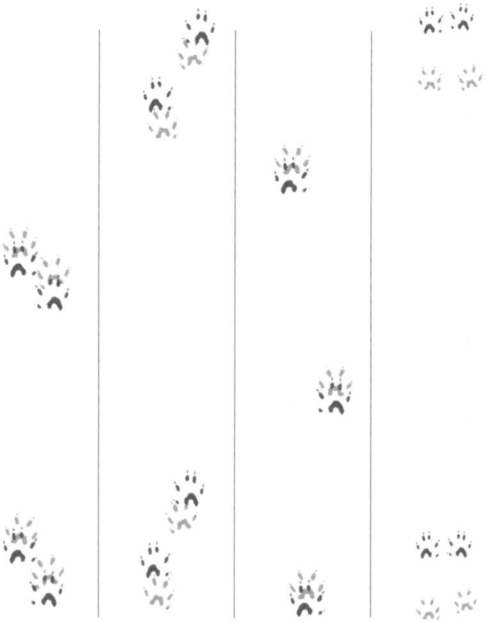

Front

Hind

A   B   C   D

WEASELS

TRACK MEASUREMENTS	Average, inches	Average, cm
Front width	1³/₁₆	3.0
Front length	1¼	3.2
Hind width	1⅜	3.4
Hind length	1¼	3.1
Trail width	2⅜	6.1
Stride	9 to 30	23 to 75

Five-toed tracks near the water, larger than weasel tracks and smaller than river-otter tracks, usually point to mink; confirm your hypothesis not only by studying the clear prints but by noticing the patterns. Mink often leave tracks in groups of four in loping or bounding gaits along a streamside (though exploratory walks may also be seen). When traveling across the snow, mink may leave bounding pairs (see A opposite page) similar to a **long-tailed weasel**'s, but with usually wider trail width and track size. In riparian areas next to streams, a **ringtail**'s five-toed track is somewhat similar, but the heel-pad shape differs substantially.

WEASELS

Doug Gaulke

A

B

C

A: Common loping pattern; sequence from bottom to top of each group is F-H-F-H.

B: Detail of a bound group, with hind superimposed over each front

C: Gallop detail, with two front tracks at bottom

If feeding were a team sport, then the mink could easily play every position. Like a river otter, it can swim easily to catch a fish or a swimming muskrat. Like a fox, it can ambush a rabbit or take a young ground squirrel. Like a raccoon, it can forage at streamside for crabs or crayfish. And like a weasel, it can poke into a tunnel to catch a muskrat or mouse. **Mink are generalists** in the most positive sense of that word, applying their many skills to seek out the most abundant food of the season and area. As trackers, we should look at a habitat from the mink's perspective, seeing what food might be focused on at this moment. A meadow vole population explosion in a field near a stream might attract mink, as might an area where fish are spawning, or a marshland where ducks, coots, or loons are nesting, or muskrat houses with young animals. Look for mink tracks, trails, and scat piles in these areas, remembering that mink often work both sides of a stream. When local food is scarce—for example, when a marshland dries up—mink may forage in drier areas, or they may travel to new food areas, up to 24 km (15 miles) in one recorded instance.

Despite their ability to hunt in meadows and brush, mink really are anchored to **shoreline habitat**, and this provides another good tracking window. Wherever they have been studied, mink always denned not far from the shoreline of a lake, marsh, or stream, in most cases within a couple of meters. This proximity guides our tracking, for we can survey the banks for dens, tracks, foraging places, and latrines. Mink tracks are commonly found going along the shoreline. Read the gait and the tracks to discover whether your mink is just traveling along or stopping to sense what opportunities present themselves in the water. Because mink cannot swim as acrobatically as otters, nor stay underwater as long, they dive and fish most easily in shallower pools with slower-moving water. Here, they often sense fish from the shore before diving, rather than surprise them from under water. Along the Pacific coast, mink are known to forage in the tide pools almost always at low tide, when they can make fairly shallow dives to snatch prey from the rich subtidal zones and not be bothered by significant wave action.

Mink do not give us many different gaits to study, preferring only walks and bounds, but their **locomotion** nevertheless is a good teacher, allowing us to become a connoisseur of their easiest gait, the bound. In it, mink push off with their two front feet, elevate, and then push off with their two hind feet. Though this gait often produces the typical paired tracks found among weasels, it can also produce, with very slight variation in foot placement and timing, patterns we might call lopes or gallops. Shun labels for these, and rather immerse yourself into the current track pattern, visualizing motion and noticing nuances of speed change and shoulder orientation dictated by the mink's intentions—for example traveling to a new hunting area or being alert for feeding opportunities. Mink also enjoy tunneling in the snow and sliding like otters.

DOUG GAULKE

D

D: In soft snow, mink often create a trough rather than bound on the surface. This tunnel in Wisconsin leads to a den.

E and F: Streamside travel in California. In E a mink explores upstream along the shore of the Eel River, leaving faint groups of four bounding tracks (arrows). In F a mink crosses a mudflat on the bank of the Cosumnes River, moving directly and quickly to a brushy area; the disks behind the toes show that this is a fast walk.

E

F

SPECIES AND WEIGHT	*Neovison vison* 15 subspecies in North America 0.5 to 1.6 kg (1.2 to 3.5 lb.) Male 50% to 80% larger than female

HABITAT Streamsides, lake and river shores, marshes, and swampland are usual habitats; areas with dense brush nearby are preferred, but some foraging occurs in meadows, open areas, or coastal tide pools.

BREEDING Breeding usually January through April; males may travel widely in search of females. Mating pairs may be together for a short time and may den together briefly. Females commonly mate with more than 1 male in a season. In some areas breeding season (e.g., autumn in Florida and Apr and May in coastal Alaska) is timed so that the raising of young coincides with local food abundance. Gestation about 51 days (may vary with delayed implantation), litters usually 3 to 6.

DEVELOPMENT Young grow rapidly, weaned at 5 to 6 weeks. Juveniles are 40% of adult weight and 60% of adult length at 7 weeks; juvenile females are adult size by late summer, juvenile males reach their larger adult size between November and February. Female and kits remain together until late August and then young usually disperse, when young siblings may travel together for a time.

SOCIAL HABITS Mainly solitary except when female travels with young in late summer. In areas near rivers or streams, home ranges are linear, following a stream for about 1.8 to 5 km (1 to 3 miles), but may encompass tributaries also. Near lakes or marshes, home ranges may have other shapes and be as large as 20 hectares (49 acres). Males' home ranges larger than females'; scent marking occurs but significant territoriality is not recorded.

FEEDING Generalist forager eating fish, crustaceans, insects, mice, muskrats, rabbits, frogs, and birds and their eggs. Streamside foraging common; mink may dive to catch fish or to bring up crustaceans. Muskrat tunnels may be entered, or voles may be caught in meadows. Local and seasonal preferences for the most available food; larger males tend to travel more widely and to take larger prey than females. Hunting and foraging primarily at night or at dusk or dawn.

Little mortality to predators, though some mink are taken by foxes, bobcats, lynxes, and owls. Significant human trapping, though most commercial mink furs now come from farm-raised animals. Mink are susceptible to environmental contaminants such as mercury and PCB in fish that they eat; this may affect mink reproduction.

Scats about 1 cm (⅜ in.) diameter, usually black or brown folded cords tapered at both ends; scats containing fish are oily and eventually disintegrate. Scats deposited on elevated places and especially near dens. Dens almost always in vicinity of water, in muskrat or woodchuck holes, among tree roots, or in brush piles. Entrances 10 to 15 cm (4 to 6 in.) diameter; some entrances may be away from water. Mink generally use numerous dens in their home ranges (up to 24 recorded) and commonly stay in a den only 1 to several nights before moving to another. One study found that mink traveled an average of 350 meters (1,148 ft.) between dens on consecutive nights. Well-worn trails to preferred feeding areas. In snow, otterlike slides and tunnels.

RIVER OTTER Track ID

WEASELS

TRACKS

Webbing between toes shows in clear prints, esp. H track.

Proximal pad often visible in F track

H track larger; inside toe large

LEFT FRONT

LEFT HIND

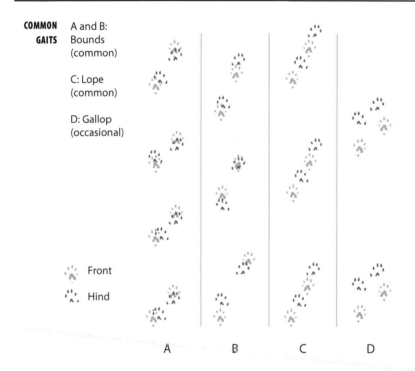

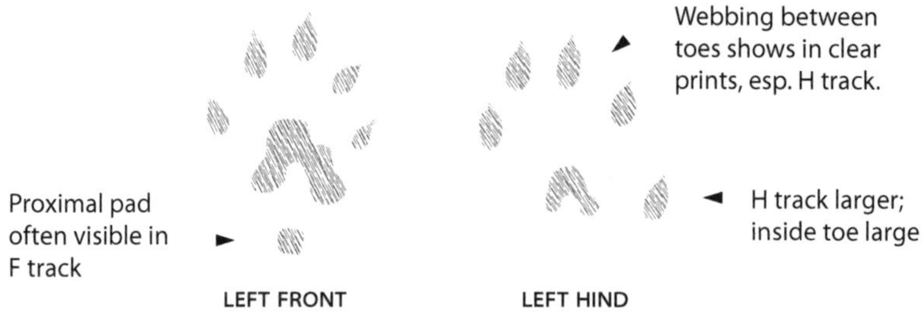

COMMON GAITS

A and B: Bounds (common)

C: Lope (common)

D: Gallop (occasional)

Front

Hind

A B C D

TRACK MEASUREMENTS

	Average, inches	Average, cm
Front width	2½	6.3
Front length	2½	6.3
Hind width	2⅞	7.2
Hind length	2¾	7.0
Trail width	4¾ to 7¾	12.1 to 19.7
Stride*	15+	38+

*Bound

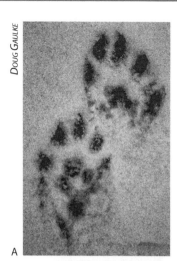

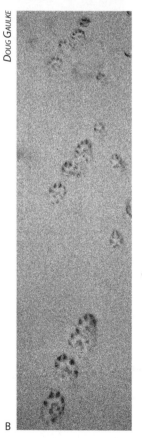

Five-toed tracks 5.1 cm (2 in.) or more in width put the river otter in the vicinity of raccoons and fishers; mink, weasel, and pine marten tracks are smaller and wolverine larger. Clear river-otter tracks, with the characteristic weasel-shaped heel pad, webbing between the toes (especially in the hind track), and a wider hind track with prominent inner toe, should withstand any confusion. If the tracks are less distinct, use other characteristics. **Vs. raccoon:** Otter toes are not as elongated as raccoon toes, and the track pattern does not resemble the pacing raccoon's (an otter lope even differs from a raccoon's). **Vs. fisher:** The inner toe of an otter track, especially the hind, is not noticeably smaller than the other toes, as is the case with the fisher. Fisher tracks show no prominent webbing, and the fisher weighs about half as much as a river otter.

FINE POINTS

WEASELS

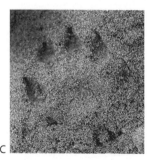

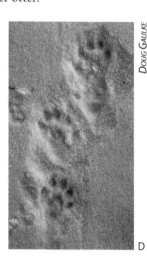

A: Left hind (top) and front tracks; note proximal pad in front track and widely positioned inner toe on hind track.

B: Loping pattern

C: Indistinct front track

D: Detail of loping pattern, LF-LH-RF-RH from bottom to top

A river otter's mobility can offer challenges to a tracker confined to shore or even traveling by canoe or kayak. Otters seen fishing in a rock pool one day may appear several miles up- or downstream the next. In part, river otters vary their fishing areas for efficiency, but some wanderlust and a love for swimming play a role too. If an otter's seasonal home range encompasses 32 km (20 miles) of a river, and if it usually travels during the dark hours, how do we find its current location? Fortunately for us trackers, river otters not only frequent **activity centers** where foraging is best, they also haul out near these places to scent-mark, communicate with one another, and thereby space themselves. Along the shore, look for otter pull-out areas, where the animals have rolled on the ground and scent-marked, sometimes pushing vegetation up into a mound. The most heavily used areas will have numerous scats deposited at their edges; here several otters, for example a mother and her young, use the same roll area, and other individuals who happen along mark there also. (Scent marking is a very strong drive; a man traveling with a family of pet otters observed that each one tried to be the last one to mark their site.) In these places, also look for slides down into the water. Some biologists studying otters visited otter roll spots daily, mashing down previously deposited scats so that new ones could be recognized the next day. If the soil permits, try to identify how many otters recently used a roll area.

Heavily used scent stations point to good foraging nearby, which is your cue to learn about otters' **choice of habitat**. Otters prefer fish to all other foods (fish remains being found commonly in 90% of scats), and they select the most abundant, slowest-moving fish in the area. If you have found otter sign on the shore, examine scats (without touching them, of course) to determine the recent diet. If there are fish scales and bones, study the nearby water for prime fishing spots such as quiet pools, logjams, and undercut banks; the area's profile will help you find otters in other places. If you haven't found otter sign yet, imagine how they would fish or forage at this time of year, and then look for appropriate habitat. In midsummer a female with young may take them to sloughs or backwaters where they can most easily learn to fish. Later in the year a family may cooperate to "herd" fish for easy catching. Where fish are spawning, otters concentrate their fishing. And during winter otters may dig up hibernating frogs from marsh bottoms.

Otter **land travel** is another tracking window. Because otters don't forage out of the water, they move on land only for other reasons: to travel to another lake or stream; to go to a den away from water; to find a mate during breeding season in spring; or to disperse to a new area after leaving their mother's home range. If possible, follow a trail to narrow down the possibilities, and, of course, consider the time of year. Dispersal of young to new areas may occur from November until spring, and siblings sometimes travel together for a short time.

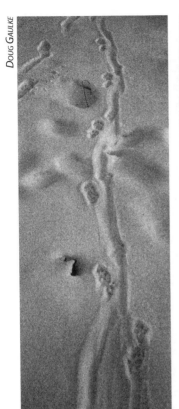

E

F

E and F: River-otter trails in Wisconsin. In E an otter ends a slide and lopes, dragging its tail. In F an otter alternately slides and bounds.

G: A group of otters has gathered near a scent pile (arrow), leaving numerous tail drags.

G

SPECIES AND WEIGHT

Lontra canadensis

7 subspecies in
North America

5 to 14 kg (11 to 31 lb.)

Male somewhat larger
than female

HABITAT   Rivers, streams, lakes, ponds, reservoirs, marshes, and coastal habitats, where fish and crustaceans provide abundant food and where adequate shoreline cover is available for resting, scent marking, and denning. In areas with permanent winter freeze, otters select sites where water can be accessed from land through the ice. Otter trails may cross dry land between lakes or stream drainages. Heavy human use may discourage otter activity.

BREEDING   Breeding in December to April; female is in estrus for about 45 days beginning shortly after giving birth. Males travel extensively during breeding season, seeking out females. Young are sexually mature at 24 months. Gestation of 2 months after delayed implantation, so that birthing occurs about 10 to 12 months after copulation (usually Mar to Apr). Litters 1 to 4, natal dens may be up to several hundred meters from water in secure burrows often dug by other animals.

DEVELOPMENT   Young emerge from den at 10 to 12 weeks; female may move litter to new den prior to that time. Mother's training of young in fishing and foraging begins in early summer; otter families may prefer backwaters and slower-moving streams at this time. Young grow rapidly for 1st 10 months, approach adult weight by 1 year, and are fully grown by 2 years. Mother and young remain together at least until November, but young may also disperse as late as the following spring. Dispersing otters may explore habitat for a month or 2 before establishing new home range; travels of up to 193 km (120 miles) are recorded. Dispersing siblings may travel together for a period.

SOCIAL HABITS   An otter group is usually a female with young, sometimes joined by a nonbreeding female. Adult males, and yearling males and females, are often solitary. Home ranges often overlap, though a female raising young may keep adult males away. An otter's range usually follows shorelines and can cover from 8

WEASELS

to 80 km (5 to 50 miles) in a season (male ranges larger than females'). Otters' home ranges contain 1 to several "activity centers," where fishing and foraging are concentrated. Activity centers may be used by unrelated otters but usually not at the same time. Coastal river otters who fish for large ocean fish during spawning season are known to form adult male groups for cooperative fishing.

FEEDING

Fish comprise most of diet in all habitats; otters prefer slow-swimming fish including sculpin, perch, bass, sunfish, carp, suckers, catfish, and whitefish among many other species. Otters tend to fish in coves, near shorelines, under cutbanks, around logjams, and in slow-moving pools; cooperative herding of fish by 2 or more otters sometimes occurs. During spawning season for salmon or other species, many otters may congregate in one area. Otters also commonly eat crayfish and other invertebrates such as large diving beetles, stonefly nymphs, and dragonfly nymphs. Insects, frogs, and turtles are dug out from their hiding places in mud at lake and stream bottoms. In some areas otters are known to eat mussels or to prey on muskrats and beavers. Swimming birds such as grebes, cormorants, teals, and widgeons are taken from below, especially during birds' molting season. Rarely, otters may eat fruit such as blueberries. Otters are active primarily at night and near dusk and dawn; they are least active at midday.

WEASELS

SURVIVAL

Otters are vulnerable on land but have few natural enemies except wolves. Habitat loss is their most serious threat. Commercial trapping is allowed in 27 states.

SIGNS

Pull-out locations onshore where otters roll and scent-mark; pushed-up vegetation, musky odor, and often many scats in these places. Scats crumbly and often oily, commonly with fish and crustacean remains; also deposited on sandbars, logjams, and other elevated places near shore. Slides into water on grass, mud, or snow are common. Dens usually in bank burrows, logjams, or abandoned beaver lodges, but dens as far as 0.8 km (½ mile) away from water are recorded, and otters may temporarily den in riparian vegetation near shoreline. Regularly used routes between bodies of water.

H: A fresh, dark otter scat has been deposited on a log in the middle of Big River, California, where older scats have begun to crumble.

H

TRACKS Front claws prominent, but not as long ►
as striped skunk's

Six heel pads
show in clear track ►
(F and H).

◄ Hind claws
often do not
show.

LEFT FRONT   LEFT HIND

COMMON
GAITS

A: Pace
(common)

B: Irregu-
lar pace
(common)

C: Diago-
nal walk
(occasional)

D: Lope
(common)

E: Lope/
gallop
(occasional)

Front

Hind

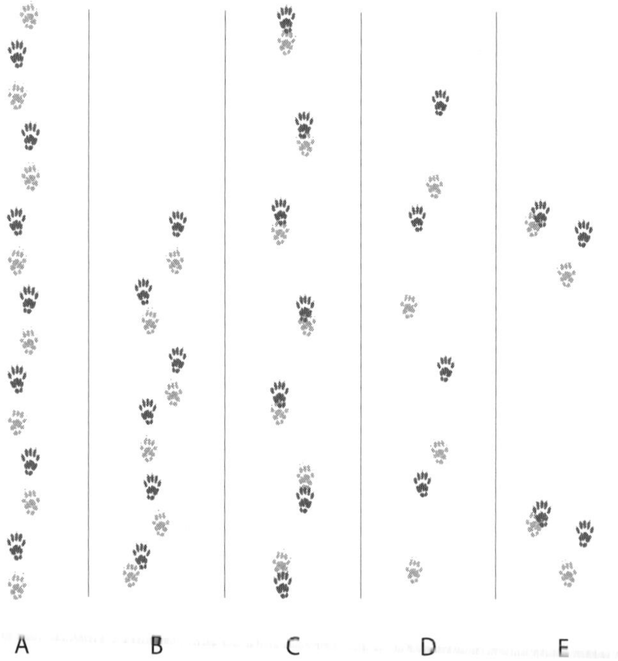

A   B   C   D   E

SKUNKS

TRACK
MEASUREMENTS

	Average, inches	Average, cm	Usual range, inches*
Front width	$^{15}/_{16}$	2.4	¾ to 1$^{1}/_{16}$
Front length	1$^{3}/_{16}$	3.0	1 to 1½
Hind width	⅞	2.2	$^{9}/_{16}$ to 1$^{5}/_{16}$
Hind length	1⅜	3.4	1⅛ to 1¾
Trail width	2¼	5.7	1½ to 3⅝
Stride	4⅝	11.7	3⅛ to 6⅞

*More than 90% of my measurements fall within this range.

A

B

In a pace- or diagonal walk pattern, as shown in A, B, and C on the opposite page, spotted-skunk tracks can be distinguished from a striped skunk's by the "knobbiness" or segmentation in front and hind heel pad areas, which the **striped skunk** lacks; spotted-skunk tracks are also generally smaller and the front claws not so long as the striped skunk's. The trail of a spotted skunk is often more irregular in where the feet land than a typical striped skunk's. A gallop pattern, though, most resembles a **ground squirrel**'s trail, both in track placement and the "knobbiness" of the clear prints. Confirm the ID by finding the inside toe on the front track (squirrels have only four toes). **Hognose skunk** tracks are larger with much longer claws, and **hooded skunk** tracks do not show as much clear segmentation in the heel-pad area. Both of these skunks have a limited range in the southwestern United States.

FINE POINTS

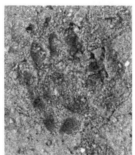

C

D

A: Typical irregular pace-walk pattern

B: Diagonal walk

C: Right front track

D: Right hind track

SKUNKS

Unlike its plodding, waddling cousins—the striped, hooded, and hognose skunks—the spotted skunk has been described as an "acrobat" by early observers, and indeed its **agility** will become evident as you study its tracks. From a lope or gallop, the spotted skunk can turn on a dime. It can climb straight up a vertical rock face or suddenly nose into a tiny crevice after a beetle or mouse. Its gaits and track patterns have many more variations than are illustrated on page 262. One moment it can shuffle along in a typical pace walk, and in the next it can gallop across open space. It can bound like a weasel. Take the opportunity to study gaits and gait changes, for you will likely see some new ones. When you see an acrobatic movement in the tracks, really study each track and picture how each foot landed and pivoted. It may take a while to understand a movement that took a second or two, but in doing so you'll grasp the spotted skunk's remarkable agility.

This athletic prowess is also expressed in the skunk's **threat displays**, which, even more than its accurate spraying, deters potential predators. At the slightest disturbance, a spotted skunk might go into a handstand with tail raised; it has been seen to walk several yards on its hands, do a pirouette, drop to all fours to stomp its front feet, or even charge an intruder. (When it really sprays, which is relatively rarely, it usually faces the target with all four feet on the ground, and rotates its body into a horseshoe shape, with the rear end also pointing toward the target.) Especially around human habitation, where domestic dogs may elicit a threat display from a skunk, you may well find some handstand tracks. Just make sure you study the front and rear track differences when you're tracking the spotted skunk!

The use of its territory is another window to the spotted skunk's biology; this could be called irregular and opportunistic, as befits an animal walking with a deterrent wherever it goes. A single skunk may use a dozen different dens in its home range, sharing it with other skunks from time to time. For the tracker, this means rather than being able to read trails and runs radiating out from a constantly used den, you'll more likely find random trails from a whole population of skunks that use common areas for foraging and denning. Don't despair: You can still learn something about a local skunk population by measuring tracks. Males are often larger than females, and males usually den alone. Over numerous visits to an area, look for alternative den sites. Also pay attention to food resources, for a spotted skunk may spend a whole night digging for larvae at the roots of a patch of plants, or it may roam for miles among rock piles and brush on the lookout for mice.

A spotted skunk gallops across the Olancha Dunes in California's Owens Valley.

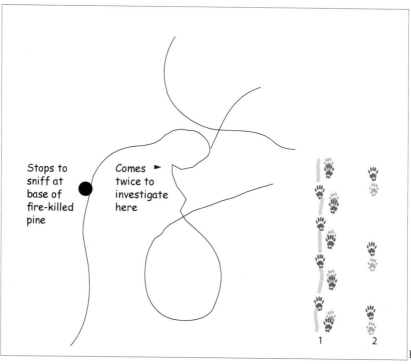

Stops to
sniff at
base of
fire-killed
pine

Comes
twice to
investigate
here

1   2

E

E: A spotted skunk's winter trail meanders through the snow at 2,438 meters (8,000 ft.) on Mount Pinos in Southern California. Tracks were quite aged in the sun, but the track pattern, and detail in shaded prints, allowed identification. From track size and stride, the skunk was probably a small female. Most often the diagonal walk pattern #1 was found, in which the left feet showed drag marks and the left hind track directly registered on top of the left front. In other places the skunk used the pace pattern #2. In sections of its trail not shown here, the skunk poked its head into the snow, making a 5 cm (2 in.) impression, sniffed the base of some trees, and investigated the base of a low shrub, walking in a few inches and then backing out. It emerged from and went into a hole in the snow at the base of a fallen log.

F: A typical spotted-skunk gallop pattern is compressed, i.e., the four tracks are close together, and the animal is not up on its toes, giving stability for quick changes of direction.

F

G

H

G: A spotted skunk has galloped along a dirt road in a riparian area near Bakersfield, California, and come to a sudden ninety-degree pivot. The two arrows show where the hind feet threw off plumes ahead of the tracks as the skunk braked and anticipated the turn, while the two white arrows show where one front and one hind foot threw off large plates during the pivot. This was just a momentary, acrobatic motion, for the skunk took just two short steps to the left, pivoted again, and galloped off in the original direction of travel.

H: In a diagonal walk pattern, a spotted skunk in the southern Sierra Nevada looks off to the left as it walks. The angled shoulders are deduced from the pitch of the right front and left rear tracks toward the left.

SKUNKS

SPOTTED SKUNK   Notes for the Tracker

SPECIES AND WEIGHT   *Spilogale gracilis* (western spotted skunk) and *Spilogale putorius* (eastern spotted skunk)

8 subspecies in North America

0.4 to 0.9 kg (7 to 30 oz.)

Male larger than female

SKUNKS

HABITAT   Sea level to 2,560 meters (8,400 ft.), in rocky, brushy, riparian, and forested areas as well as deserts. Apparently avoids wetlands and prefers areas with ground cover, brush, and rocks to completely open terrain. Has expanded its range to agricultural areas and, when around humans, often dens in or near buildings and other structures.

BREEDING   Western spotted skunk breeds in September, undergoes delayed implantation, and gives birth in April. Eastern spotted skunk breeds in March or April and gives birth in May or June. Young-of-year may breed. Litter size 2 to 5 (average 3.8); southern population of Eastern spotted skunk may produce 2nd litter in July or August.

DEVELOPMENT   Young weaned at about 54 days, reach the range of adult weight by 2 to 3 months.

SOCIAL HABITS   Not a territorial animal; numerous dens in a local habitat are used by a number of skunks at different times, and 1 skunk may use many dens. A female sometimes shares a den with other females, but males seem to den alone. Little is known about home range sizes; one California home-range average is 30 hectares (73 acres) in winter and 61 hectares (151 acres) in summer. Males travel more than females, especially in breeding season.

FEEDING   Almost exclusively nocturnal. Adult insects and larvae, especially of scarab beetles, stag beetles, and Jerusalem crickets, make up a large part of diet; millipedes and centipedes also eaten. Spotted skunks also hunt for small rodents, especially voles and white-footed mice, catching them from behind, pinning them with the feet, and killing by biting on the neck. Lizards and toads eaten sometimes. Carrion of larger mammals such as cottontails also eaten on occasion. Fruits and seeds have been found in the scats of some skunks, but these make up very small portion of diet.

Threatening display, a handstand with tail spread, is primary deterrent against predators or intruders in the spotted skunk's space. Can walk on hands for several yards in this display. Musk more acrid than striped skunk's, can be sprayed very accurately 1.5 to 1.8 meters (5 to 6 ft.). Skunk faces threat and brings its body into a horseshoe shape to spray. Audible foot stomping is another warning gesture. Most recorded mortality occurs from automobiles, trapping, or other human causes, such as domestic dogs and cats.

Dens numerous, throughout skunk's habitat, in rock piles, brush, or underground burrows excavated itself or appropriated from ground squirrels, pocket gophers, or other animals. Most dens near cover or base of rocks, trees, or shrubs, but some burrows in open areas; many dens lined with grasses. Den entrances about 10 cm (4 in.) in diameter. Dens also found under buildings and in attics. Scats usually less than 1.3 cm (½ in.) diameter, often with insect remains, sometimes tapered at end. Scats found in den chambers, along regular runways, and outside dens. Diggings for insects and larvae at base of plants or elsewhere, sometimes quite numerous. Carrion sometimes dragged to den entrance or secluded spot.

SKUNKS

SKUNKS

TRACKS

Long, prominent claws on F track ►

F heel pad smooth, not segmented ►

◄ H heel pad sometimes shows creasing

LEFT FRONT

LEFT HIND

COMMON GAITS

A: Pace walk (common)

B and C: Lopes (common)

D: Diagonal walk (occasional)

E: Gallop (occasional)

Front

Hind

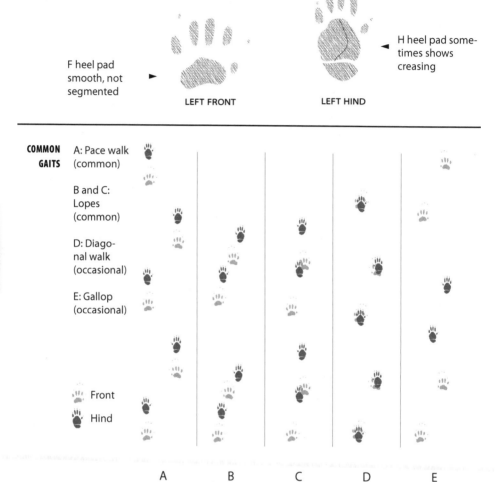

A B C D E

TRACK MEASUREMENTS

	Average, inches	Average, cm	Usual range, inches*
Front width	1⅛	2.8	¾ to 1⁷⁄₁₆
Front length	1³⁄₁₆	3.1	⅝ to 1¾
Hind width	1¹⁄₁₆	2.7	⅞ to 1⅜
Hind length	1⅝	4.1	1 to 2
Trail width	3⅛	7.9	1¼ to 4
Stride**	7½	19.1	4¼ to 12¼

*More than 97% of my measurements fall within this range.   **Pace walk

Striped-skunk hind tracks resemble miniature raccoon prints but are practically always smaller. Usually, a striped skunk's small five-toed front track with long, prominent claw marks cannot be confused with anything else. In many areas where the **spotted skunk** shares habitat, look for the smooth continuous imprint of the striped skunk's front heel pad compared to the segmented character of the spotted skunk's. In parts of Texas, Arizona, New Mexico, Colorado, and Oklahoma, **hognosed skunks** show similar tracks, but these have even longer front claws, and toes that are bulkier and less separate. **Hooded skunks**' tracks are very similar to striped skunks', but they show more creasing in the hind heel pad and taper more to the back of the foot. Hooded skunks are present only in a small part of southern Arizona, New Mexico, and Texas.

FINE POINTS

SKUNKS

A: Pace walk

B: Left front

C: Right hind

D: Loping pattern

What profundity could there be in a set of waddling-striped-skunk tracks? Well, a meandering skunk trail allows the tracker to follow an animal methodically, track by track, in slow motion as it were, and such a precise reading of a trail not only improves your tracking ability but also opens a window to the skunk's **body language**. The secret here is to pick an irregular section of a skunk trail and study each track, noticing pitch (that is, the inward or outward orientation of the track) as well as any twisting of the foot visible through pressure releases. Get down on all fours and imitate the placement and rotation of each foot. You'll find that the skunk's track pattern can have been made in only one way, with a particular sequence of foot movement and particular shoulder orientation. Once discovered, this moment in a skunk's life becomes quite positive reinforcement to your tracking ability. In addition, you'll discover in the skunk's waddling a purpose, as you notice the head sweeping back and forth to detect the scent or sound of possible prey.

The image of a meandering skunk, thus uncovered, also opens a window to its **foraging personality**. A skunk's built-in deterrence allows it to focus long and intently on whatever it is eating, without concern for danger. Studies with captive skunks have shown that once it senses a certain kind of food, such as larvae underneath the soil, a skunk's smell, hearing, and visual acuity increase with regard to that food, to the exclusion of other foods. That's why you may find dozens of little diggings in one area left by a "tunnel-visioned" skunk. This focus is also evident in creative behavior: Skunks have been known to scratch on the outside of beehives to entice its inhabitants out. The angry bees are then pinned to the ground and eaten one by one, and one skunk indeed consumed more than 150 bees at once. Amazingly, striped skunks are agile enough to catch grasshoppers; they have been observed swishing through grassland to flush grasshoppers, which are bounded after, then pinned to the ground and eaten. When you find a striped skunk's foraging area, look for feeding signs and tracks that will tell you how it has focused its awareness in this area. Because skunks often proceed quickly and directly from their day beds to a foraging area, follow a loping-skunk trail to find a current foraging site.

Tracks might also lead you to a striped skunk's den. While day beds change frequently during much of the year, a female's natal den is used for a longer time and can be a window to its **family life**. From May to early August, look for signs of a mother skunk followed—often single file—by several baby skunks.

SKUNKS

A striped skunk lopes uphill on the central California coast, sweeping its tail along the sand.

SKUNKS

E

F

G

H

Using pressure releases to illuminate gaits:

E: The flatness of this left hind track indicates a slow gait, namely a pace walk, without even seeing the track pattern.

F and G: The hind and front tracks, respectively, of this loping skunk show a dish-fissure extending from the toes to the rear part of the tracks. In the front foot, G, the rocking motion of the lope is evident by the fact that the rear part of the foot hit the ground, which it rarely does in a walk.

H: This photo shows a track pattern in which each hind track is superimposed over a front track. At first glance, this would be a diagonal walk, but the stride, long for a striped skunk, and pressure releases counter that assumption.

I: This photo is a detail of a right hind track, showing the disk-fissure behind the toes that confirms this gait as a trot.

I

J: In a common foraging pattern, a striped skunk moving from left to right has stopped suddenly to dig for food.

K: Though striped skunks are classified as "pacers," a close analysis of a track pattern can reveal more precisely how the animal is walking at any time. In this pattern, the right hind and left front tracks are both pitched to the right (arrows), while the left hind and right front tracks point in the direction of travel. By visualizing and imitating the motion that would create this pattern, it is discovered that this skunk is meandering with its head swinging twice to the right, then back to the center in this sequence.

SPECIES AND WEIGHT   *Mephitis mephitis*

13 subspecies in North America

1.2 to 6.6 kg (2.4 to 14.5 lb.)

Male slightly larger than female

HABITAT   Generally from lowlands to 1,981 meters (6,500 ft.), in coastal dunes, marshland, chaparral, grassland, forest edges, meadows, brushlands, croplands, and urban areas. Prefers foraging areas with abundant insects, larvae, or small rodents; requires nearby protected denning sites in burrows, rock outcrops, or brush.

BREEDING   Breeding between late January and late March, 1st-year females later in this period. Males travel farther seeking mates; male-female pairs may travel together. Gestation 59 to 77 days, averaging 63, earlier mating associated with longer gestation. Birth April through early June (May through June in more northerly climates). Litters usually 4 to 8.

DEVELOPMENT   Young emerge from den after 40 days, first travel with mother from 6 to 8 weeks after birth. Juveniles usually accompany mother until late July or early August, then disperse. Recorded dispersal distances range from 0.4 km to 9.7 km (¼ to 6 miles).

SOCIAL HABITS   Solitary foragers except when female rears young. However, skunks may den together, especially during winter in northern climates, apparently most often in groups of females or 1 male to several females. Short-range sensory awareness and lack of competition for food results in little territoriality. One skunk's home range often overlaps with 1 to 4 others'. Home ranges are usually 1 km² to 5 km² and are often elongated; ranges often expand during breeding season.

FEEDING   Insects including grasshoppers, beetles, and larvae are staple food where available; small mammals such as meadow voles are also frequently dug from nests or caught in their meadow runways. Seasonally and opportunistically, skunks also consume some wild and cultivated fruits, carrion, and birds' eggs or

SKUNKS

nestlings. Most foraging begins shortly after dusk and continues until just before dawn, sometimes with rest breaks. Skunks often travel directly from day bed to foraging area, then rely on hearing, eyesight, and smell to flush or dig out insects or other prey. Some tests suggest that skunks focus on a single food after they first encounter it.

SURVIVAL

Conspicuous coloration and defensive displays, including front-foot stomping, arched back, and raised-tail deter most predators, and unpleasant musk can also be sprayed from anal gland either in stream of fluid or mist, up to 3 meters (10 ft.) in a 30- to 45-degree arc. Nevertheless, some predation by coyotes, mountain lions, foxes, owls, and other predators. Significant mortality from human vehicles and some from trapping. Disease affects skunk populations; striped skunks have highest rabies incidence of any domestic or wild mammal. Survival in wild normally less than 6 years.

SIGNS

Scats 1.6 to 1.9 cm (⅝ to ¾ in.) in diameter, often containing insect remains, deposited along runways and especially in piles in or near dens. Dens in rock cavities, hollow logs, brush, culverts, buildings, and in burrows dug by other animals. Female prepares natal nest by scraping leaves, grasses, or other debris between feet to den entrance and then pushing it in. Dens sometimes shared by more than 1 skunk, especially in cold weather. Shallow, often locally abundant diggings for insects and larvae, especially in meadows, fields, and grassland; also eggshell remains from raided nests of ground-nesting birds during spring.

SKUNKS

L

L: Along California's central coast, wire fences like this one are erected to protect nests of the endangered snowy plover from predation by striped skunks and other predators. These tracks show that a juvenile skunk can nevertheless squeeze through the 4.8 cm (1⅞ inch) opening.

WEASEL   Track ID (Short-Tailed and Long-Tailed)

TRACKS

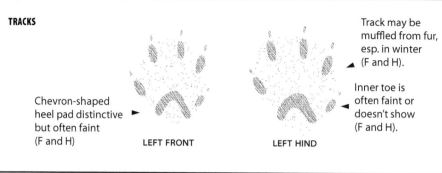

Chevron-shaped heel pad distinctive but often faint (F and H)

LEFT FRONT

Track may be muffled from fur, esp. in winter (F and H).

Inner toe is often faint or doesn't show (F and H).

LEFT HIND

COMMON GAITS

A: Bound (common)

B: Alternating length bound with foot drag in snow (common)

C: Slow bound (occasional)

D: Gallop to lope (occasional)

(B is smaller scale)

Front

Hind

A   B   C   D

WEASELS

TRACK MEASUREMENTS

	Usual range, inches*	Usual range, cm
Front width	7⁄16 to 13⁄16	1.1 to 2.1
Front length	7⁄16 to 1¼	1.1 to 3.2
Hind width	½ to ⅞	1.3 to 2.2
Hind length	⅝ to 1⅝	1.6 to 4.1
Trail width	1 to 2⅜	2.5 to 6.0
Stride	8½ to 22	22 to 56

*These ranges combine both species. Short-tailed measurements average smaller than long-tailed, but males of the former are the same size as females of the latter.

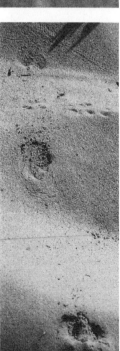

A

B

A weasel's **track pattern** is the best identifying characteristic; this is most often a bound, with the hind (H) feet landing more or less on top of the front (F) tracks, one pair of F/H slightly ahead of the other. Measuring a trail width of 2.5 to 6 cm (1 to 2⅜ in.), and considering track size, will almost always separate weasels from larger bounders such as mink, pine martens, and fishers. If your suspected weasel isn't bounding, the tracks may resemble a rodent's. Study the trail and pay attention to the "trail width" of the two F tracks vs. the two H ones. A weasel's body build usually causes these pairs to be almost equal, in contrast to a rodent's whose F tracks are usually placed inside the H straddle. Weasel clear prints often don't show clear detail, especially the inner toe. Look closely for the chevron-shaped heel pad, which helps ID. Amazingly, long-tailed weasel tracks may most resemble those of **kangaroo rats**, which can also create pairs of muffled tracks sometimes offset from one another and without a tail drag. Of course, in a weasel's pattern the pairs are actually four tracks, not two as with a k-rat, so look for the F tracks hiding beneath the H ones.

FINE POINTS

WEASELS

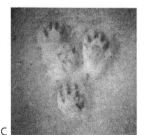

C

D

A: Typical bound of a short-tailed weasel

B: Close examination of each track group reveals four prints, with front pairs and hind pairs showing the same trail width—ruling out a rodent.

C: Gallop pattern of a short-tailed weasel. Note faint inner toe and faint heel pad.

D: Two hind tracks of a long-tailed weasel in sand. Front tracks are underneath.

There are three important things to know about the weasel: **metabolism, metabolism, and metabolism.** A weasel's compact, tubular body, with its large surface area, little fat, and little underfur, requires a constant supply of food. Weasels seem to always be on the hunt, and when they have filled their small stomachs, they hunt some more, caching kills for future meals. For the tracker, a weasel's metabolism has several implications. The first is habitat choice. In order for a female weasel, which is half the size of the male, to raise a litter, she usually lives where there is an abundance of voles, mice, or shrews, which she, with her small size and maneuverability in small spaces, is supremely adapted to catch. Look for weasel scats, tracks, and remains of kills in meadows or brushy areas with concentrations of small rodents. Another implication of the weasel's metabolism is mobility. Rather than radiate their movements out from a permanent den, weasels go where the food is, making kills and then taking over their prey's nests. Look for weasel nests, lined with the fur of their prey, that are used for possibly only a few days. Because the larger male weasel may not be able to follow rodents into their tunnels, it must range more widely to catch a baby rabbit, surprise a pocket gopher, or flush a mouse from hiding. So, also be alert for weasel tracks and temporary dens far from the "ideal" habitat. Finally, high weasel metabolism means that local populations fluctuate along with their prey; weasels may disappear from an area and then suddenly reappear.

Tracking weasels over snow reveals their superb **winter adaptations**. Voles and mice are active under the snow all winter, and weasels can easily access their tunnels and runways. Larger weasels cruise the snow, suddenly diving beneath it when they hear or smell a rodent; smaller weasels tend to patrol areas near trees or shrubs where they can find an access tunnel under the snow. As you follow a weasel's trail on snow, look for hesitations or changes of direction that indicate its hunting alertness. Prey that is killed is often taken to a hole in the snow to be consumed or cached. Look for signs of prey drags in the snow; look for spots of blood of prey at a snow tunnel entrance. Longer, straighter trails may lead hundreds of meters from a den to a hunting area; follow them until the tracks reveal a change of behavior into the hunting mode. Especially after a snowstorm, weasels may restrict their hunting movements from their dens. Because territories don't overlap much in winter, take these times to assess how many weasels reside in an area. You may even be able to tell species and gender by measuring trail width. Where both short-tailed and long-tailed weasels live, there are typically three sizes of weasels: the short-tailed female (smallest); the short-tailed male and long-tailed female (same size); and the long-tailed male (largest).

In Yosemite National Park a weasel interrupts its travel with burrowing beneath the snow and exploratory digging.

E

E: A long-tailed weasel, denning in a cairn along a Colorado hiking trail at 3,962 meters (13,000 ft.), greets backpackers with considerable scolding.

F: In Switzerland numerous trails radiate to and from an underground den of a short-tailed weasel or ermine, the same species as is found in North America.

F

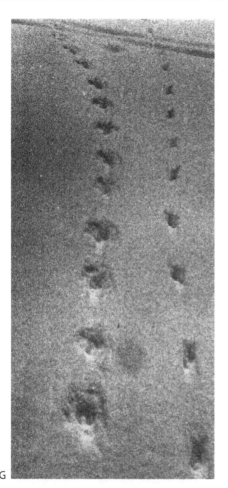

G: In Colorado's Routt National Forest, a weasel bounds one direction and returns carrying its prey, whose tail drags on the right and its nose on the left.

H and I: Unlike short-tailed weasels, long-tailed weasels commonly alternate bounds, with a high-energy leap followed by a leg-dragging one when traveling long distances in the snow. This weasel's trail was photographed at 2,743 meters (9,000 feet) near Fraser, Colorado. The tail, held straight behind, doesn't usually drag.

SPECIES AND WEIGHT   *Mustela frenata* (long-tailed weasel), male 160 to 450 g (5.6 to 15.9 oz.), female 80 to 250 g (2.8 to 8.8 oz.); *Mustela erminea* (short-tailed weasel), male 67 to 116 g (2.4 to 4.1 oz.), female 25 to 80 g (0.9 to 2.8 oz.); *Mustela nivalis* (least weasel) not shown here

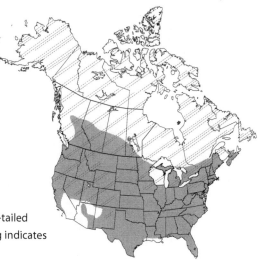

Solid shading indicates long-tailed weasel range, while hatching indicates short-tailed weasel range.

HABITAT   Forests, meadows, grassland, shrubland, riparian areas, marshes, and tundra, from sea level to 3,962+ meters (13,000+ ft.); generally absent from desert areas without water. Prefers local habitats with high concentrations of small rodents such as voles and mice that allow easy hunting by smaller females. Short-tailed weasel is especially adapted to northern areas with prolonged winter snow cover; long-tailed-weasel range does not extend into boreal forests of Canada and Alaska.

BREEDING   Most breeding in July or August; female who has given birth mates again, and female young-of-the-year mate with a resident male at 3 months, often before leaving their mother. Male weasels, however, are sexually mature only at about 15 months. Delayed implantation of egg, and variable overall gestation from 7 to 11 months, resulting in births usually mid-April to May. Litters usually 4 to 8.

DEVELOPMENT   Young first play outside their den at 5 to 8 weeks (usually early to mid-June), can kill prey at 10 to 12 weeks. Young males are the size of their mother at about 7 weeks, become full size at 1 year. Young females reach adult size at 6 months (late fall). Family groups tend to split up in early fall, but some young may remain near their mother's territory. Young males, especially, may travel widely the spring after their birth.

SOCIAL HABITS   Weasels space themselves by scent marking. Females' home ranges generally overlap little with one another, while larger male home ranges may overlap or adjoin several females' ranges. Most home ranges are between 10 and 80 hectares (24.7 to 198 acres), but some (especially males') are larger. Home ranges fluctuate with prey density and with season; weasels travel less in winter when there is snow cover.

WEASELS

FEEDING

Voles, mice, and shrews make up most of diet in most areas, but chipmunks, pocket gophers, rabbits (especially juveniles), and birds are also hunted. Small body size, especially of females, allows concentrated hunting in vole tunnels and under snowpack and therefore may lead to diet specialization. Larger males, especially long-tailed weasels, may need to travel farther and hunt larger prey because they cannot fit into some small rodent tunnels. Smaller prey are killed with a bite to the back of the neck; larger prey, often weighing more than twice as much as a weasel, are immobilized with a bite to the neck muscles and killed later. Weasels eat a small amount of food at a time, especially preferring brains and internal organs, and numerous prey may be stashed in a nest for later consumption. Mice or voles may be entirely consumed.

SURVIVAL

Tubular body shape, low fat reserves, and lack of dense underfur cause high metabolism needs, especially in cold climates; hence weasel populations may fluctuate with local prey density. Weasels are themselves vulnerable to owls, hawks, foxes, and other predators. Winter coats turn white for camouflage in areas of consistent snow cover. Weasels are legally trapped for their pelts in some areas.

SIGNS

Scat usually 0.3 to 0.6 cm (⅛ to ¼ in.) in diameter, twisted cords, deposited on elevated surfaces such as rocks, near dens, or in latrines within dens. Nests in holes or tunnels of prey species, often lined with grasses and fur of prey; natal nests may also be in rock crevices or under logs. Nests may be used for many days, with runs emanating from them, or may be used for a short time only. Caches of uneaten prey in or near dens. Remains of partially eaten prey (skulls, feet, tails, or skin) may be found in nest.

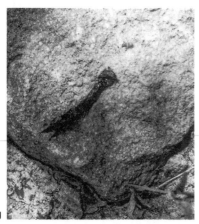

J: Weasel scat on a hiking trail in Colorado

J

WEASELS

RACCOONS, OPOSSUMS, AND BEARS

TRACKS

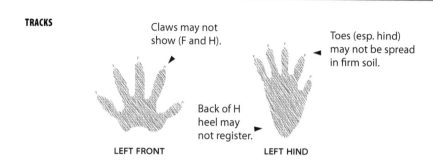

Claws may not show (F and H).

Toes (esp. hind) may not be spread in firm soil.

Back of H heel may not register.

LEFT FRONT

LEFT HIND

COMMON GAITS

A: Pace (common)

B: Lope (common)

C: Running pace (occasional)

D: Slow pace (occasional)

E: Gallop (occasional)

Front

Hind

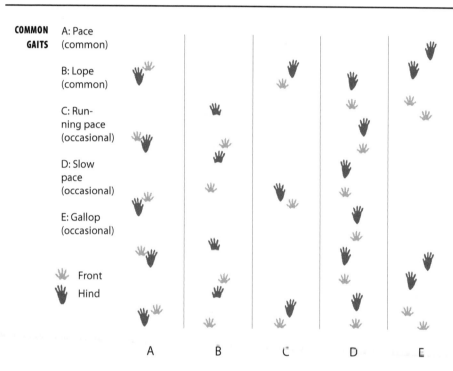

A   B   C   D   E

TRACK MEASUREMENTS

	Average, inches	Average, cm	Usual range, inches*
Front width	1¹⁵⁄₁₆	4.9	1½ to 2¾
Front length	2⅜	6.1	1½ to 3
Hind width	1⅞	4.8	1⁵⁄₁₆ to 2⁹⁄₁₆
Hind length	3¹⁄₁₆	7.9	2 to 4¹⁄₁₆
Trail width	4⅜	11.1	2¾ to 5¾
Stride	13¾	35.0	8¼ to 17

*More than 95% of my measurements fall within this range.

RACCOONS

The walking pattern with paired front and hind tracks, depicted in A on the opposite page as well as figure A at left, is unique to the raccoon and helps ID immensely. If the tracks are in a different pattern, use other clues. **Coati** tracks show shorter toes and more segmentation in the heel-pad area; in the United States the coati's range is also confined to southeastern Arizona. A **river otter**'s tracks will show webbing in clear prints, and a **fisher**'s tracks most often form a bounding pattern not seen with raccoons. Badger tracks show shorter toes and much longer claw impressions. Check habitat and range of these animals to narrow down the choices.

A: The vast majority of raccoon trails are "pace" patterns.

B: Left front track at left, paired with right hind track at right

C: When the hind heel pad doesn't fully register, front and hind can be distinguished by relative toe position. These tracks are left front (above) and right hind (below).

RACCOONS

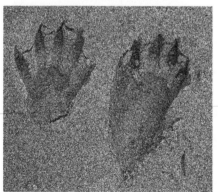

Think of a raccoon and you immediately picture those long, agile fingers probing under rocks in a stream for crayfish or trying to open someone's cooler in a campsite. Indeed, raccoons' brains are jammed with circuitry supporting that forepaw dexterity as well as extraordinary sensitivity in all parts of the hand. For the tracker, this **forepaw sensitivity** becomes a window into the raccoon's life. Even when a raccoon walks, those long toes seem to feel the ground and express the animal's very thoughts. Thus raccoons, more than any other mammal, offer you a chance to read **toe-movement pressure releases**. Though it may sound intimidating, this reading is accessible to any serious tracker because it's self-taught anyway. Start by making your own barefoot tracks, learning how the toes move in anticipation and compensation of every movement. When you've begun to understand toe-movement principles, settle down with some good raccoon tracks. Imitate how it walks, read the larger pressure releases, and then see what those toes are doing for balance and anticipation. You may well be sucked into a level of tracking that you thought impossible.

The raccoon offers the tracker the very best opportunity to distinguish individual animals' tracks from one another, because each animal's **unique walking personality** is reflected quite obviously in the positioning of the front/hind pairs, the pitch of each foot, and indicator pressure releases. Quirks such as foot drags and limps are also common. When you find tracks of several raccoons traveling together, draw each raccoon's patterns and then picture exactly how each one walks—getting down on all fours definitely helps!

Seemingly every waterside habitat at medium or low elevation will eventually produce raccoon tracks, but the tracker misses a window into this animal's **foraging behavior** by focusing just on water. Raccoons most often concentrate their feeding in the richest areas, and while these can certainly be wetlands, they can also be orchards, wild fruiting trees far from water, or urban food sources. Raccoons may travel miles directly from bedding areas, up over dry and dusty terrain to feeding areas, or from one feeding area to another. This is your cue to step back to the larger view and notice what current food in your landscape might attract raccoons as well as where bedding or denning areas might be. Once in a feeding area, zero in once more on the detailed view. Look for feeding signs such as remains of crustaceans or fruits, and notice scats, their location, and contents. A family group may travel together, then fan out to forage separately. Distinguish individuals' tracks and find out how a family is foraging.

Three raccoons walk next to a coastal California estuary.

RACCOONS

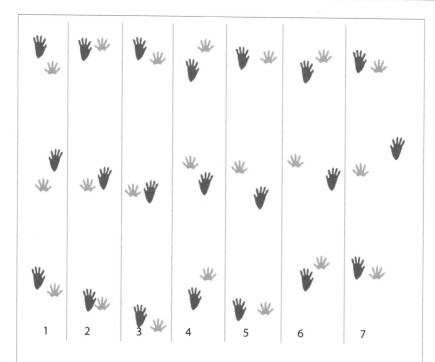

1   2   3   4   5   6   7

D: Raccoon walking patterns vary by individual animal and are relatively easy to distinguish. Different stride lengths on left and right sides for each animal cause the unique front/hind pairings; these are seven examples from my notebooks and photos. Even when two raccoons' patterns are similar, the pitch of each foot as well as the exact placement of each track will help distinguish individuals' trails from one another.

D

E: An opportunistic raccoon leaves ashy claw marks and prints after exploring a campfire pit.

E

F and G: These two left hind/right front pairs come from different sections of one raccoon's walking trail and show how numerous "indicator" pressure releases repeat themselves in each track. The six arrows in photo F point to pressure releases that can be found in exactly the same places in photo G; they were created by foot and toe movement identical in each step. (Many more indicator pressure releases are evident in the photos but are not marked with arrows.) The number and severity of the pressure releases are unusual even for a raccoon and suggest a considerable injury or deformity.

RACCOONS

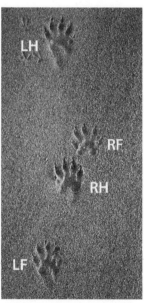

H and I: These two raccoon loping patterns are both "rotary" lopes, but there is a big difference in the angling of the shoulders. Photo H's raccoon is facing to the left, as evidenced by the position of the right front track; the plate-fissure on the right hind shows the swivel of the body back to the direction of travel. In photo I the raccoon is facing almost straight ahead.

SPECIES AND WEIGHT

Procyon lotor

14 subspecies in North America

3.5 to 13 kg (8 to 28 lb.)

Male 10% to 15% larger than female

HABITAT Fresh- and saltwater marshland, forests, and woodland where standing or running water occurs; agricultural areas; suburban and urban open spaces and greenbelts; and deserts with open water; from sea level to 2,438 meters (8,000 ft.). Range has expanded dramatically since the 1940s through most of the United States, coinciding with extirpation of wolves and expansion of agriculture and suburban development.

BREEDING Most breeding peaks in March; 2nd breeding in May or June possible for females that fail to mate earlier or lose a litter. Males may fight during breeding season to establish dominance. Female travels and rests with 1 male for 1 to 3 days but may also breed with other males; dominant (usually heavier) males tend to mate with more females in an area. Gestation usually 63 to 65 days, litters average 3 to 4, birth usually in May in natal den in tree hollow, ground burrow, brush pile, or other protected spot.

DEVELOPMENT Female may move den after birthing. Young accompany mother on short foraging trips at about 7 to 10 weeks. By 12th week young accompany her throughout the night, continuing this for 2 months. Young may rest alone sometimes by 5th to 9th month. Juvenile males disperse to new range, usually after 1 year; females usually remain near mother's range, but may also disperse as yearlings; dispersal often in straight lines, from 2.4 to more than 32 km (1.5 to 20+ miles). Juveniles reach close to adult weight at 14 to 15 months.

SOCIAL HABITS Mothers and young travel as a group from summer through fall, the group gradually loosening and forming varying temporary mother-offspring or sibling alliances. Yearlings and adult males generally travel alone, but in some areas male raccoons form bands of 3 to 5 unrelated individuals with an internal dominance hierarchy that travels together and defends its territory from other male bands. Even when raccoons travel in small groups, they usually space themselves apart from one another while foraging. Concentrated food sources such as garbage dumps, however, may attract large groups of raccoons. Adults share daytime resting beds only about a third of the time, usually with a raccoon of the same gender. Female home ranges typically overlap one another's, the neighboring females often related. Male ranges often do not overlap each others' but overlap several females'. Home ranges vary by available water and food and usually average from 4 to 250 hectares (9.75 to 618 acres) for females and 16 to 600 hectares (40 to 1,482 acres) for males.

FEEDING

Raccoons forage throughout the night, often moving among concentrated food sources some distance apart. Eats wide variety of fruits, nuts, and seeds, including wild grapes, manzanita berries, acorns, and elderberries, and cultivated fruits and grains including corn and wheat where available. Along wetland edges and streams, forages for crayfish and other crustaceans, small fish, and shellfish. Insects, earthworms, and eggs of nesting birds, especially waterfowl, taken seasonally.

SURVIVAL

High juvenile mortality from predation before emergence from natal den. Human hunting, trapping, and vehicle kills cause most adult mortality; canine distemper, rabies, and starvation, especially in colder climates, contribute. Average life span in the wild probably under 3 years in most areas.

SIGNS

Scats 1.3 cm (½-in.) diameter even-diameter cords with blunt ends, deposited individually or sometimes in latrines, at base of trees, on large tree limbs, on rocks or logs, or on ground near feeding areas. Scats containing crayfish remains reddish, highly pulverized. Dens aboveground in tree hollows where available, otherwise in ground burrows dug by other animals, brush piles, or in rock outcrops. Feeding signs include remains of crustaceans or shellfish at streamside, diggings for ground bees or yellow-jacket nests, and remains of fruits and nuts.

J: Raccoon scat

K: A raccoon has foraged in the dunes of California's central coast, changing direction often in between its numerous diggings.

RACCOONS

TRACKS

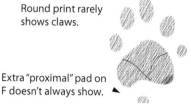

Round print rarely shows claws.

Extra "proximal" pad on F doesn't always show. ◀

Inside toe ◀ barely registers (F and H).

LEFT FRONT   LEFT HIND

COMMON GAITS

A: Diagonal walk, indirect register (common)

B: Fast walk (occasional)

C: Slow walk (occasional)

D: Lope (occasional)

E: Bound (occasional)

Front

Hind

A   B   C   D   E

RACCOONS

TRACK MEASUREMENTS

	Average, inches	Average, cm	Usual range, inches*
Front width	1⅛	2.9	¾ to 1½
Front length	1⅜	3.5	1¹¹⁄₁₆ to 1⅝
Hind width	1¹⁄₁₆	2.7	⅞ to 1½
Hind length	1⁵⁄₁₆	3.3	1 to 1⁹⁄₁₆
Trail width	2⅞	7.3	1¹¹⁄₁₆ to 4⅛
Stride**	8	20.3	5⅜ to 11

*More than 93% of my measurements fall within this range.   **Diagonal walk

A

B

Ringtail tracks may be quite variable. The tiny inside toe, especially in the hind track, may barely register, making many tracks appear to be four-toed. On the front track the "proximal" or extra little heel pad may not always register. Finally, parts of the creased heel pad on both front and hind feet may or may not show in the tracks, depending upon soil and the ringtail's movement. But the size and shape of the tracks leave few other possibilities. **Vs. domestic cat:** Look carefully at the heel-pad shape and look for the inside toe, which is very small in a ringtail and usually absent in a cat. **Vs. spotted skunk:** The skunk's tracks usually show prominent claws and the hind track's heel pad is more elongated.

A: Left front track

B: Left hind track

C: The ringtail's bushy tail brushed over its tracks. Note that the inside toe barely shows on the hind track (bottom), while the front track (top) doesn't register the extra heel-pad impression.

D: Diagonal walk pattern

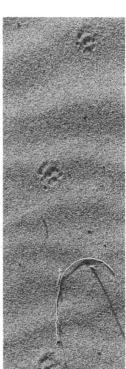

C

RACCOONS

D

297

If you looked at rocky or brushy terrain through the dark round eyes of a ringtail, you would see a jungle gym of opportunity, for this animal is truly the **gymnast among foragers**. The ringtail's rear feet can pivot 180 degrees, partly from the hip and partly from the ankle, allowing it to point its feet and claws backward as it runs down a rock face or momentarily hangs one-footed from a tree. Rotated just ninety degrees, the feet can grasp a limb (or in the case of one pet ringtail, the sides of a door) to ascend or descend in perfect control. On rock faces these feet can be inserted into tiny cracks, and indeed the ringtail uses other tricks of the rock climber: It can stem up or down a crevice supporting itself with its feet on one surface and its back on the other; and it can quickly ricochet from one surface to another (even though the surfaces may be positioned at ninety-degree angles). Going one better than the human climber, a ringtail can execute an accurate "power leap" up, down, or laterally into a tiny target space (even a small crevice). While most trackers would find rock-tracking a ringtail beyond their skills, it is still possible to appreciate some of the steep terrain they inhabit. Around caves and rock outcrops, do some scrambling. Look for ringtail scats and dens, and look for tracks on dusty ledges, which most other animals would avoid. Become the gymnast and discover where you would hunt if you could climb anywhere—looking out for rattlesnakes as you do.

This ability to "go anywhere" allows the ringtail to **forage in a free-spirited way**, unbound by methodical routines. It makes full use of all of the resources in a given season, perhaps snatching up some grasshoppers, climbing into a bird's nest to catch a roosting bird, nimbly scaling a cactus to eat its fruit, ambushing a mouse or woodrat, scaling a rock face to grab a bat, and even licking nectar from an agave blossom. Survey a ringtail's habitat to see what food it might provide and where the animal would thus be traveling. If you find scat, pick it apart (using tweezers in your track pack) and see what the current diet is.

Observers have noticed that the **ringtail shows different postures** when traveling through its territory, and some of these can be read in tracks. There is the low-slung crouching walk (perhaps when sensing prey or caused by the ringtail's own vulnerability to owls and other enemies); there is a high-stepping confident fast walk, and there is a "glide" with tail stretched out behind, barely above the ground. When you find ringtail tracks, try to read its personality through the gait and pressure releases.

A ringtail scurries across a dried-up playa in Death Valley's sand dunes, far away from the rocky terrain often associated with ringtail habitat.

RACCOONS

E

F

G

E: A ringtail makes a kill in the sand dunes near Stove-pipe Wells, Death Valley. The tracks show a series of struggles.

F: Detail of bottom left portion of photo E, the ringtail is facing the drag marks of its prey, shown by each ringtail front foot coming down three times in this location.

G: This sequence of bounding tracks shows pairs of double prints, created by the ringtail hitting both front feet in quick succession, then swinging the two rear feet to land on top of the front tracks.

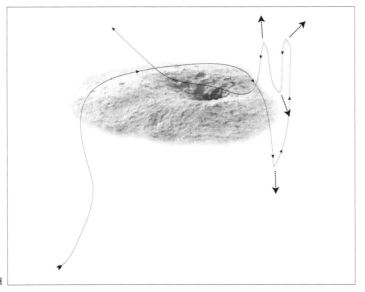

H

H: A ringtail hunts near a kangaroo-rat burrow, skirting the entrance and then making four changes of direction after stopping and looking (dotted line arrows).

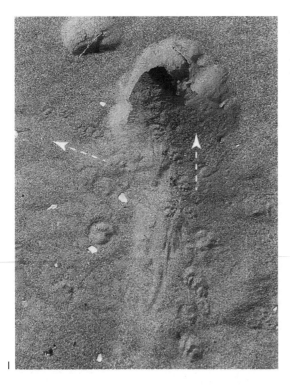

I: A ringtail walks directly toward a kangaroo rat burrow, investigates with the front feet planted at the entrance, and then makes a ninety-degree left turn.

I

RACCOONS

301

SPECIES AND WEIGHT   *Bassariscus astutus*

7 subspecies in North America

0.9 to 1.4 kg (1.9 to 3 lb.)

HABITAT   Wide variety of habitats from sea level to above 1,829 meters (6,000 ft.), including desert; chaparral; riparian areas; montane conifer forests; oak, piñon, and juniper woodland; and dry tropical areas. Usually not present in highly developed agricultural areas. Highest densities may occur in riparian areas with a dense midstory of vegetation but also common in rocky areas.

BREEDING   Usually February to May, concentrated in March and April. Gestation 51 to 54 days, litter size 1 to 4.

DEVELOPMENT   Young eat solid food after 1 month, accompany parents on nightly hunts after 2 months, at which time they have excellent agility. Appear like small adults at 4 months and fully grown at 7 months. Both parents may feed young, according to some reports.

SOCIAL HABITS   Generally dens solitarily at numerous sites within home range, usually spending no more than 3 consecutive days in 1 den. Some male-female pairs may stay together during gestation, but no tendency toward monogamy. Home ranges recorded from 5 hectares (12.4 acres) in riparian areas to 136 hectares (336 acres) in canyon lands; males' larger than females'. No overlap of home range within gender, but male and female ranges may overlap.

FEEDING   Opportunistic forager, eating insects, fruits, mammals, arthropods, birds, and reptiles. Within its home range, hunts locally abundant mammals such as woodrats, mice, and squirrels and eats seasonally abundant fruits such as juniper berries, mistletoe berries, catcus, madrone, and hackberry. Uses climbing ability to hunt nesting birds and roosting bats. Grasshoppers, crickets, beetles, and moths included among many other insects. Carrion sometimes eaten. Active almost entirely during darkness but may begin and end foraging in twilight.

Vulnerable to great horned owl. May be caught by other nocturnal animals including coyotes, bobcats, and raccoons.

Scats about 1 cm (⅜ in.) in diameter and 3 inches long, usually unsegmented but may have up to 4 segments. Scat odor not musky like weasel or fox, often deposited on elevated surfaces such as rock ledges, tree branches, or boulders. Sometimes deposited over time in concentrated areas. Often contains remnants of several kinds of foods. Dens in rock crevices, tree cavities, brush piles, buildings, and other animals' burrows; dens usually not lined with bedding.

J: Ringtail scat in the Chiricahua Mountains of Arizona

K: Ringtail tracks enter a temporary den in Death Valley, California.

RACCOONS

TRACKS

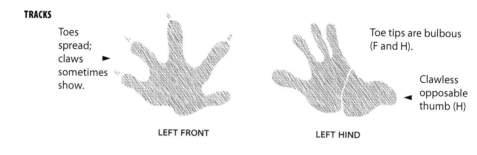

Toes spread; claws sometimes show. ►

Toe tips are bulbous (F and H).

Clawless opposable thumb (H) ◄

LEFT FRONT   LEFT HIND

COMMON GAITS

A: Diagonal walk (common)

B: Pace walk (occasional)

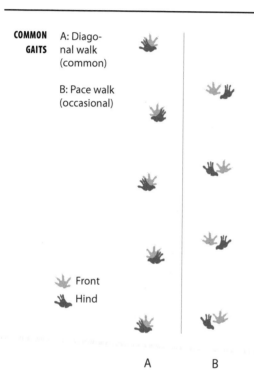

Front
Hind

A   B

TRACK MEASUREMENTS

	Average, inches	Average, cm	Usual range, inches*
Front width	2¹⁄₁₆	5.2	1½ to 2½
Front length	1¾	4.4	1⅞ to 2¼
Hind width	1⁵⁄₁₆	3.4	1 to 1¾
Hind length	2¼	5.8	1⅝ to 2⅝
Trail width	4⅛	10.5	2¼ to 5¾
Stride**	9¹⁄₁₆	23.0	5¾ to 13

*More than 96% of my measurements fall within this range.   **Diagonal walk

OPOSSUMS

A

B

Once encountered, the alien-looking double print of a walking opossum cannot be forgotten. The hind track shows a unique opposable thumb pointing inward. In a walking pattern the front track is usually partially covered, and thus often shows only four toes. Only the front track could be confused with anything else, namely a raccoon's front track. But the opossum's front track usually shows more of a toe spread and more bulbous toe tips than a raccoon's. Most opossum walking patterns show a negative straddle.

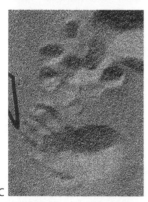

C

D

E

A: Right front track

B: Right hind track

C: Left front (top) and hind tracks in loose sand

D: Common double print, the left hind over the left front

E: Common diagonal walk pattern

OPOSSUMS

An opossum trail is the path of a **true survivor**. Despite its reputation as dim-witted, this marsupial species—the only one in North America—was dealt a full deck of survival adaptations that have enabled it to expand its range northward to New England since colonial times, and through-out much of California since introduction there about a hundred years ago. Here are some adaptations. Opossums are fully immune to bites of rattlesnakes and water moccasins. The opossum has a high birth rate. Because she carries her young in her pouch, the female is highly mobile and can exploit food resources without being tied to a natal den. Opos-sums can avoid danger by climbing, swimming, or feigning death. An opossum's prehensile tail allows it to gather abundant nest materials and thus survive cold winters in northern habitats. As you discover opossum tracks in places "where they shouldn't be," you're given a chance to appre-ciate the species' overall success. But if you're lucky, you may also find an occasional sign of a specific survival event, as we have: the tracks of an opossum who turned to face a predator, then a body-plop impression, the trotting-off tracks of the predator, and the get-up-and-walk-away tracks of the opossum.

The opossum's **development and dispersal** offer an excellent tracking window. Opossums mate twice a year, normally in February and May, and about ninety days after that, the young, who are then the size of wood-rats, emerge from their mother's pouch to give the tracker little opossum tracks to study. For about ten days to two weeks, the young may still nurse, but they also explore near their den while the mother forages more widely. Then, the mother often transports her brood on her back to a new territory, where they are let loose to begin their lives away from competi-tion with other opossums. This is the only time the young ride on her back. In May and August begin looking for juvenile opossum tracks. The ambitious tracker may also look for changes in a female opossum's tracks late in her youngs' development; she may then be carrying an extra two pounds of weight in her pouch.

The waddling tracks of an opossum, at first glance, show little variation. The opossum's primitive skeletal structure, adapted more for climbing than for terrestrial movement, allows only a walk and a seldom-used trot about the speed of a fast-walking human. Nevertheless, an opossum's meandering trail can reveal its **foraging personality**, which may be described as "eat anything you can find." Beetles, carrion, grapes, slugs, earthworms, vole nestlings, or a snake may be on a night's menu. When you follow an opossum trail, discard any ideas about concentrated food resources or regular foraging routes. Look for stops and starts, changes of direction, sniffing, and eating.

F

G

F: Size variations in opossum tracks. Shown actual size, the opossum front track at top is the largest I have measured, while the tracks at bottom were made by a baby opossum that apparently fell off its mother's back as she strode through a tracking box.

G: The hind toe drags of this walking opossum create tracks that are a challenge to identify. This animal has a large negative straddle, i.e., the right and left pairs cross over the center line.

H: An opossum walks up to a crest of a little hillock, hesitates, and walks down the other side. At the crest it is balanced on the right front and the two hind feet (arrows). As it leans to the left to walk downhill, the toes of three feet drag out.

H

OPOSSUMS

SPECIES AND WEIGHT   *Didelphis virginiana*

3 subspecies in North America

1 to 6.4 kg (2 to 14 lb.)

Male up to 50% larger than female

HABITAT   Riparian areas, deciduous forests, marshlands, agricultural areas, grasslands, and suburban areas from sea level to 3,000 meters (9,000 ft.). Prefers edge habitat and requires adequate denning sites. Intolerant of extreme heat or cold but has steadily moved northward in the United States since colonial times. Eastern opossums have been introduced into areas of the West, including New Mexico, Arizona, and the Pacific coast states.

BREEDING   Two breeding periods per year, February and May (earlier in southern states). Males expand their range, continually visit females' areas until an estrous female is located; several males are attracted to the same areas. Hissing and fighting among males, the heaviest males prevailing and doing most mating. Mating pair are usually together only 1 day. Gestation 13 days, young crawl to maternal pouch to nurse. Litters usually 7 to 9; some females breed only once per year but most breed twice, coming into estrus immediately after 1st litter is mature.

DEVELOPMENT   Young remain in mother's pouch for more than 2 months, emerge at about 80 days, when they each weigh about as much as a chipmunk. They remain in the mother's den or venture only a short distance away until they are weaned at 90 to 100 days, each then the size of a woodrat. At this time female may carry young on her back to a new den and feeding area. Female then breeds again and young begin to forage on their own. For about 3 months, the young gradually expand their foraging range. Young females may themselves breed at 8 months.

SOCIAL HABITS   Opossums usually sleep, travel, and forage alone. Daytime dens, located near forage areas, may be used by several opossums at different times. An opossum normally uses a den for 1 or 2 nights only before moving to another; nevertheless, a particular animal often has a few preferred dens it uses continually. Rarely, 2 opossums share the same den. The home range expands as an opossum

OPOSSUMS

ages and becomes familiar with new forage areas. Some home-range estimates are 20 to 150 hectares (49 to 371 acres); males' ranges are larger than females'. Males are usually agonistic toward other males, and females toward other females, only in the breeding season.

Opossums are omnivorous but depend upon significant amounts of animal food. Insects, including grasshoppers, ground beetles, and larvae, are routinely eaten. Opossums often eat carrion or consume nestlings of voles and rabbits. Earthworms, snails, slugs, salamanders, toads, snakes, millipedes, crayfish, moles, and shrews are common in the diet. Fruits such as mulberry and grape are foraged for. Some birds are consumed, especially as nestlings, and in urban areas pet food and garbage form part of the diet.

FEEDING

Opossums are most vulnerable in the first few weeks after weaning; perhaps only 30% survive. Adults succumb to great horned owls, dogs, and vehicle collisions but are not a large part of other predators' diets. Tens of thousands are hunted or trapped annually in the United States also. To escape danger, opossums seek cover in brush or underground, or stand their ground, hissing and baring their teeth. When severely threatened an opossum "feigns death," rolling onto its side, curling its lips back, becoming rigid, and excreting foul odors from its anus. Opossums may also swim to escape danger and they swim well underwater. They are immune to bites from eastern and western diamondbacks, copperheads, and water moccasins. A high reproductive rate and the ability of a mother to transport newly weaned young on her back to a new area have enabled a rapid expansion in the United States.

SURVIVAL

Scats rarely found, nondescript, difficult to distinguish from those of similar-size mammals. Dens most often underground where available, in burrows of woodchucks or other animals, also in tree stumps, debris piles, hollow logs, outbuildings. Some appropriate and expand the arboreal nests of tree squirrels and crows. Nest material including leaves and debris gathered with mouth, pushed under belly, and grasped with tail; an opossum may make numerous trips to its den with nest materials.

SIGNS

OPOSSUMS

TRACKS

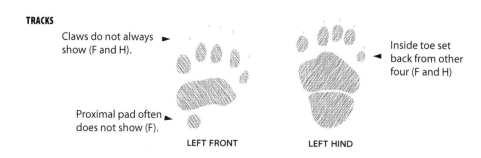

Claws do not always show (F and H). ►

◄ Inside toe set back from other four (F and H)

Proximal pad often does not show (F). ►

LEFT FRONT   LEFT HIND

COMMON GAITS

A: Pace walk (common)

B: Diagonal walk (occasional)

C: Lope (occasional)

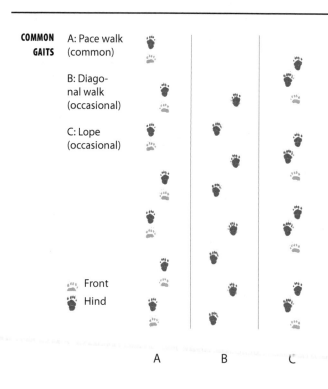

Front

Hind

A   B   C

TRACK MEASUREMENTS

	Average, inches	Average, cm	Usual range, inches*
Front width	4¹³⁄₁₆	12.2	3¾ to 6
Front length	4¾	12.1	3³⁄₁₆ to 6
Hind width	4¾	12.0	3⅝ to 5⅞
Hind length	7¼	18.4	5 to 9
Trail width	11⁷⁄₁₆	29.1	7 to 19
Stride**	23⁵⁄₁₆	59.2	15¾ to 30¼

*More than 96% of my measurements fall within this range.   **Pace walk

A

B

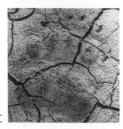

C

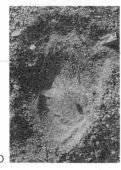

D

The size and heavy compression of black-bear tracks leave few other choices. In habitats where **grizzly** and black bears coexist, the species' tracks may overlap in size. Look at the position of the inner toe on the front (F) tracks; it is set back considerably from the other four toes in a black-bear track, while a grizzly's toes form an even arc. Also, a grizzly's F claws are much longer. A small bear's tracks might also overlap in width with a **wolverine**'s, but the latter's stride would be much smaller, and a wolverine's H track shows a different shape. In certain terrain (for example in deep snow and walking uphill) bears will create a diagonal walk pattern not unlike a human walking. Make sure you look carefully at the shape of the track in difficult substrate such as pine needles.

E

A: Left front track

B: Right hind track

C: Left front showing claws

D: Even when toes aren't distinct, the enormous weight in the heel area makes a bear track obvious.

E: Pace walk pattern

The bear's gift to the tracker is a string of deeply compressed, usually obvious tracks, with little variation of gait, that begs to be followed. But following that trail is often an adventure, for this original All-Terrain Mammal may lead you straight down a cliff, through a thicket, or down the middle of a creek. When you walk with the bear, you sense that only one of you knows why it's going where it is, and it isn't the tracker. Bears, actually, know their territory very well, have good memories of the best feeding places, and know where other bears are. Hence the **purpose of the trail** is a good window for bear tracking, and this may be revealed in several ways. If your bear is a large, old resident, it may be taking a direct route to a favorite meadow or berry patch to forage. If it's a subadult, it may take a circuitous route purposely to avoid contact with a bigger bear. If it's June, the trail is very long, and the tracks are big, you may be following a male bear out looking for females. If it's late fall, a long trail of any size tracks might lead from the final prehibernation foraging area back to the bear's core area where it will den. When interpreting a trail's purpose, pay attention to what size bear you have, the time of year, and where the bear's food is. A very serious caution: Be very alert and careful when you encounter fresh tracks of a mother black bear with cubs; consider backtracking rather than trailing them.

Because black bears have low reproduction and mortality rates, their **local stable population** offers an excellent tracking window. A given area might support only two or three females and a couple of males whose territories overlap or adjoin. Because bears grow slowly, there will be a whole range of track sizes, from tiny cubs to yearlings to subadults to dominant breeding adults. As a tracker, you should therefore start a notebook with current measurements of track sizes, trail widths, and left and right strides. A family unit of mother and cubs, or mother with yearlings, will for the most part keep other bears away from their favorite feeding places. Dominant males' home ranges may overlap a couple of females'; they may use common feeding areas but usually not at the same time. And subadults (2½- to 4½-year-olds) squeeze in between, generally avoiding contact with other bears. The best time to take a reading of a local population is before the June breeding season or in midsummer when wide-scale wandering is least.

A bear's **fall feeding push** cannot be ignored by the tracker who wants to understand bear biology. Weight gain before hibernation, for example, governs whether young bears will survive, when a female first conceives, and whether she successfully completes a pregnancy. The ripest patches of berries, acorns, or other fattening foods may attract bears from great distances. They then forage in the same area but nevertheless space themselves according to dominance. In these places look for bear trails back and forth between foraging areas. Notice track sizes, ages, and locations, and be alert because bears most often forage during daylight hours.

At an elevation of 1,981 meters (6,500 ft.), most bears in Sequoia National Park would be hibernating by late December, when this photo was taken. This adult was probably either changing dens after being disturbed or was a late male hibernator (females typically den earlier). The depth of the snow caused the bear to use a diagonal walk; the gait was very regular whether on level ground, uphill, or downhill.

F

G

Black-bear beds:

F: A freshly used bed on the edge of Clover Meadow in Sequoia National Forest is punctuated by a scat pile.

G: Another bed in pine needles, 0.8 km (½ mile) from the same meadow, has numerous scat piles on its edges. Some of the piles have remnants of pine-nut shells.

H: Excavated pine needles (arrow) lie below a bed excavated to about 20 cm (8 in.); it is 76 cm (30 in.) long.

BEARS

H

I   J

Juvenile bears:

I: In early July a small cub (trail on right) walks next to its mother in the Sierra Nevada.

J: In mid-March in the Sierras, a cub born the previous year travels by itself in the vicinity of a ski resort. Its fresh tracks cross older ones of an adult bear.

K: A frisky bear cub lopes and bounds up a slope.

L: The same bear detours to climb up on a stump.

K   L

BEARS

315

BLACK BEAR   Notes for the Tracker

SPECIES AND WEIGHT   *Ursus americanus*

14 subspecies in North America

Usually 40 to 145 kg (88 to 320 lb.)

Male 10% to 70% larger than female

HABITAT   Deciduous and coniferous forests and chaparral, where abundant growth of grasses, sedges, and forbs provides spring food and where shrubs and trees provide ample berries and nuts for summer and fall food. Seasonally preferred habitats include lush meadows, riparian areas, fruiting shrub patches, and oak and hardwood nut groves. Core habitat must provide secluded winter denning areas.

BREEDING   Most mating in June or early July. Males travel long distances through numerous females' territories, follow scent trails of estrous females. Breeding pairs may travel together for several days. Fighting and chases among males during breeding season; increased marking of trees with claws and teeth, especially by larger, dominant males with established territories who breed most. Gestation 60 to 70 days after delayed implantation; birth in January or February during mother's hibernation. Litters usually 1 or 2. Females normally breed only after 4½ years or more, and often skip 2 to 3 years between litters.

DEVELOPMENT   Mother and newborns leave den in late March to April but commonly remain in immediate vicinity of den for 1 to 3 weeks. Young about 11 kg (25 lb.) in 1st summer, travel close to mother throughout year and den with her during next winter. Yearlings accompany mother until June, when they disperse, weighing about 18+ kg (40+ lb.). Female young tend to stay within or near mother's home range; males disperse farther (up to 217 km/135 miles recorded), some as 2-year-olds and some not until age 4.

SOCIAL HABITS   Male home ranges (usually 30 to 135 km²) generally overlap with some other males'; female home ranges (usually 10 to 50 km²) may or may not overlap with some other females'. Male and female ranges do overlap with each other. Where there is overlap, bears of both genders avoid contact and usually space themselves more than 100 meters (328 ft.) apart even when feeding in the same area. Dominant bears may chase subordinate ones, or initiate fighting, when there

BEARS

is contact; subordinate bears such as subadults often take circuitous routes to avoid contact. Home ranges are stable from year to year, especially where bear hunting has little impact. In late summer and fall, bears may travel great distances to commonly used berry- or nut-producing locations, where dominance hierarchy regulates spacing. At hibernation time most bears return to the core of their home range. Hibernation begins from October to January depending upon climate; pregnant females den earlier. Bears usually emerge in March or April after hibernation of 2 to 6 months. In warm climates a small percentage of bears may be active throughout the winter.

New growth of grasses, sedges, and forbs are primary spring and early summer diet. From mid-July, bears seek out foods high in protein and fat to gain weight before hibernation, roaming their territory to find currently ripening fruits such as manzanita berries, blackberries, coffee berries, chokecherries, acorns, pine nuts, and other locally abundant fruits and nuts. Especially when these are unavailable, bears may spend considerable time tearing open dead logs looking for ants or bees' nests. Rarely, bears eat carrion or prey upon mammals such as marmots. Most foraging activity during the day, especially in summer, with peaks in early morning and around dusk, and with frequent rest periods. Human garbage may attract bears from adjacent home ranges and may make up more than ⅓ of diet seasonally.

FEEDING

Poor nut or berry crops cause substantial mortality, especially of young and yearlings, and inhibit successful reproduction by breeding females. Human hunting is a major cause of mortality in some areas. Cubs and young bears may be vulnerable to attack by a large adult male bear.

SURVIVAL

Scat 3.2+ cm (1¼+ in.) diameter, in very large piles, usually containing remnants of grasses, berries, or insects. Hibernation dens in hollow trees, excavated ground cavities, rock cavities, brush piles, or dug-out depressions on open ground, usu-

SIGNS

BEARS

ally with bedding material added; pregnant females usually have most-protected dens. Dens reused only a small percentage of the time. Summer beds may be shallow depressions in the ground. Marking trees and posts, most often in summer, showing claw marks, bite marks, and fur remnants, located in open areas at the edge of trails; made by adult residents, primarily males.

M

M: Bear scat containing grasses

GRIZZLY BEAR Track ID

TRACKS

Very long claws (esp. F) ►

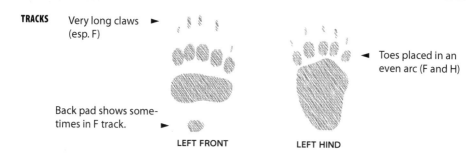

◄ Toes placed in an even arc (F and H)

Back pad shows sometimes in F track. ►

LEFT FRONT　　　**LEFT HIND**

COMMON GAITS

A: Pace walk (common)

B: Diagonal walk (occasional)

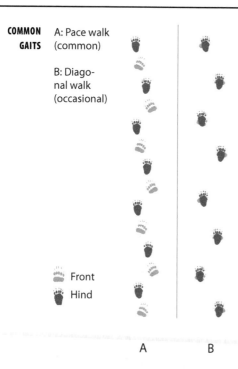

Front

Hind

A　　　B

TRACK MEASUREMENTS

	Usual range, inches	Usual range, cm
Front width	4¼ to 8¼	10.8 to 21
Front length	4⅜ to 8	11.1 to 20.3
Hind width	4½ to 7	11.4 to 17.8
Hind length	6⅜ to 11⅜	16.2 to 28.9
Trail width	10⅛ to 19½	25.7 to 49.5
Stride*	21¾ to 33¾	55.2 to 85.7

*Pace walk

BEARS

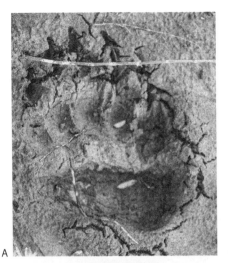

Grizzly or brown-bear tracks sometimes overlap in size, trail width, and stride with black-bear tracks, although on average they are larger. If you are in a habitat where both species are found, look at the position of the toes. In a grizzly's front tracks the five toes are positioned in a consistent arc, and the inside toe, unlike the black bear's, is not set back from the other four. This is especially noticeable in the front track. Also, the claws, especially in the front track, are much longer in relation to the overall track than is the case with black bears.

FINE POINTS

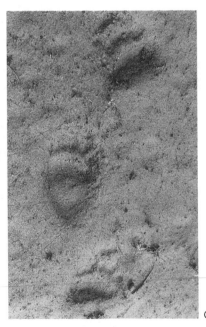

A: Right front track

B: Left hind track of a 430 kg (950 lb.) Kodiak bear, showing a length of 29 cm (11¼ in.)

C: Common pacing pattern with front tracks pitched substantially inward

BEARS

319

If the hair on your neck stands up when you encounter fresh grizzly bear tracks, then your innate alarm system is working just fine. Tracking grizzly bears is serious business because of the animal's unpredictable and sometimes violent reaction to an invasion of its personal space. This is where settling down with some older prints makes perfect sense, and here you can work on basics of **individual animal identification** through tracks. Since at least the 1930s, field biologists have tried to count the number of individual bears in an area by measuring and recording their tracks at common-use areas—with mixed results. Generally, measurement of front-pad widths turned out to be a good indication of the size and gender of a bear: For example, in Yellowstone a measurement of less than 12.5 cm ($4^{1}/_{10}$ in.) meant an 80% chance of a female, and greater than 14.5 cm ($5^{7}/_{10}$ in.) a 90% chance of an adult male. If you've found an area with numerous grizzly tracks, you can practice your holistic tracking by measuring not only tracks but also trail width and stride; also notice unique pitch and placement of the front and hind feet. The larger the track, the more evident are individual variations among them such as squat vs. elongated heel-pad shape in bear hind tracks. Record track measurements and patterns in your notebook, then try to visualize the walking animals. Tracks of a female with cubs are especially interesting, but be on special alert then. Managers of wild areas properly try to keep humans away from active grizzly areas as much for the bears' space as for our own safety.

A bear's **large appetite** will leave some pretty big signs for trackers. In some areas one grizzly, male or female, may kill three or four adult elk or moose per year (pretty easily at that) and will stay two days to a week around the carcass because it can eat "only" 29 kg (65 lb.) of meat a day. Hence, numerous bear beds and piles of scats are left nearby. In fall a bear could consume 100,000 berries in a day's feeding, leading to impressive scats. From summer foraging, also look for diggings in meadows where roots are consumed or ground squirrels dug up.

SPECIES AND WEIGHT

Ursus arctos

80 to 600+ kg (175 to 1,320+ lb.)

Males 125% to 220% larger than females

BEARS

Mountains, plains, and coastal areas of the West and North, where ample feeding and denning sites exist. Stable populations require considerable remote habitat. Within a home range, bears often move seasonally to the best foraging areas, which may include old-growth forests, coastal and mountain meadows, salmon-spawning streams, and berry-producing shrublands.

HABITAT

Breeding normally begins in May or early June and ends before the end of July. Male follows estrous female; pair may remain together for a few hours to several weeks. Male posturing and fighting during breeding season. Both genders sexually mature at 3½ years or later; largest males breed most. Gestation 6 to 8 weeks after delayed implantation; litters of 1 to 3 born during hibernation (Jan through Mar). Females breed every 3 years on average.

BREEDING

Family often remains near hibernation/natal den for several weeks after emergence. Young remain with mother for 2 to 4 years. Dispersal often a gradual process; however, some rapid, direct dispersal movements to 340 km (211 miles) recorded. Males generally disperse farther than females. Weight triples in first summer; females approach maximum weight at about 9 years, males at about 14.

DEVELOPMENT

Shared usage of overlapping home-range areas common. However, at concentrated food sites, a hierarchy plays out in which adult males dominate, females with small cubs are next, and other bears are last. Home ranges vary by area and food availability, usually 50 to 400 km² for females, 200 to 1,500 km² for males.

SOCIAL HABITS

Seasonal feeding cycles. In spring, grasses, forbs, and sedges heavily consumed, also ungulate carrion, especially bison and elk. Summer foods include roots and bulbs; juvenile ungulates such as moose, elk, or caribou that are killed; insects; and small terrestrial mammals including voles and ground squirrels. In fall locally abundant fruits including huckleberries, blueberries, and serviceberries used; salmon streams heavily fished. Pine seed caches of red squirrels raided.

FEEDING

Hibernation begins around October, often timed with temperature drop and significant snowfall, emergence usually April or May. Some cubs killed by competing adult male grizzlies; most adult mortality from hunting or conflict with humans.

SURVIVAL

BEARS

Scat is huge pile containing plant or animal remains. Diggings for tubers or insects. Carrion remains with numerous beds and scats nearby. Hibernation dens excavated and lined with branches, entrance 0.3 to 0.6 meter (1 to 2 ft.) wide and 0.9 to 1.2 meters (3 to 4 ft.) high, usually in remote location. Bough beds in snow near den, used for several weeks after emergence. Day beds in spring-through-fall feeding areas, shallow to 46 cm (18 in.) scrapes.

SIGNS

INSECTIVORE

SHREW Track ID

TRACKS

Five toes on F ►

◄ Five toes on H

LEFT FRONT   LEFT HIND

COMMON GAITS

A: Gallop (common)

B: Bound (common)

C: Bound in snow with tail drag (common)

D: Trot

※ Front
※ Hind

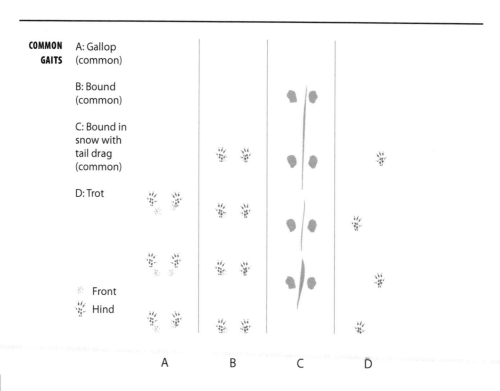

A   B   C   D

TRACK MEASUREMENTS

	Example, inches	Example, cm
Front width	3/16	0.5
Front length	3/16	0.5
Hind width	1/4	0.6
Hind length	1/4	0.6
Trail width	3/4 to 1	1.9 to 2.5
Stride**	1 3/4 to 2 5/8*	4.4 to 6.7

These examples are for an Ornate shrew.   *Gallop

INSECTIVORE

DOUG GAULKE

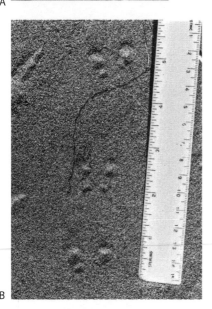

A

Very small tracks showing five toes on the front feet and five on the hind definitely belong to a shrew. Without clear prints, trail width and track size will usually distinguish tracks of most shrew species from those of voles, harvest mice, *Peromyscus* mice, and grasshopper mice, because shrews generally weigh half as much or less than these gallopers. Look for a shrew trail width of 2.5 cm (1 in.) or less. That leaves a few species of pocket mice that may approach a shrew's small size. The best strategy is to list all of your local mouse and shrew species by size and to study detail in clear prints when you have them. Note also that shrews, unlike mice, often trot rather than bound or gallop. In snow they often create furrows as they walk or trot.

FINE POINTS

MARK ELBROCH

C

Shrew species and ranges: Shrews are found throughout North America. Of the 35 species in the genera *Sorex, Notisorex,* and *Cryptotis,* 33 weigh less than 11 g/²⁄₅ oz. (many 2 to 6 grams); water shrews and marsh shrews are larger. Three species in the *Blarina* genus are also larger.

B

A: Shrew trail in Wisconsin

B: Gallop pattern from California's central coast

C: Right front (left) and hind tracks

INSECTIVORE

UNGULATES

TRACKS

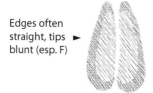

Edges often straight, tips blunt (esp. F) ►

◄ Concave hoof creates raised area in track (F and H).

COMMON GAITS

A: Diagonal walk (common)

B: Trot (common)

C: Lope (occasional)

D: Pace walk (occasional)

E: Slow walk (occasional)

Front

Hind

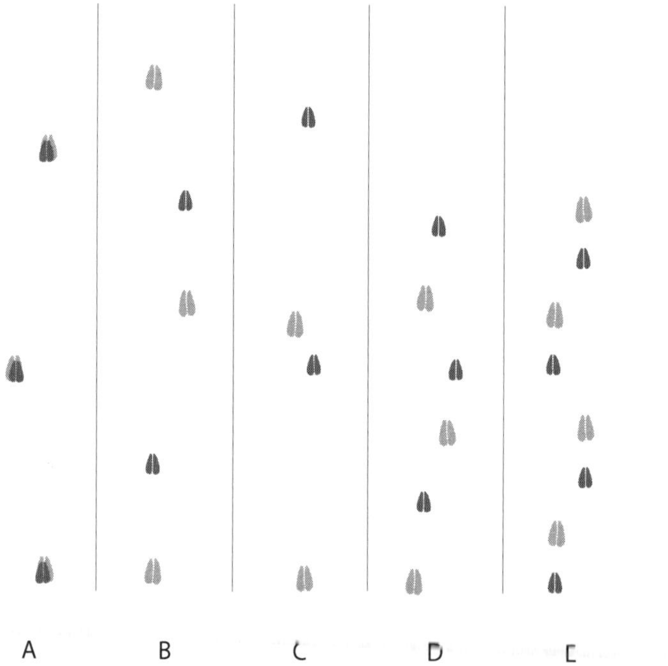

A   B   C   D   E

TRACK MEASUREMENTS

	Average, inches	Average, cm	Usual range, inches*
Front width	2	5.0	1⅝ to 2⅜
Front length	2⅞	7.3	2¼ to 3⅜
Hind width	1⅝	4.2	1½ to 2⅛
Hind length	2⁵⁄₁₆	6.0	1⅞ to 2¾
Trail width	5	12.7	3⅞ to 5⅝
Stride**	20⁹⁄₁₆	52.2	17⅜ to 28

*More than 93% of my measurements fall within this range.   **Diagonal walk

A

B

C

Where sheep have come down from steep rocky areas, their tracks may be confused with those of **mule deer**, which may be of similar size. While most bighorn tracks are blockier, with straighter edges and blunter tips than deer, some are remarkably deer-like. Look at the center of the track; a sheep's cup-shaped hoof often leaves a raised area, while deer tracks are flatter. **Domestic or feral sheep** tracks are of similar size and shape. Check the habitat closely; in their grazing, domestic sheep make their presence far more evident than do bighorn. Remember also that **wild burros** introduced into the West make obvious trails in bighorn habitat; their tracks are one-toed, however, and have an overall round shape.

FINE POINTS

A: Classic front track shows blockiness and rounded tips, unlike other ungulates.

B and C: Right front and right hind tracks, respectively. The hind especially resembles deer in overall shape, but both tracks show the rise in the forward two-thirds of the track from the sheep's cupped hooves.

D: Slow gallop pattern

D

UNGULATES

The tracker lured to the bighorn sheep's domain will learn the importance of **habitat dependence**. The bighorn is marvelously adapted to steep, rocky, wide-open terrain where it can use its outstanding eyesight, short legs, and stocky build to spot and then evade potential danger. It can run straight up a forty-degree slope with about a third the excess effort it would take a human. Here, predators have little chance to take a bighorn, but conversely on the flatlands, mountain sheep are quite vulnerable. Travel routes, resting sites, and forage areas are thus chosen for safety. Feeding, especially for groups of females and young, usually takes place near "escape cover," and night beds are high up on the ridges with commanding views. Finding evidence of sheep activity can be a challenge where the rocky substrate yields few "clear prints." Start by taking the large view, perhaps from a high vantage point. Faint sheep trails begin to pop out, and ever-so-faint depressions in the rocks reveal themselves as beds. Confirm their identity by switching to the detailed view. Look for scats around beds, in feeding areas, and along trails. Drop into a very relaxed state of mind, then begin walking a rocky sheep trail, letting subtle stone dislodgments and disturbed vegetation reveal sheep tracks. As you follow bighorn trails, note what terrain is preferred; saddles between feeding areas or between bedding and feeding areas are good places to start.

The bighorn's **social structure** is another good tracking window. For most of the year, mountain sheep separate themselves into social groups of adult rams on the one hand and ewes, lambs, and yearlings on the other. Socialization helps bighorn survival by providing more eyes to sense danger, therefore increasing feeding efficiency. Typically, female-young groups inhabit the steepest, safest terrain while male groups choose more rolling terrain. By location and track size, try to identify the kind of sheep group you have found. Rams' tracks are larger than ewe tracks, and the largest rams have 14 kg (30 lb.) of extra weight just from their horns. Group size may also show something about the quality of bighorn habitat; poor forage causes groups to be smaller, while scarce water sources in the desert draw larger groups.

Occasionally, sheep must cross flatlands to access "islands" of better forage, or in the case of breeding males, to find female groups. **Fragmented habitat** is common among many sheep populations. Crossings are usually very direct and may be up to 10 km (6.2 miles). If you find tracks in the flats, try to determine the source, destination, and the reason for travel. Look at the size of the group, whether they are males or females and young, and note whether it is breeding season. A final caution about tracking bighorn: Keep your distance if you see them, because human encounters may stress a local population.

UNGULATES

A bighorn trail is often subtle, evident only from stone dislodgments, bruised green vegetation, and occasional fresh scat deposits (arrow).

E

E: Bighorn beds are scrapes in rocky substrate, often very faint and often with a commanding view. Scats on the edges of these scrapes confirm their identity.

F: This bighorn trail originated at a small cave (star and inset) where sheep had sought refuge from a spring rainstorm in the Mojave Desert. There were large and small scats there. The trail was picked up at a saddle and backtracked. Sheep trails often cross saddles and then skirt the sides of outcrops, avoiding the ridgetops.

F

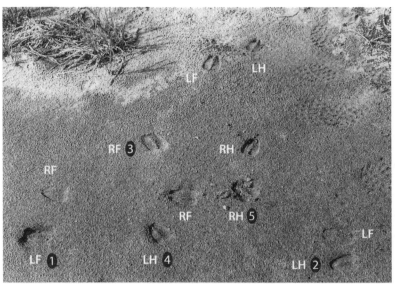

G

G: A bighorn stops and turns to its right. Where the left front (LF) and right front (RF) are planted at the left of this photo, the sheep looks out over a large lake in the East Mojave Desert, with rugged mountains—and primary bighorn habitat—26 km (16 miles) away, past the opposite lakeside. Lone sheep that occasionally cross the lakebed when it is dry are usually mature rams. As the turn is made, the bighorn leans to its left, supporting itself momentarily on that side (1–2) as its RF is replanted to 3. Then the left hind (LH) (4) moves and the right hind (RH) (5) is planted for the pivot and direction change.

H: Bighorn feed on the flesh of barrel cacti after pawing and butting away the spines with hooves and horns.

H

BIGHORN SHEEP   Notes for the Tracker

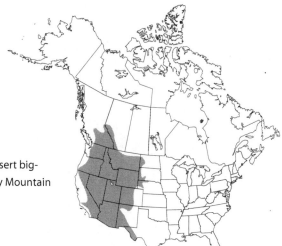

SPECIES AND WEIGHT   *Ovis canadensis*

5 subspecies in North America

34 to 135 kg (75 to 300 lb.)

Male 50% to 100% heavier than female, desert bighorn smaller than Rocky Mountain bighorn

HABITAT   Open, rocky areas of the West with good visibility and nearby precipitous escape terrain are preferred. Bands of females with young and yearlings generally stay closer to steep terrain, while male groups may drift into rolling hills and canyons. In Southwest desert, regular water sources shape summer habitat, bighorn not straying far from them. In many areas bighorn habitat is fragmented into "islands."

BREEDING   Breeding usually November and December for northern and high-elevation populations, July through October for southern and desert populations. Rams may travel widely among ewe groups, and large male-female groups form. Some fighting including head butting among rams; largest rams win most battles and are most successful breeders. Chases of ewes by rams common prior to breeding. Gestation 6 months. Pregnant ewes wander alone to steep, inaccessible site 10 to 14 days prior to giving birth. Lambs 1 per ewe, born May through July in north, January through April in south. Southern populations may have significant numbers of out-of-season births.

DEVELOPMENT   Ewes feed away from resting newborn lambs. Ewes and new lambs gradually move from their isolated sites to form larger "nursery" groups of ewes, lambs, and yearlings, where ewes take turns watching lambs while others feed. In some populations lambs may suckle with more than one female, including ewes that have lost lambs. Much play among lambs including jumping, chases, butts, threats, and mounts. Males are about 20% larger than females at end of 1st year. Rams reach maximum growth at about 7 years, ewes at 1 to 3 years. Ram hind foot length peaks at about 4 years. Young rams disperse to bachelor groups in 2nd to 3rd year.

SOCIAL HABITS   Outside of breeding and lambing season, ewes travel with other ewes and young, while rams travel in bachelor groups. Size of these groups usually varies from 2 to 10, with poor forage quality causing smaller groups. Water sources in summer may cause larger groups to congregate in desert populations. Among rams, a linear hierarchy is established through fights, spatial displacements, front-leg kicks, and face or horn rubbing by subordinates; oldest rams with biggest horns are almost always dominant. Home ranges vary from about 0.5 km² to 28 km²; in the north the winter range is smaller, while in the south the summer range is smaller.

FEEDING

In most areas, grasses such as fescue, galleta, and needlegrass make up majority of diet; forbs such as filaree and Indian wheat important especially when they are green. Many shrubs and trees browsed for leaves and/or buds and flowers, including mountain mahogany, ceanothus, brittlebrush, desert mallow, jojoba, saltbush, ephedra, paloverde, yucca, and Joshua tree among many others. Dried vegetation sometimes eaten; whole green plants dug up with hooves and eaten. In desert, flesh of cacti including saguaro and barrel cactus eaten after spines pawed or butted off; fruit of prickly pear and cholla also eaten. Primarily daytime feeders, moving downslope in early mornings, taking rest breaks during the day, and moving upslope before nightfall. Some nighttime feeding in desert. Much foraging done within 100 meters (328 ft.) of escape cover. Mineral licks important for phosphorus, especially when diet includes much new green vegetation.

SURVIVAL

Excellent eyesight and ability to move efficiently straight up and down steep slopes, contribute to survival. Lamb mortality in a herd may be 40% to 90% in first year, principally from predation. Coyotes, mountain lions, eagles, and other predators may take young or adult bighorn; adult rams are killed more than ewes due to choice of habitat. Fragmentation of habitat by human encroachment and lack of good forage in some areas limit populations.

SIGNS

Scats deposited singly or in groups, about 0.8 cm (⁵⁄₁₆ in.) in diameter, often with nipple on one end and with flattened places on sides; very similar to mule-deer scats at times. Browse signs and pawings from feeding. Pawings at mineral licks. Night beds are usually scrapes in open, often with commanding view, close to escape cover, and with scat piles at their edges. Day beds in foraging areas, often numerous and less clustered than night beds due to movement of herd. Rock outcrops and caves used for shade in desert. Well-used trails between bedding and feeding areas and between habitat "islands."

I and J: Bighorn scats. The samples in J resemble deer scats.

J

I

TRACKS

One-toed tracks
(F and H) ◄

Rim sometimes
shows (F and H). ◄

LEFT FRONT

LEFT HIND

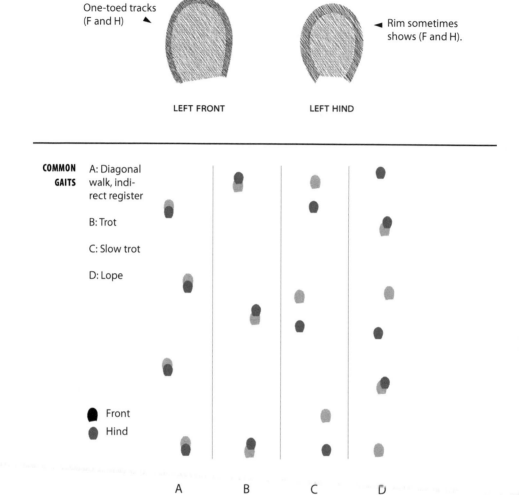

COMMON GAITS

A: Diagonal walk, indirect register

B: Trot

C: Slow trot

D: Lope

● Front
● Hind

A   B   C   D

TRACK MEASUREMENTS

	Average, inches	Average, cm
Front width	2⅜	6.0
Front length	3¼	8.3
Hind width	2¼	5.7
Hind length	3⅜	8.5
Trail width	6³⁄₁₆	15.7
Stride**	20⁷⁄₁₆	51.9

The only other one-toed ungulate in North America is the horse, which has a considerably larger track. Even indistinct compressions could be distinguished from elk or bighorn-sheep tracks, which might be about the same size, by their very round front edge. The burro is an African wild ass, *Equus assinus,* that has become feral in the southwestern United States.

A

B

A: Trotting burro tracks at the Colorado River

B: Front (bottom) and hind tracks

C: Horselike scat

C

Wild burros have become feral in many areas of the arid Southwest.

UNGULATES

337

TRACKS

Track edges ► round (F and H)

◄ Substantial space between toes (F and H)

LEFT FRONT

LEFT HIND

COMMON GAITS

A: Diago-nal walk (common)

B: Slow walk (common)

C: Calf trot-ting pattern (common)

Front

Hind

A   B   C

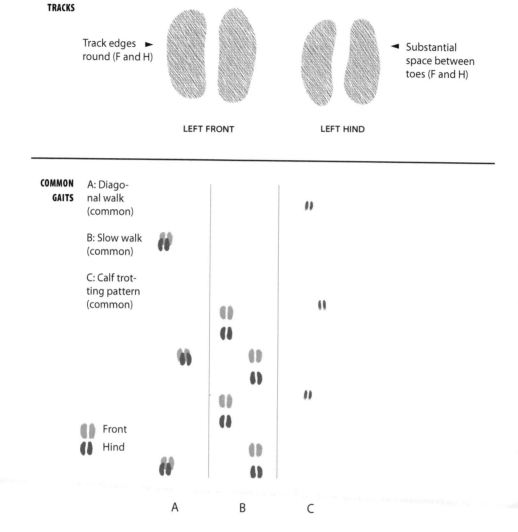

TRACK MEASUREMENTS

	Example, inches	Example, cm	Calf example, inches
Front width	4½	11.4	3¼
Front length	5⅜	13.7	3⅛
Hind width	3⅝ to 4½	8.6 to 11.4	2¾
Hind length	3⅞ to 5⅜	9.8 to 13.7	3
Trail width	10½ to 15¼	26.7 to 38.7	7⅛
Stride	34¹⁄₁₆	86.5	20⅛ to 22⅝

UNGULATES

Domestic-cow tracks may be confused with those of **bison** where these are present; track size, trail width, and stride would overlap. An adult cow's track is much rounder than any other wild ungulate's. However, a domestic calf track's shape and size do compare to that of an **adult elk**. The calf's much shorter legs, though, cause a walking stride several inches shorter than an elk's stride for the equivalent size track.

FINE POINTS

A: Domestic calf hind track below an adult's track

B: Hind (left) and front tracks of an adult

C: Slow walking pattern of a domestic calf

UNGULATES

TRACKS

Rounded sides and tips (F and H) ►

Deep compressions at base of toes (F and H) ►

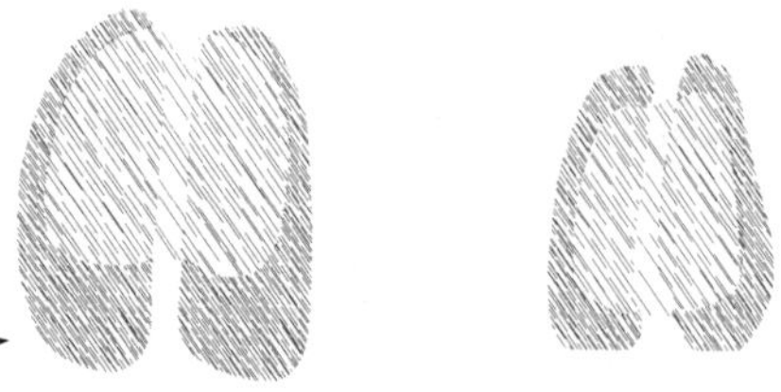

◄ Frequently seen raised area in center of track (F and H)

LEFT FRONT   LEFT HIND

COMMON GAITS

A: Diagonal walk (common)

B: Diagonal walk with slight overstep of H beyond F (common)

C and D: Trots (common)

E: Lope (occasional)

Front

Hind

A   B   C   D   E

TRACK MEASUREMENTS

	Average, inches	Average, cm	Usual range, inches*
Front width	3³⁄₁₆	8.1	
Front length	4⅜	11.1	
Hind width	2¾	7.0	2⁵⁄₁₆ to 3¼
Hind length	3¹¹⁄₁₆	9.3	3¼ to 4¼
Trail width	7⁷⁄₁₆	18.9	3 to 11½
Stride**	26⅝	67.6	22½ to 30

*More than 94% of my measurements fall within this range.   **Diagonal walk

A

B

Being much larger than deer tracks and smaller than moose tracks, elk tracks usually withstand confusion with those of any indigenous ungulates in their habitat. Note the round shape of the track sides *and* tips, which helps distinguish even a small juvenile elk track from that of a deer. Elk hooves have large pads at their back ends, which, imprinting strongly along with the hoof edges, often leave a raised area in the center of a track; the ridge between the toes is therefore often obscured. **Domestic calf** tracks, though, can strongly resemble adult elk tracks in shape and size. Use these aids: A domestic calf's much shorter legs will create a shorter stride, and, like all inbred mammals, a calf's track pattern will tend to be irregular. That is, in a diagonal walk, the RF-RH pair will rarely be a mirror of the LF-LH pair as it usually is in wild diagonal walkers.

C

D

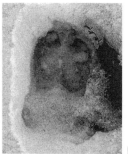

E

A and B: Front (top) and hind (bottom) tracks both show strong impressions from the pads at the back of the toes, leaving a raised area in the center of the track.

C: Diagonal walk pattern. Elk often drag their feet even in shallower snow.

D: Left front/left hind pair

E: Dewclaws show in deep snow or mud.

UNGULATES

The natural instinct to herd, which provides elk the safety to graze in open spaces, gives the tracker an interesting challenge about group identity. Except in the fall breeding season, elk travel either in female-led herds (containing females, yearlings, and sometimes a few young males) or in all-male bands. Tracks can reveal the number in a herd if elk are traveling close together in a walk and if the herd is not too large. Use a method adapted from jungle explorer Jim Corbett: Pick a section of the trail 66 cm (26 in.) long, the average walking stride of an elk. Count every full or partial track, including front tracks underneath hind ones. Divide by two for the number of elk; you will probably be within one. From spring to early winter, small calf tracks in a group will identify a female-led band, while a group of large tracks will probably be a herd of the oldest bulls. Subgroups of families, including a female, a yearling, and a calf of the year, may also travel together.

A herd's **use of habitat** may also be revealed through tracks and signs. A herd may drift from a fraction of a mile to several miles in a day, alternating between foraging and resting, often with little territorial expansion. Remember that besides good forage, elk need shade or cover for resting times, thus preferring edge habitat when it is available. Look for regularly used corridors (elk often do not use the same individual trails). From the age of tracks and the orientation of the landscape, try to read routine daily patterns—for example, a drift to windy ridges in early evening to avoid insects or a migration to riparian areas to seek midday shade. Within foraging areas look for browse signs, including remnants of grass or plant clumps that have been pawed from the ground for their roots. Both female and male elk debark and rub posts or trees, especially in heavily used forage areas. Look for incisor scars on trees; these may be made either in spring or fall. Grazing elk use a slow walk. A stiff trot, with head erect to detect motion, is used to scope out potential danger. A herd may also lope or gallop at a steady rate of about 22 mph when it is alarmed. When you find groups of tracks, study the gait and pressure releases to read the mood of a herd.

The breeding and birthing cycle leaves good evidence for the tracker too. The rut begins when bulls shed the velvet from their antlers; in doing so they thrash and mutilate bushes and patches of ground. Wallows of pawed earth where bulls scent-mark themselves with urine and roll around may also be found. While a "herd master" constantly defends his harem from challenges, the herd continues to browse and graze. Frequent bugling of bulls throughout the rut, especially in early morning and late afternoon, may lead one to observe some of the drama. In April or May you may come across tracks of a female and newly born calf apart from the herd for two weeks. As soon as a few days after birth, the calf may follow its mother on her feeding circuit. Look for deer-size tracks of calves that are more rounded and blockier than deer tracks.

UNGULATES

Groups of female and young elk usually defer to one mature cow for leadership, especially when the herd passes through narrow passageways. Here, an older cow leads a band of transplanted tule elk to their new home on the Wind Wolves Preserve in Southern California. They trotted, loped, and then galloped.

UNGULATES

343

F: With most diagonal walkers, a hind track placed slightly ahead of the front track would tend to have been created by a fast walk or a trot, but elk commonly produce this pattern while walking.

G: A loping pattern

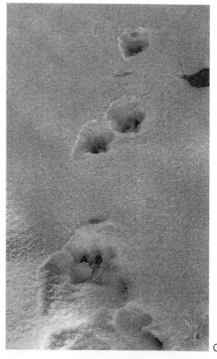

F

G

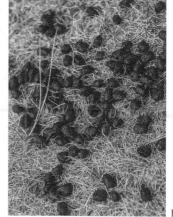

H

H and I: Two forms of elk scat at a golf course in Arizona, a winter feeding spot for local elk

I

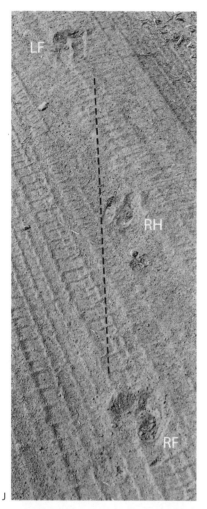

J: A pregnant female elk, trotting, pitches out her hind tracks in relation to the direction of travel (dotted line), showing the weight she is carrying in her womb.

K: In the beginning of the birthing season, an elk calf only days old left a hind track about 3.5 cm (1⅜ in.) wide.

L: Track size suggests that these three elk traveling together in northern Arizona are a cow, a yearling, and a calf.

SPECIES AND WEIGHT   *Cervus canadensis*

4 subspecies in North America

170 to 497 kg (375 to 1,095 lb.)

Male averages 37% larger than female

HABITAT   Open forested land and bottom- lands and selected coastal areas of the Northwest. Prefers edge habitats where brush or dense understory pro- vides calving areas and weather protection, and where meadows and riparian areas provide sufficient browse. In the Rockies elk commonly migrate between lowland winter "pastureland" and summer high-elevation forests and meadows. Selectively reintroduced into other small areas, including Tule elk of California, where herds were once large.

BREEDING   Breeding season or "rut" begins in September in the Rockies, late July or August in most California habitats. Bulls thrash the ground or low bushes with antlers as they shed velvet from them, urinate on themselves, and wallow. A mature bull of 4+ years attempts to join a herd of cows and young, herding them and con- tinually rebuffing other male challengers through threat gestures and occasional serious fights. This "harem master" eats and sleeps little for about a month. Smaller, younger males may fight each other, and especially bulls of 3+ years mount continuous challenges, occasionally defeating a harem master. Most breeding is by largest bulls with largest antlers, and harem size is often 10 to 40. Bugling by males, except yearlings, throughout the rut. Gestation 250 to 265 days, almost always 1 calf. Birthing usually May to early June; female goes away from herd to brushy area hours before birth. In a migratory herd, calving often occurs during upward migration, at intermediate altitude.

DEVELOPMENT   Mother and newly born calf usually remain in a small area apart from the herd for about 2 weeks; calf hides in low brush while mother feeds in vicinity. Nurs- ing occurs about 5 times per day, less than 2 minutes each time. Calves move well within 5 days, can run at the normal herd speed of 22 to 24 mph by 14 days. In the herd one adult female sometimes "babysits" several calves while their mothers feed. Calves begin to feed significantly on vegetation at about 4 weeks; usually weaned by November. Males grow single spike antler at 1 year, 4 to 6 spikes at 2 years, and usually 6 thereafter; thickness of antlers is an indicator of age. Mature females have longer manes than younger females.

UNGULATES

Outside of breeding season, elk form female herds (with females and 1-year-old males) and looser, usually smaller male herds. Female herds are "led" by a dominant older cow, the leadership especially evident when the herd crosses water or moves through a narrow passageway. Female herds may break into family subgroups at times. Male herds have no consistent leadership, but the oldest bulls often form a herd away from younger males, and very old bulls may be solitary. Some 2- and 3-year-old bulls temporarily join a female herd. When moving, herd members constantly call. Gestures of dominance such as charges and foot pawing occur to space elk while feeding and to vacate a subordinate elk from a preferred bedding place. Dominance hierarchy is established by the age of 6 months.

Grasses and sedges comprise majority of the diet for most of the year, supplemented with forbs (including plantain, sunflower, evening primrose, globe mallow) and browse (including blackberry, willow, shad scale, ephedra, maple, alder, sagebrush). In some seasons and areas, forbs and browse become most important. Elk may travel several miles per day, drifting among forage areas and alternating feeding with resting and ruminating in the shade. Feeding peaks are early morning and evening. Elk are more generalist feeders than deer, though calves are selective. Elk may paw up grass bunches to eat roots, dropping clumps to the ground.

Calves vulnerable to predation, especially by coyotes, sometimes by bears and golden eagles, until they join the herd. Mother may drive off coyotes. Adults and juveniles preyed upon by grizzly bears and wolves where these exist. Herd alertness, through hearing and smell, and herd running speed provide safety. Some mortality from malnutrition and rutting battles.

Scats 1.9 cm (¾ in.) long, often with irregular or flattened surfaces, resembling deer scats but larger and usually more abundant. Softer scats congeal and may resemble those of domestic cattle. Posts or trees marked by both males and females, showing debarking with lower incisors; these are also rubbed with the face. In breeding time, bushes rubbed and mutilated from bulls' antler de-velveting; also wallows showing hoof scrapes. Beds usually not prepared, generally in cover close to forage areas. Regular corridors where migration occurs.

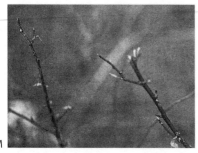

M

M: Elk browse

TRACKS

Toes usually spread (F and H) ►

Prominent dewclaws (F and H) ►

LEFT FRONT   LEFT HIND

COMMON GAITS

A: Diagonal walk (common)

B: Trot (common)

Front
Hind

A   B

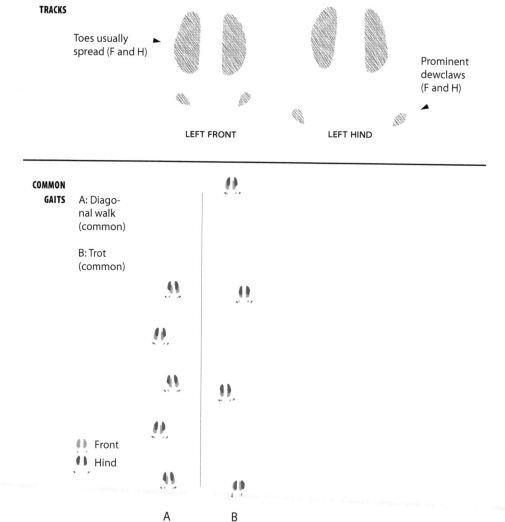

TRACK MEASUREMENTS

	Range, inches	Range, cm
Front width	2¼ to 3	5.7 to 7.6
Front length	2½ to 3	6.4 to 7.6
Hind width	2 to 3+	5.1 to 7.6+
Hind length	2 to 3+	5.1 to 7.6+
Trail width	5 to 7	12.7 to 17.8
Stride**	13 to 15	33.0 to 38.1

*Diagonal walk

UNGULATES

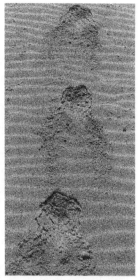

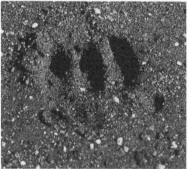

Feral pig tracks resemble deer tracks in shape and size, but several characteristics aid in track ID. Pig tracks are rounder and the toes more separated than deer tracks, and a pig's dewclaws are prominent in soft soil even in a walking gait (not just in fast gaits as usually is the case with deer). If substrate conditions make for confusion, remember that the walking stride of a feral pig is much shorter than a deer's because of the pig's short legs. In this case, use soil movement to confirm the pig's gait as a walk and not a trot.

FINE POINTS

A: Walking pig tracks

B: Trotting pattern

C: Hind track (right) superimposed over front in a walk

The feral pig or wild boar, *Sus scrofa,* was introduced from Europe, and its range is growing rapidly in the United States including areas of Arizona, Oregon, Vermont, Pennsylvania, and New Hampshire not shown on this range map. Regional populations are variable in size.

UNGULATES

TRACKS

Spread toes, F more than H ▶

LEFT FRONT

LEFT HIND

COMMON GAITS

A: Pace walk

Trots, lopes, and paces occur also.

 Front

Hind

A

TRACK MEASUREMENTS

	Average, inches	Average, cm
Front width	3¹¹⁄₁₆	9.4
Front length	4¹¹⁄₁₆	11.9
Hind width	3¼	8.3
Hind length	4½	11.4
Trail width	12	30.5
Stride*	23¼	59.1

*Pace walk

Llama tracks may be found especially in the western United States, where the South American natives are used as pack animals on hiking trails. The tracks are much larger than those of deer, antelope, or bighorn sheep and are roughly elk size. Because the toes, especially of the front tracks, are spread even when walking, llama tracks are usually easily identified. Like other members of the camel family, llamas are perfect pace walkers, the hind stepping beyond the front track on the same side with every step. Other gaits are seldom seen on hiking trails, but in captivity or in the wild, you may see trots, lopes, or gallops.

FINE POINTS

A

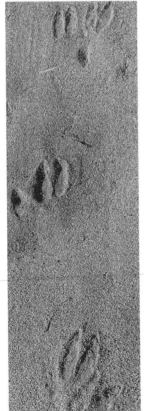

A: Hind (top) and front (bottom) tracks within a pace pattern

B: Llama front track next to black-tailed-deer tracks (above)

C: As is common with domesticated animals, individuals may show quirks in their track patterns.

D: The feet of Richter, a 159 kg (350 lb.) male

B

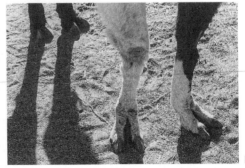

D

C

UNGULATES

TRACKS

Toes spread and dewclaws show when walking in soft substrate or when running (F and H). ▶

LEFT FRONT   LEFT HIND

COMMON GAITS

A: Diagonal walk (common)

B and C: Trots (common)

D: Gallop (occasional)

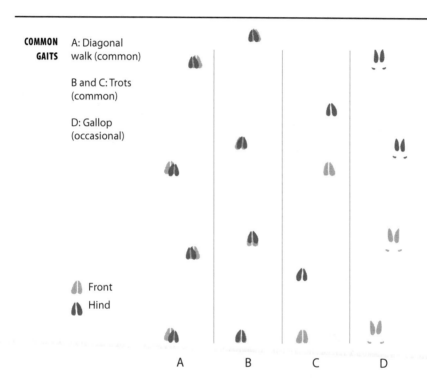

🐾 Front

🐾 Hind

A   B   C   D

TRACK MEASUREMENTS

	Range, inches	Range, cm
Front width	4¼ to 5	10.8 to 12.7
Front length	5⅞ to 6½	14.9 to 16.5
Hind width	3½ to 5	8.9 to 12.7
Hind length	4¼ to 6½	10.8 to 16.5
Trail width	9½ to 14⅛	24.1 to 35.9
Stride*	28 to 37	71.1 to 94.0

*Diagonal walk

UNGULATES

Moose tracks are the largest North American ungulate tracks, and those of an adult would usually withstand confusion with any other hoofed-animal tracks. However, a juvenile's tracks, especially in summer to fall of their first year, fall in the size range of adult elk tracks and might be confused where the two species share habitat, especially in the Rockies. While adult moose tracks are more pointed and deer-like than their rounder elk counterparts, moose-calf tracks tend to be round also. Note that elk tracks show a large, prominent pad area toward the back of each toe that is absent in moose tracks.

FINE POINTS

A

A: Diagonal walk pattern

B: Hind (left) and front tracks

C: Front track in a gallop, showing spread toes and dewclaws

B

C

UNGULATES

There is an irony in the moose's wonderful **adaptations to northern living**. Yes, a moose's very long legs allow it to travel easily in reasonably deep snow, and the metabolism of such a large body keeps the moose comfortable even in high winds at down to minus two degrees F. But when snow depth approaches a moose's chest height—about 71 cm (28 in.)—this animal's vulnerability emerges, causing behavioral changes interesting to us trackers. In the mountainous West as well as some lowland habitats of the North, moose may migrate miles every winter to an area with lesser snow depth, often timed with the year's first big storm. And even within its local winter habitat, moose respond to an unusually deep snowpack by retreating to sheltered areas with shallower snow, even choosing to browse on inferior food and risk malnutrition. A tracker on backcountry skis or snowshoes can find evidence of these adaptations. Look for migratory corridors used in the late fall; a large number of moose may be on the move. In a local wintering area, look for regular trails frequented by groups of moose walking single file to conserve energy—including trails of a female and her calf. Notice how browse choices have changed from earlier preferences.

Having evolved in the dense boreal forest, moose have developed some interesting **communication methods** to find one another during the fairly short mating season. In some areas cows coming into estrus scent-mark small trees in the forest to advertise their availability. Five-centimeter-diameter (2 in.) trees, generally with smooth bark, are scored with the cow's incisors and then marked with glands on the head; bulls score with their antlers and then scent-mark. Elsewhere, cows scrape and urinate on the ground to attract bulls. If you find such evidence, also look for wallows scraped out by a bull's front feet and then urinated upon. A cow will wallow in the depression. As early as August you might also find signs of the pre-rut, when bulls thrash trees with their antlers and chase and fight one another to establish dominance. Whenever you track moose, use utmost caution, because both sexes may have tempers and can be quite dangerous.

SPECIES AND WEIGHT	*Alces alces*
	4 subspecies in North America
	270 to 700 kg (600 to 1,540 lb.)
	Males larger than females

UNGULATES

Boreal forests, tundra, and river courses of the North; mixed conifer-deciduous forests of the Northeast; and mixed forest and riparian areas of the mountain West; requires relatively low summer temperatures and abundant forage. Nearby coniferous stands commonly used for resting and safety. Well adapted to cold winters, snow, bogs, lakes, and ponds.

HABITAT

Breeding usually late September to early October. In August and September bulls establish dominance through displays, fights, and tree thrashing. Cows scent-mark in scrapes or on small saplings to attract bulls; bulls create wallows and urinate in them. A pair may stay together for several days; largest bulls mate with numerous cows. Gestation 215 to 240 days, 1 to 2 calves born in late May to early June. Birthing in secluded area, often near water.

BREEDING

Female and calf travel close to each other throughout the summer. Mother fiercely protective. Weaning in mid-September, dispersal of calf usually at 1 year, in some populations to distant areas, in others close by.

DEVELOPMENT

Not territorial; home ranges may overlap and moose may forage and travel together in small groups during most of the year (though cow-calf pair remains by itself). Larger aggregations may form during winter. Seasonal home ranges usually 0.4 km² to 44 km², smallest in winter and in early stages of calf rearing.

SOCIAL HABITS

Browse, especially willow in North and West, and balsam fir and birch in Northeast, make up most of food for most of the year; dogwood, *Ribes, Prunus,* aspen, service-berry, and other shrubs also eaten. In summer forbs and in some areas aquatic plants including pondweed, horsetail, and bur reed consumed. Conditions such as deep snow or high winds may cause foraging of nonpreferred food where there is better cover. Moose alternate resting and feeding during both day and night.

FEEDING

High mortality (to 80%) of calves, especially from 5 days old to mid-July, from predation by black and brown bears and wolves. Older moose also vulnerable to wolf predation. Persistent snow deeper than 71 cm (28 in.) restricts movement and may cause starvation. Superbly adapted to cold, but threat of summer heat stress causes behavior changes.

SURVIVAL

Scats amorphous piles or dry pellets greater than 2.5 cm (1 in.) long. Wallows dug by bulls during rut, and scent-marking scrapes on small trees from cows' incisors or bulls' antlers.

SIGNS

UNGULATES

D

D: Scat

TRACKS

Ridge between toes clearly visible; entire track is "flat" (F and H) ►

◄ Heart-shaped track (F and H) with uniform convex curve on edges

LEFT FRONT   LEFT HIND

COMMON GAITS

A: Diagonal walk (common)

B: Trot (common)

C: Trot (occasional)

D: Lope (occasional)

E: Bound or stot (common)

(Illustrations C, D, and E are smaller scale.)

3.2 meters (10¹/₂+ feet) between groups

Front

Hind

A   B   C   D   E

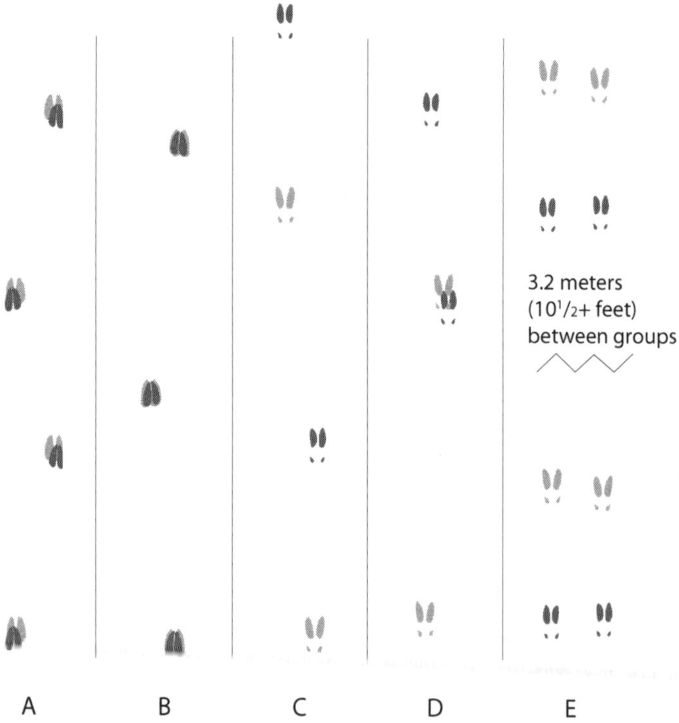

TRACK MEASUREMENTS

	Average, inches	Average, cm	Usual range, inches*
Front width	1⅝	4.1	1⁵⁄₁₆ to 2³⁄₁₆
Front length	2⁵⁄₁₆	5.9	1⅞ to 2⅞
Hind width	1⁷⁄₁₆	3.6	1⅛ to 1⅞
Hind length	2¹⁄₁₆	5.2	1½ to 2⅝
Trail width	4⅞	12.4	2⅝ to 7⅝
Stride**	20⁷⁄₁₆	51.9	15 to 29

*More than 95% of my measurements fall within this range.   **Diagonal walk

UNGULATES

356

A

B

C

D

E

First, know your habitat because it's unlikely that mule deer will share it with more than one or two other hoofed animals in a given area. Track size and stride will usually distinguish deer from the elk, which is larger, and the feral pig, which is smaller. The following are a little more difficult. **Vs. bighorn sheep:** Bighorn front tracks especially are blockier and more blunt-tipped than a deer's; the cup-shaped bighorn track also leaves a raised area in the forward two-thirds of the track while the deer track is "flatter." **Vs. pronghorn:** Pronghorn tracks also show a raised area due to the cup-shaped hoof, and a pronghorn track's widest part is farther back than the deer track's. Pronghorn do not have dewclaws and tracks sometimes show concave edges. **Vs. white-tailed deer:** In some areas where they share habitat, white-tails are smaller, but many trackers cannot tell their tracks apart consistently.

FINE POINTS

A and B: Typical hind-over-front tracks. Front toes may or may not splay.

C: Hind (left) and front tracks, showing variation in shape from photos A and B

D: Common diagonal walk pattern

E: Close-up of running track with toes spread and dewclaws show-ing. Dewclaws register in stots, gallops, lopes, and some trots, and also sometimes with steep terrain or an injury.

UNGULATES

357

Behind every deer trail is a story—well, at least a choice, and the tracker who studies these **travel preferences** will learn about nuances of the land, weather patterns, and other factors essential to a deer's survival. This deer walks along the side of a dirt road closest to cover; another takes a trail into the prevailing wind; three deer go into a trot as they cross an open area. These examples, and others you will discover, show that temperature, wind direction, time of day, humidity, phase of the moon, and cover density all influence where and when deer travel and what gait they use. (For example, in temperatures above sixty-five degrees, deer tend to seek out shade or breezy areas.) The key is not to overanalyze each deer trail you see but to look widely and store information in your mind. With each deer trail you pass, widen your awareness to see the trail's origin and destination; notice cover, bedding, and feeding areas. Notice the wind direction and temperature when the tracks were made. Now and then, walk some of these trails "becoming" the deer; notice where you feel safe, where you feel the need to hurry or be especially alert. Eventually these patterns you've noticed become part of your own consciousness, and you'll find yourself predicting deer trails even before you see them.

A fresh deer print in fine dust tempts the tracker like no other track, with unsurpassed **raw material for track reading**. The deer's large weight distributes itself in a tiny surface area, magnifying every motion. The slightest change of direction or head turn screams out with bold pressure releases. Start by paying attention to the ridge between the toes in a string of tracks; a consistently straight ridge, with each track uniformly deep, suggests a direct, purposeful walk with head level, perhaps to the deer's day bed. Fractured, tilted, or twisted ridges suggest sideward motion and should prompt you to read pressure releases to interpret the tracks. Move your thumb in the soil to re-create the motion in each track, and get down on all fours to imitate the deer's movement.

To a novice tracker, a browse is a browse is a browse, but to the deer it's survival. A mule deer uncannily selects the vegetation with most protein at every point in time, and indeed the choice will vary from week to week and even from day to day. These **forage choices** determine whether a doe will have two fawns or one, how successfully she can nurse her young, whether fawns will survive their first drought or heavy snow season, and how a buck's vitality, expressed by antler growth, will play out in the breeding season. Begin to follow the seasonal browse preferences—from spring grasses to forbs to new shrub growth to marginal older growth to highly nutritious acorns—and within these seasons, notice weekly preferences that will dictate travel routes and bedding areas. In your area notice "last-resort" browse during plants' dormant season; heavy browsing on these (juniper or sagebrush, for example) may presage heavy die-offs of the deer population from malnutrition.

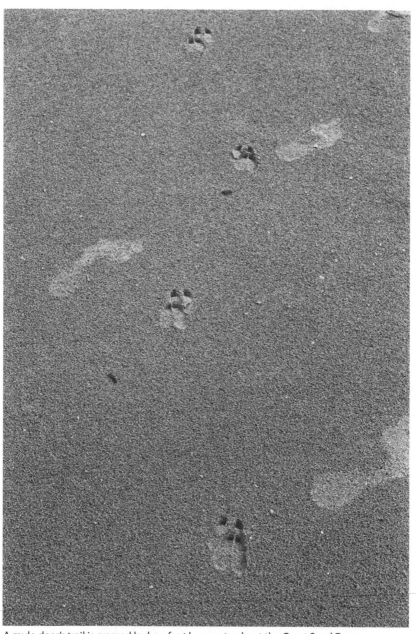

A mule deer's trail is crossed by barefoot human tracks at the Great Sand Dunes, Colorado.

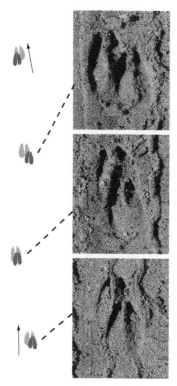

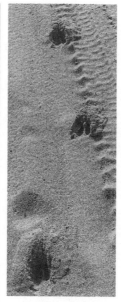

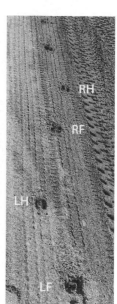

G: Understanding deer trots. Trot 1 at upper left (see B on page 356) can be distinguished from a diagonal walk by the severe forward-motion pressure releases caused by each hoof diving down and in. Trot 2 at upper right (C on page 356) is faster, causing both front and hind toes to spread and the dewclaws to show; the front toes spread more than the hind ones. Below, a LH track where a deer accelerated from trot 1 to trot 2; notice the plate-fissure (arrow) associated with the speed change.

F: From bottom to top, reading a slight direction change in a sequence of mule-deer tracks. In the bottom photo both the right front (RF) and right hind (RH) tracks point straight ahead, but the ridge between the hind toes is already sloping to the left in anticipation of a turn. In the middle photo the left front (LF) is pitched slightly to the left and the left hind (LH), which would ordinarily register outside the front track with this particular deer, swings to the inside as the deer's shoulders turn toward the left. A ridge to the left side of the hind track also points in that direction. In the top photo the RF foot has swung to the left, and the RH shows the toe ridge pushed toward the right as weight shifts. The actual change of direction doesn't take place until the next pair of tracks.

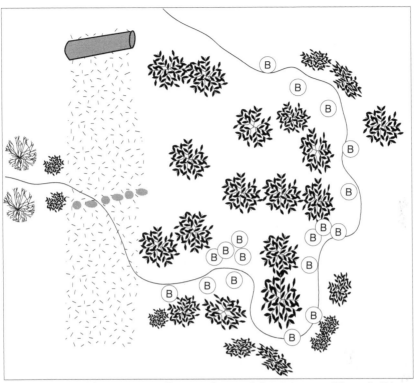

H

H: A deer emerged from an open Jeffrey-pine forest at left, using cover of firs and wild currant to cross an old road and enter a favorite browse area among snowberry and ceanothus shrubs. The letters show fresh browse evidence in this forest at about 2,500 meters (8,200 ft.).

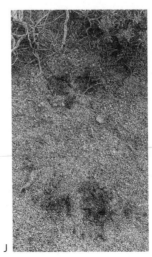

I: Scarcity of water can cause a local deer population to concentrate activity, as in the high desert of Joshua Tree National Park in California.

J: A stotting track pattern

I

J

SPECIES AND WEIGHT   *Odocoileus hemionus*

9 subspecies in North America

Usually 48 to 95 kg (105 to 210 lb.)

Male 25% larger than female

HABITAT   Open brushland, conifer, and hard-wood forests, chaparral, high desert, stream bottoms, and meadows where cover is nearby; sea level to 3,048+ meters (10,000+ ft.). Avoids dense, unbroken forest canopy, arid deserts with little cover, and grassland without trees and shrubs. Newly burned areas attract deer for its nutritious and abundant new growth.

BREEDING   Breeding season lasts 6 to 8 weeks in a local area, this period usually beginning from mid-September to mid-December depending upon latitude and elevation. Bucks and does normally first breed in their 2nd year. Sparring among bucks, especially younger ones, but few serious fights; thrashing of vegetation with antlers and pawing ground with hooves common. At estrus, does urinate often. Males do not "herd" females, a single buck generally follows a single doe until mating. Nevertheless, older, more dominant bucks breed most often. Gestation about 7 months, birthing usually April to June, 1 or 2 fawns per female; older females tend to have twins if diet is adequate.

DEVELOPMENT   Female usually rests away from fawn(s) while they are very young, and twin fawns often rest apart from each other. Fawns begin to browse vegetation at 1 month, weaned by 3 to 5 months. Much play among fawns during summer. Male fawns show visible bump, precursor to antler, at 5 months; antler growth to spikes or sometimes forks by first spring. Antler fork development depends upon diet as well as age. First-year young remain with female through fall breeding season to next spring, when she drives them away as she gives birth again. Second-year bucks may then disperse many miles, while 2nd-year does often rejoin their mothers until they themselves bear young the next spring.

SOCIAL HABITS   Most frequently seen social unit, except at breeding time, is doe with fawn(s) and yearling(s); 2+ such groups may travel together. Older, dominant female in a group often guides timing and location of feeding and travel. Bucks may be

UNGULATES

solitary or form small bachelor herds. In winter, especially after large snowstorms, large numbers of deer may congregate temporarily ("yarding"). Home ranges usually from about 35 hectares (86 acres) to 7 km²; in arid climates such as Arizona, to 120 km². Migratory herds have high-elevation summer ranges and low-elevation winter ones, separated by well-used, relatively narrow corridors in which there are temporary feeding areas during migration. Where mixed groups travel together, males are submissive to dominant females except during breeding season.

FEEDING

Deer alternate between browsing for up to 2 hours at a time and resting to chew their cud. Feeding times depend upon season and temperature; browsing at dusk and dawn is common and midday feeding occurs primarily in fall and winter. A local population may feed on 70+ species, but often only 5 or 6 plants are preferred at any moment as deer seek out plants with most protein: new grasses for several weeks in spring, then forbs, then new growth in shrubs and trees. Diet includes ceanothus, mountain mahogany, serviceberry, rose, snowberry, willow, oak, juniper, elderberry, chamise, sagebrush, dogwood, aspen, many other shrubs, and dozens of grasses, forbs, and sedges. Freshly dropped acorns are relished in fall, and fungi are dug up and eaten in summer and fall.

SURVIVAL

Fawn mortality, especially in 1st month, vulnerable to coyotes, bears, and other predators; adult deer always vulnerable to mountain lions. Malnutrition a major mortality factor for fawns and for whole populations in some years; drought causes poor forage during late summer and fall in low areas, while heavy winter snows may restrict access to good forage in mountains.

SIGNS

Scats in pellet form, about 0.5 cm (³⁄₁₆ in.) wide by 1 to 1.6 cm (⅜ to ⅝ in.) long with dimple on one end and nipple on other; scat from spring browse clumped together. Scats deposited especially in browse areas. Beds in grasses, under trees, or in brush, selected for wind, sun, and shade factors, often with commanding view of danger in 1 or 2 directions; summer beds sometimes scraped to bare soil. Browse pinched off, often with jagged end, contrasted to clean cut of rabbit or rodent browse. Bruised branches from rubbing antlers in late summer and fall.

K: Deer browse often shows jagged or scraped ends because deer lack upper incisors.

L: Scat pile

UNGULATES

PRONGHORN Track ID

TRACKS

Track edges are often concave (F and H).

Widest part of track is toward rear.

LEFT FRONT

Center of track is usually raised (F and H).

No dewclaws show when running (F and H).

LEFT HIND

COMMON GAITS

A and B: Trots (common)

C: Lope (common)

D: Gallop (common)

E: Pace walk (occasional)

Walks and slow walks are also common.

Front

Hind

A B C D E

TRACK MEASUREMENTS

	Average, inches	Average, cm	Usual range, inches
Front width	2	5.0	1⅛ to 2⁷⁄₁₆
Front length	2⁹⁄₁₆	6.5	2³⁄₁₆ to 3
Hind width	1¾	4.4	1⁷⁄₁₆ to 1¹⁵⁄₁₆
Hind length	2⅜	6.0	2⅛ to 2¹⁵⁄₁₆
Trail width	5⅜	13.7	
Stride**	19³⁄₁₆	48.7	

*Diagonal walk

UNGULATES

364

A

B

Tracks resemble those of **mule deer**, with which pronghorn sometimes share small portions of their habitat. Several characteristics help: Pronghorn tracks are often, but not always, concave on their outer edges, not convex as with deer. The widest part of a pronghorn's track is farther toward the rear of the track than the widest part of a deer track. Pronghorn tracks tend to show a raised portion in the center of the track, while deer tracks are flatter. Finally, pronghorn do not have dewclaws, so a running trail without dewclaws showing is almost certainly a pronghorn's.

FINE POINTS

A and B: Right front and right hind tracks, respectively

C: Tracks of a group of pronghorn traveling together at different speeds

D: Pronghorn tracks sometimes strongly resemble mule-deer tracks.

E: Detail of galloping track, which conspicuously doesn't show dewclaws.

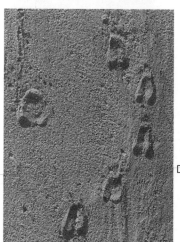

C

D

E

UNGULATES

If it's best to learn from the master, then there is no better teacher of **gaits and motion** than the pronghorn, whose athletic superiority stands above all other land mammals currently on earth. A combination of speed and endurance, made possible by a large heart, huge lung capacity, a high volume of blood with greatly elevated hemoglobin, and a windpipe the diameter of a vacuum-cleaner hose, allows the pronghorn to maintain high speeds for miles. Perhaps because there are no predators left who could challenge them (the North American cheetahs and hyenas having become extinct 10,000 years ago), pronghorns seem to flaunt their abilities. Groups, including fawns, have raced cars for miles at nearly 40 mph, periodically cutting in front of them. Two were observed running 1.2 km (¾ mile) up a ridge, with an elevation gain of 244 meters (800 ft.), in 90 seconds. The pronghorn's athleticism plays out in challenges of territoriality, in breeding-season chases, in fawns' developmental play, and in easy but rapid movements through their landscape. While it is entertaining and instructive just to watch a herd's movements, it is truly an honor to study their tracks.

Find a dirt road or wash with a few sets of pronghorn trails, and begin studying each animal's tracks. A pronghorn's fast-moving repertoire includes several speeds of trots, transverse and rotary lopes, and gallops of different speeds. Record not only the track patterns but notice also pressure releases and sequence changes. Some gallops are so smooth that the expected explode-off pressure releases are absent. Biologists studying film of running pronghorn have noticed frequent lead changes of front and hind legs in lopes and gallops. (This refers to the sequence of left or right feet landing first or second.) Front and hind leads may change in different strides, and track patterns would vary accordingly. Also, when a pronghorn changes gaits from a lope or gallop to a trot, one of the four feet may not land in the transitional stride. Add to all of these variables the factor of body language or posture (for example, an "elegant" vs. efficient trot), and the master has given us a lot to learn from. Don't forget to measure the awesome stride lengths!

A tracker can evaluate dynamics of pronghorn **social interaction** and how it's manifested in different habitats by reading tracks and signs. In classic pronghorn terrain a dominant male "protects" a group of females and fawns from March through early October and marks this territory with scrapes, scats, urination, and scent-marked vegetation. Look for concentrations of sign especially at boundaries between two territories. In September a buck will make many marking trips each day, especially to sides of the territory where encroachment by another male is most likely. Nonterritorial males will also mark in other places. In other habitats, though, sparse forage and a low-density pronghorn population may cause territoriality to erode. Here, a male and his harem of females and fawns still travel together, but there is more overlapping of boundaries between groups. Scent marking still peaks in spring and fall, though, and can be studied by the tracker.

F: Male pronghorn scent-mark in a habit called S.P.U.D. (sniff-paw-urinate-defecate).

Trails of two pronghorn loping together are depicted here. The spacing of tracks shows they were traveling at the same speed, and each prong- horn hits first with its left front. The left trail is a transverse lope, though, while the right one is a rotary lope, showing a turn of the shoulders to the left that caused debris to be thrown off. The right hind is severely pitched back toward the direction of travel.

G

H: At first glance this pronghorn trail appears to be separated in groups of four, as in a gallop. However, because the bottom two tracks are pitched identically to the left, and the next two tracks are pitched in the direction of travel, the gait must be a trot, in which alternative front/hind pairs act in unison. The pitch of the right-front/ left-hind pair at bottom, as well as the lean of each track to the left, shows that the pronghorn's head is turned to the left this whole time, in a wide-stanced, stable trot.

UNGULATES

367

SPECIES AND WEIGHT *Antilocapra americana*

4 subspecies in
North America

41 to 59 kg
(90 to 130 lb.)

Male slightly larger than
female

HABITAT Grassland and open shrubland
with high visibility and adequate
forage. Nearby rolling hills and water
sources add to ideal habitat; low broken
vegetation necessary for birthing. Fences without
enough bottom clearance and roads with substantial traffic inhibit movement.

BREEDING Breeding period usually mid-September to early October. Territorial males
attempt to maintain a harem by herding females, preventing individual females
from running away, and challenging would-be male intruders through displays
and chases. These males feed and rest little for the duration of the rut. Serious
fights between males occur only in presence of a female in estrus; injuries and
fatalities are common. Meanwhile, females "test" males by attempted escapes or
approaches to a male intruder, always selecting and mating with only successful defenders or fighters. Increased scent marking with urine, scat, and cheek
rubs during rut, by territorial males and 3-year-old+ challengers who may try to
establish their own temporary adjacent territories. Younger males also harass
and intrude upon harems. Gestation 250 days, birth of twins in late May to mid-
June. Females seek protected areas with high visibility to give birth.

DEVELOPMENT For first 10 days after birth, mother feeds apart from her hiding fawns. Brief
nursing reunions are each followed by relocation to new hiding places, usually
100 meters to 1 km (328 ft. to 0.6 mile) away. This occurs at least several times
per day, and fawn beds are not reused. From 11 to 20 days, mothers and fawns
begin to congregate, and by 30 days, maternal herds have formed. Fawns can
outrun a human when a week old and can run with the herd before 3 weeks.
Fawns are weaned by late August; males separate from mothers and usually join
bachelor herds at 12 weeks.

SOCIAL HABITS Winter aggregations of pronghorn, after the rut, may number to more than 100;
individuals space themselves, and overt competition is relatively mild. In March
individual territorial males each associate with and "protect" a herd of females

UNGULATES

with fawns and do so through summer to the fall breeding season. Within these herds, females reinforce dominance hierarchy through sparring, head butts, and displacement, while the male actively patrols and marks the edges of his territory with cheek rubs on vegetation and S.P.U.D.s (see "Signs" below). Meanwhile, subordinate males form bachelor herds apart from these and continually test and reinforce dominance hierarchy among themselves through direct stares, broadside displays, chases, sparring, and scent marking. Competitive behavior peaks in early spring and again during the fall rut. Solitary males may also be found—older males who have lost territorial defenses or dominant males in winter avoiding contact with other pronghorn. Where forage is poor and pronghorn density is low, territoriality is less pronounced and boundaries less defined.

FEEDING

Primarily forbs preferred, secondarily browse from woody plants; the latter more important in fall and winter. Hundreds of species eaten, including some grasses and sedges. Pronghorn do a slow feeding walk, nose along vegetation, or they become selective, walking purposefully from one preferred plant to the next. In winter pronghorn may paw the snow to reach forage underneath. Feeding and resting/ruminating alternate throughout day and night, generally with feeding peaks after sunrise and just before sunset.

SURVIVAL

Pronghorn easily outrun any predator, can cruise at 35 to 40 mph for more than 9.7 km (6 miles) without exhaustion, and can sprint at 55 to 60 mph. Causes of adult mortality are principally starvation in severe winters and fatalities from male combat during the rut. High fawn mortality from coyotes, golden eagles (who can carry off a fawn even 1 month old), and occasionally other predators. Females and other herd members may chase and attack a prowling coyote. Inadequate habitat restricts population in some areas.

SIGNS

Scats in pellets or clumps, resembling mountain sheep or deer scats. Beds in open, or in low shrubs, usually not prepared. During summer and especially during the rut, scent marking by adult males including cheek rubs of vegetation, thrashing of divots from ground, and S.P.U.D.s (sniff-paw-urinate-defecate). Scent marking most concentrated at boundaries between male territories.

I: Pronghorn scat on the Carrizo Plain in California

TRACKS

Outside toe often
protrudes farther
forward (esp. F). ►

◄ H track smaller

LEFT FRONT　　　　　LEFT HIND

COMMON GAITS

A: Diagonal walk (common)

B: Trot (common)

C: Lope group (common)

D: Gallop

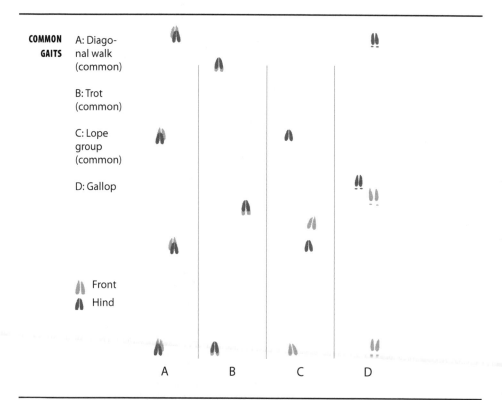

Front
Hind

A　　B　　C　　D

TRACK MEASUREMENTS

	Average, inches	Average, cm	Usual range, inches
Front width	2	5.1	1⅝ to 2⅛
Front length	2⁹⁄₁₆	6.5	2⅛ to 3
Hind width	1¹³⁄₁₆	4.6	1⅝ to 2⅛
Hind length	2½	6.3	1⅞ to 2¾
Trail width	5¹⁵⁄₁₆	15.0	3¼ to 9¼
Stride*	20⅝	52.4	15⅛ to 26

*Diagonal walk

UNGULATES

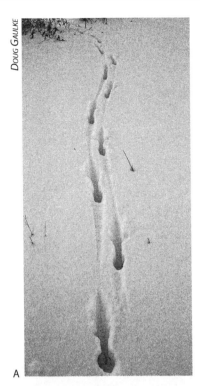

A

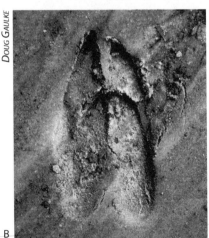

B

Other ungulates within white-tailed-deer geographical range include elk and moose, whose tracks are larger; and pronghorn, mule deer, and feral pig, whose tracks may overlap in size. **Vs. pronghorn:** Besides using a different habitat type, pronghorns have tracks that show a raised area in the center; antelope also lack dewclaws. **Vs. feral pig:** Pig tracks will show shorter strides, the toes are often spread more, and dewclaws are more prominent when walking. **Vs. mule deer:** Know the habitat, because the two species may be found together primarily in the Southwest and the Rockies; even here, elevation and habitat type often separate them. Where they are together, southwestern whitetails are smaller than mule deer, while in the Rockies they tend to be the same size. There, it may take close study to tell the tracks apart.

FINE POINTS

A: Common diagonal walk pattern

B: Left front/left hind pair from diagonal walk

C: Right front track in a run, showing dewclaws

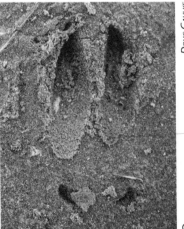

C

UNGULATES

The white-tailed deer's agenda for the fall breeding season is full: establish hierarchy and dominance, continually mark one's presence in the local habitat, find mates, and deter rivals. While physical sparring and body language accomplish some of this, much of the **communication among individual deer** occurs primarily at night through scent and visual marking, leaving some interesting study possibilities for us trackers. Our first task is to establish the phase our local rutting season is in by studying signs. Before the rut, bucks shed the velvet on their antlers, sometimes leaving velvet fragments on branches. Then, bucks begin to rub branches on trees and shrubs with their polished antlers and foreheads, leaving broken branches, lightly scored bark, and sometimes fragments of hair. These rubs retain scent and, when made in the presence of other bucks, communicate dominance. One or two weeks before the height of actual breeding, the signs become more dramatic. At conspicuous places, dominant bucks begin to make scrapes; a branch just above head level is mouthed and rubbed with the forehead to leave scent, and beneath it a scrape is made with the front hooves. The buck often urinates over glands on its rear legs to leave a strong scent, sometimes noticeable even to humans when fresh. If you find a fresh scrape, look for tracks there. By studying the front-hoof impressions and the height of the rubbed branch, you can sometimes determine the size of the buck who made the scrape. The buck may revisit a scrape, sometimes re-marking it, but a doe also frequently comes to investigate, leaving smaller tracks there. You may also be able to understand the size of a buck's range by looking for rubs and scrapes, which tend to be clustered in groups. One buck is known to have created 108 rubs and 27 scrapes over seven weeks in his territory, which extended about 6.4 km (4 miles).

The white-tail's **response to danger** is another good tracking subject. Depending upon scent and hearing more than vision, and backed up by an ability to outrun most predators, a white-tail exhibits some interesting behavior when encountering a threat. A deer may stomp one or both of its front feet, in part to elicit a response from an unknown threat. Or it may circle around the threat until it gets a scent reading. If you observe a white-tail making a foot stomp, study the front tracks so that you can later recognize this action in tracks. Unlike mule deer, who tend to cluster and even stand their ground when encountering predators such as coyotes, white-tailed deer tend to scatter, flagging their tails as an alarm signal and exhibiting an easy gallop with occasional "spy hops" of greater elevation. Follow galloping or bounding tracks to get an appreciation of the gracefulness of this deer. In contrast to the easy escape gallop, you may find tracks of a flat-out sprint, occurring when white-tails are startled at close range. One white-tail was observed to cover 8.8 meters (29 ft.) in one leap, clearing a brush fence 2.3 meters (7½ ft.) tall. Older bucks, rather than fleeing, may glide away in a head-down, quiet trot in which the hind feet land outside the front tracks.

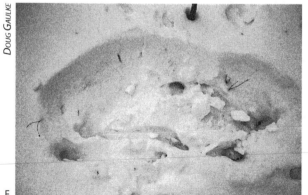

D: Buck antler rub

E: A deer startled from its day bed has created this track pattern (RF-LH-LF-RH). While the pattern is technically a lope, the proximity of the two hind tracks and the common pressure releases within them show that the deer is jumping for elevation as well as speed.

F: A day bed in snow

SPECIES AND WEIGHT

Odocoileus virginianus

17 subspecies in
North America

22 to 137 kg
(48 to 300 lb.)

Male about 20% larger
than female

HABITAT Wide range of habitats including
deciduous and coniferous forests,
riparian areas, swampland, high
desert grassland, desert oak woodland,
and prairies where woodland patches pro-
vide cover. Has thrived in some habitats that have changed from human activity,
including wooded corriders and patches near urban areas or adjacent to agricultural land.

BREEDING Breeding generally October to December in most northern locations; variations,
both earlier and later, occur in the southeastern states. During the "pre-rut," and
after velvet has been removed from antlers, bucks thrash antlers usually on trees
1.3 cm to 10 cm (½ to 4 in.) in diameter, rubbing off bark or breaking branches.
Sparring occurs among bucks at this time and throughout the rut. Bucks, especially older ones, begin to scent-mark at conspicuous areas, rubbing antlers on
tree branches, marking these with facial and oral scent, and pawing the ground
beneath, sometimes scent marking these scrapes with urine excreted over tarsal
glands. Scrapes may be visited by younger bucks and by does during the rut. A
breeding buck follows a single doe for up to several days and commonly beds and
waits nearby until she is ready to breed. After copulation the pair usually remains
together for a time; the buck may continue to repel other males in the vicinity.
Gestation about 200 days, 1 or 2 fawns born usually May to June.

DEVELOPMENT Does usually remain within 91 meters (300 ft.) of their fawn(s) shortly after
birth, and twins are kept separate from each other by their mother for the first
few weeks. Fawns begin eating plant food by about 3 to 4 weeks and thereafter
follow their mother at least until the following spring. Dispersal varies with
habitat and local density.

SOCIAL HABITS Most white-tailed deer associate in small maternal groups (a doe, fawn[s], and
yearling[s]), or in bachelor groups, but deer may also be found individually or in
small yearling groups. Open habitat and wintering areas with significant

UNGULATES

snow or a high-density deer population cause groups to be larger and often mixed with both males and females. A hierarchy, with the largest deer dominant, may play out in group feeding situations. Home ranges, usually 25 to 450 hectares (62 to 1,112 acres), depend upon density, season, and food supply. In some populations generally short migrations to wintering area providing lower snow depth and greater cover for thermoregulation. "Yarding" of larger groups common in these areas.

FEEDING

Wide variety of forage including browse, forbs, grasses, fruits, acorns, mushrooms, lichens, sedges, and ferns. In a given area, though, white-tailed deer are selective feeders, especially when there is adequate variety, preferring a relatively small number of foods at a given time. Agricultural fields and mast-producing areas such as oak woodlands strongly attract deer seasonally.

SURVIVAL

Fawn mortality commonly up to 70%, most within their first month. Fawn predation often by coyotes, occasionally bobcats and other predators. Adult whitetails vulnerable to some predation by coyotes and to starvation or accidents. Most adult mortality where populations are not stressed occurs from hunting. Alarm behavior includes snorting, foot stomping, and running at moderate speed with conspicuous tail wags; sudden startling by a threat close by causes flat-out galloping without tail wags. White-tails tend to separate, rather than group, when alarmed.

SIGNS

Scats are discrete pellets often with "dimple" and "nipple"; also may be clumped and more amorphous when diet contains much moisture. Beds usually on dry, smooth ground, in sunny spots when temperature is low and shady spots when temperature is high, sometimes with vantage points. "Loitering sites," open areas with scats and numerous tracks, where deer have lingered after feeding and before bedding. In breeding season, antler rubs on small trees, scent-marked branches, and scrapes beneath them. Odor of urine/tarsal gland secretions may be noticeable to humans. Well-used runs, especially in times and locations of heavier snowfall where large numbers of white-tails have congregated.

G

G: White-tailed-deer scat

UNGULATES

APPENDIX A: MAMMAL LIST

Following is a list of terrestrial mammals found in the United States and Canada. Entries in boldface type are included in this guide.

Cats

Bobcat	*Lynx rufus*
Domestic cat	*Felis catus*
Jaguarundi	*Puma yagouaroundi*
Lynx	*Lynx canadensis*
Mountain lion	*Puma concolor*
Ocelot	*Leopardus pardalis*

Dogs

Arctic fox	*Alopex lagopus*
Coyote	*Canis latrans*
Domestic dog	*Canis familiaris*
Gray fox	*Urocyon cinereoargenteus*
Gray wolf	*Canis lupus*
Island gray fox	*Urocyon littoralis*
Kit fox	*Vulpes macrotis*
Red fox	*Vulpes vulpes*
Swift fox	*Vulpes velox*

Rabbits and Hares

Alaskan hare	*Lepus othos*
Arctic hare	*Lepus arcticus*
Antelope jackrabbit	*Lepus alleni*
Black-tailed jackrabbit	*Lepus californicus*
Cottontail	*Sylvilagus* **spp. — 8 species**
Pika	*Ochotona princeps* and *Ochotona collaris*
Pygmy rabbit	*Brachylagus idahoensis*
Snowshoe hare	*Lepus americanus*
White-sided jackrabbit	*Lepus callotis*
White-tailed jackrabbit	*Lepus townsendii*

Rodents

Antelope squirrel	*Ammospermophilus* **spp. — *4 species***
Beaver	*Castor canadensis*
Chipmunk	*Tamias* **spp. — 29 species**
Cotton rat	*Sigmodon* spp. — 4 species
Flying squirrel	*Glaucomys* spp. — 2 species
Fox squirrel	*Sciurus niger*
Gray squirrel	*Sciurus* **spp. — 4 species**
Ground squirrel	*Spermophilus* **spp. — 21 species**
Kangaroo mouse	*Microdipodops* spp. — 2 species
Kangaroo rat	*Dipodomys* **spp. — 17 species**
Lemming	*Synaptomys* spp. — 2 species
	Lemmus trimucronatos
	Dicrostonys — 3 species
Marmot/Woodchuck	*Marmota* **spp. — 6 species**
Mice	Florida deer mouse, *Podomys floridanus*
	Grasshopper mice, *Onychomys* spp. — 3 species
	Golden mouse, *Ochrotomys nuttalli*
	Harvest mice, *Reithrodontomys* spp. — 5 species
	House mouse (introduced), *Mus musculus*
	Jumping mice, *Zapus* spp. — 3 species and *Napaeozapus* sp. — 1 species
	Northern pygmy mouse, *Baiomys taylori*
	***Peromyscus* mice, *Peromyscus* spp. — 15 species**
	Pocket mice, *Perognathus* spp. — 9 species, and *Chaetodipus* spp. — 11 species
Mountain beaver	*Aplodontia rufa*
Muskrat	***Ondatra zipethicus* and *Neofiber alleni***
Pocket gopher	***Thomomys* spp. — 10 species, and *Geomys* spp. — 8 species**
	Cratogeomys castanops
Porcupine	***Erethizon dorsatum***
Prairie dog	*Cynomys* spp. — 4 species
Rats (introduced)	*Rattus* spp. — 2 species
Red squirrel	***Tamiasciurus dougasii* and *T. hudsonicus***
Rice rat	*Oryzomys* spp. — 2 species
Vole	*Arborimus* **spp. — 3 species**
	Microtus **spp. — 20 species**

Synaptomys cooperi and *Synaptomys borealis*
Phenacomys intermedius
Lemmiscus curtatus

Woodrat   ***Neotoma* spp. — 10 species**

Armadillo

Armadillo   *Dasypus novemcinctus*

Weasels

Badger   ***Taxidea taxus***
Black-footed ferret   *Mustela nigripes*
Fisher   ***Pekania pennanti***
Hognosed skunk   *Conepatus leuconotus* and *C. mesoleucus*
Hooded skunk   *Mephitis macroura*
Least weasel   *Mustela nivalis*
Long-tailed weasel   ***Mustela frenata***
Marten   ***Martes americana***
Mink   ***Neovison vison***
River otter   ***Lontra canadensis***
Short-tailed weasel   ***Mustela erminea***
Spotted skunk   ***Spilogale gracilis* and S. *putorius***
Striped skunk   ***Mephitis mephitis***
Wolverine   *Gulo gulo*

Raccoons and Allies

Coati   *Nasua narica*
Raccoon   ***Procyon lotor***
Ringtail   ***Bassariscus astutus***

Opossum

Opossum   ***Didelphis virginiana***

Bears

Black bear	*Ursus americanus*
Grizzly bear	*Ursus arctos*
Polar bear	*Ursus maritimos*

Shrews

Shrew	*Sorex* **spp. — 22 species**
	Cryptotis parva
	Blarina spp. — 3 species
	Notiosorex crawfordi

Moles

Shrew mole	*Neurotrichus gibbsii*
Mole	*Scapanus* spp. — 3 species
	Parascalops breweri
	Condylura cristata

Ungulates

Bighorn sheep	*Ovis canadensis*
Bison	*Bison bison*
Burro	*Equus assinus*
Caribou	*Rangifer tarandus*
Dall's sheep	*Ovis dalli*
Domestic Cow	*Bos taurus*
Elk	*Cervus canadensis*
Feral pig (introduced)	*Sus scrofa*
Llama (domesticated)	*Lama glama*
Moose	*Alces alces*
Mountain goat	*Oreamnos americanus*
Mule deer	*Odocoileus hemionus*
Muskox	*Oribos moschatus*
Peccary	*Pecari tajacu*
Pronghorn	*Antilocapra americana*
White-tailed deer	*Odocoileus virginianus*

Source: Kays, Roland W., and Don E. Wilson, *Mammals of North America*. Princeton: Princeton University Press, 2002.

APPENDIX B: RECOMMENDED READING

For trackers who wish to delve more deeply into the behavior and biology of the mammals they track, I have compiled a reading list of journal articles and books most relevant to field research. These include studies from the 1930s through the present and range from old-fashioned snow tracking of mammals to the sophisticated radio telemetry research of today. Over the past eighty years, biologists have recorded a wealth of information about animals' foraging and hunting styles, social interaction, breeding behavior, diet, and movement patterns, and I think the following resources in particular will greatly enrich a tracker's perspective. There are some real gems here for the serious tracker! A full bibliography of the 900+ articles and books used for this guide is available by writing the author.

Tracking Technique, Gaits, and General Mammal References

American Society of Mammalogists. Accounts of individual species, summarizing biology and including bibliographies, can be accessed via mammalsociety.org/publications/mammalian-species.

Brown, Tom Jr. *Tom Brown's Field Guide to Nature Observation and Tracking.* New York: Berkley Books, 1983.

———. *The Science and Art of Tracking.* New York: Berkley Books, 1999.

Elbroch, Mark. *Mammal Tracks & Sign: A Guide to North American Species.* Lanham, MD: Stackpole Books, 2019.

Elbroch, Mark, and Kurt Reinhart. *Behavior of North American Mammals.* New York: Houghton Mifflin, 2011.

Evans, Jonah. iTrack Wildlife, smartphone application.

Feldhamer, George A., Bruce C. Thompson, and Joseph A. Chapman, eds. *Wild Mammals of North America: Biology, Management and Conservation.* Baltimore: Johns Hopkins University Press, 2003.

Harris, Susan E. *Horse Gaits, Balance and Movement.* New York: Maxwell Macmillan, 1993.

Hildebrand, Milton. "Symmetrical gaits of horses," *Science,* 150:701–708 (1965).

———. "Analysis of asymmetrical gaits," *Journal of Mammalogy,* 58:131–156 (1977).

Kays, Roland W., and Don E. Wilson. *Mammals of North America.* Princeton, NJ: Princeton University Press, 2002.

Moskowitz, David. *Wildlife of the Pacific Northwest.* Portland, OR: Timber Press, 2010.

Rezendes, Paul. *Tracking & the Art of Seeing.* New York: HarperPerennial, 1999.

Young, Jon, and Tiffany Morgan. *Animal Tracking Basics.* Mechanicsburg, PA: Stackpole Books, 2007.

Antelope Squirrel

Belk, Mark C., and H. Duane Smith. *"Ammospermophilus leucurus," Mammalian Species No. 368,* American Society of Mammalogists, 1991.

Bradley, W. Glen. "Food habits of the antelope ground squirrel in southern Nevada," *Journal of Mammalogy,* 49:14–21 (1968).

Jaeger, Edmund C. "The white-tailed ground squirrel," pp. 110–117 in *Desert Wildlife,* Stanford, CA: Stanford University Press, 1961.

Badger

Messick, John P., and Maurice G. Hornocker. "Ecology of the Badger in Southwestern Idaho," *Wildlife Monographs,* 76:1–53 (1981).

Minta, Steven C., Kathryn A. Minta, and Dale F. Lott. "Hunting associations between badgers (*Taxidea taxus*) and coyotes (*Canis latrans*)," *Journal of Mammalogy,* 73:814–820 (1992).

Sargeant, Alan B., and Dwain W. Warner. "Movements and Denning Habits of a Badger," *Journal of Mammalogy,* 53:207–210 (1972).

Beaver

Brady, Charles A., and G. E. Svendsen. "Social behaviour in a family of beaver," *Biology of Behaviour,* 6:99–114 (1981).

Rue, Leonard Lee, III. *The World of the Beaver.* Philadelphia and New York: J. B. Lippincott, 1964.

Svendsen, G. E. "Seasonal change in feeding patterns of beaver in southeastern Ohio," *Journal of Wildlife Management,* 44:285–290 (1980).

Tevis, L. Jr. "Summer behavior of a family of beavers in New York State," *Journal of Mammalogy,* 31:40–65 (1950).

Bighorn Sheep

Jones, Fred L. "Sign reading and identification," in Monson, Gale, and Lowell Sumner, eds., *The Desert Bighorn.* Tucson, AZ: University of Arizona Press, 1990.

Leslie, D. M. Jr., and C. L. Douglas. "Desert bighorn sheep of the River Mountains, Nevada," *Wildlife Monographs,* 66:1–56 (1979).

McCann, L. J. "Ecology of mountain sheep," *American Midland Naturalist*, 56:297–324 (1956).

Warrick, G. D., and Paul R. Krausman. "Barrel cactus consumption by desert bighorn sheep," *Southwestern Naturalist*, 34:483–486 (1989).

Black Bear

Brooks, Robert T., Ronald McRoberts, and Lynn L. Rogers. "Predictive relationships between age and size and front-foot pad width of northeastern Minnesota black bears, *The Canadian Field-Naturalist*, 112:82–85 (1998).

Jonkel, C. J., and I. M. Cowan. "The black bear in the spruce-fir forest," *Wildlife Monographs*, 27:1–57 (1971).

Piekielek, W., and T. S. Burton. "A black bear population study in northern California," *California Fish & Game*, 61:4–25 (1975).

Reynolds, D. G., and J. J. Beecham. "Home range activities and reproduction of black bears in west-central Idaho," in Martinka, Clifford J., and Katherine L. McArthur, *Bears—Their Biology and Management*, Bear Biology Conference Series, U.S. Government Printing Office, 1980.

Rogers, L. A. "Effects of food supply and kinship on social behavior, movements, and population growth of black bears in northeastern Minnesota," *Wildlife Monographs*, 97:1–72 (1987).

Black-Tailed Jackrabbit

Carnier, David R. "Ontogeny of jumping performance in the blacktailed jackrabbit," *Zoology*, 98:309–313 (1995).

Costa, W. R., R. A. Nagy, and V. H. Shoemaker. "Observations of the behavior of jackrabbits in the Mojave Desert," *Journal of Mammalogy*, 57:399–402 (1976).

Lechleitner, R. R. "Certain aspects of behavior of the black-tailed jack rabbit," *American Midland Naturalist*, 60:145–155 (1958).

Smith, Graham W., L. Charles Stoddart, and Frederick F. Knowlton. "Long-distance movements of black-tailed jackrabbits," *Journal of Wildlife Management*, 66:463–469 (2002).

Bobcat

Anderson, Eric M. "Bobcat diurnal loafing sites in southeastern Colorado," *Journal of Wildlife Management*, 54:600–602 (1990).

Koehler, G. M., and M. G. Hornocker. "Influences of seasons on bobcats in Idaho," *Journal of Wildlife Management*, 53:197–202, 1989.

McCord, Chet. "Courtship behavior in free-ranging bobcats," *The World's Cats*, 2:76–87, 1973.

Rollings, Clair T. "Habits, foods and parasites of the bobcat in Minnesota," *Journal of Wildlife Management*, 9:131–145, 1945.

Ryden, Hope. *Bobcat Year*. New York: Lyons & Burford, 1981.

Chipmunk

Best, Troy L., and Nancy J. Granai. "Tamias merriami," in *Mammalian Species, No. 476*, American Society of Mammalogists, 1994.

Broadbrooks, H. E. "Home ranges and territorial behavior of the yellow-pine chipmunk," *Journal of Mammalogy*, 51:310–326 (1970).

——. "Tree nests of the chipmunks with comments on associated behavior and ecology," *Journal of Mammalogy*, 55:630–639 (1974).

Martinsen, D. L. "Temporal patterns in the home ranges of chipmunks," *Journal of Mammalogy*, 49:83–91 (1968).

Vander Wall, Stephen B. "Mechanisms of cache recovery by yellow pine chipmunks," *Animal Behaviour*, 41:851–863 (1991).

Cottontail

Connell, J. H. "Home range and mobility of brush rabbits in California chaparral," *Journal of Mammalogy*, 35:392–405 (1954).

Fitch, H. S. "Ecology of a cottontail rabbit population in central California," *California Fish & Game*, 33:159–184 (1947).

Ingles, L. G. "Natural history observations on the Audubon cottontail," *Journal of Mammalogy*, 22:227–250 (1941).

Verts, B. J., and Steven D. Gehman. "Activity and behavior of free-living *Sylvilagus nuttallii*," *Northwest Science*, 65:231–237 (1991).

Coyote

Camenzind, F. J. "Behavioral ecology of coyotes on the National Elk Refuge, Jackson, Wyoming," in Beckhoff, M., ed., *Coyotes: Biology, Behavior and Management*. New York: Academic Press, 1978.

Gese, Eric M. "Scent-marking by coyotes: the influence of social and ecological factors," *Animal Behaviour*, 54:1155–1166 (1997).

Gese, Eric M., and Scott Grothe. "Analysis of coyote predation on deer and elk during winter in Yellowstone National Park, Wyoming," *American Midland Naturalist*, 133:36–43 (1955).

Lehner, Philip N. "Coyote communication," in Bekoff, M., ed., *Coyotes: Biology, Behavior and Management*. New York: Academic Press, 1978.

Messier, F., and C. Barrette. "The social system of the coyote in a forested habitat," *Canadian Journal of Zoology*, 60:1743–1752 (1982).

Ozoga, John J., and Elsworth M. Harger. "Winter activities and feeding habits of northern Michigan coyotes," *Journal of Wildlife Management*, 30:809–818 (1966).

Domestic Cat

Horn, Jeff A. et al. "Home range, habitat use, and activity patterns of free-roaming domestic cats," *Journal of Wildlife Management*, 75:1177–1185 (2011).

Leyhausen, Paul. *Cat Behavior: The Predatory and Social Behavior of Domestic and Wild Cats*. New York and London: Garland STPM Press, 1979.

Turner, Dennis C., and Patrick Bateson. *The Domestic Cat: The Biology of Its Behaviour*. Cambridge, England: Cambridge University Press, 2000.

Domestic Dog

American Kennel Club. *Dog Steps*. Raleigh, NC: AKC Video Series.

Hildebrand, Milton. "Symmetrical gaits of dogs in relation to body build," *Journal of Morphology*, 124:353–359 (1968).

Elk

Altman, Margaret. "Social behavior of elk in the Jackson Hole area of Wyoming," *Behaviour*, 4:116–143 (1952).

Harper, James A., Joseph H. Harn, Wallace W. Bentley, and Charles F. Yocum. "The status and ecology of the Roosevelt elk in California," *Wildlife Monographs*, 16:1–143 (1967).

McCullough, Dale R. *The Tule Elk: Its History, Behavior, and Ecology*. Berkeley: University of California Press, 1971.

Fisher

Kilpatrick, Howard J., and Paul W. Rego. "Influence of season, sex, and site availability on fisher rest-site selection in the central hardwood forest," *Canadian Journal of Zoology*, 72:1416–1419 (1994).

Powell, Roger A. *The Fisher: Life History, Ecology and Behavior*. Minneapolis, MN: University of Minnesota Press, 1993 (2nd ed.).

Raine, R. Michael. "Winter habitat use and responses to snow cover of fisher and marten in southeastern Manitoba," *Canadian Journal of Zoology*, 61:25–34 (1983).

Zielinski, William J., and Richard L. Truex. "Distinguishing tracks of marten and fisher at track plate stations," *Journal of Wildlife Management*, 59:571–579 (1995).

Fox Squirrel

Allen, D. L. "Populations and habits of the fox squirrel in Allegan County, Michigan," *American Midland Naturalist*, 27:338–379 (1942).

Baumgartner, L. L. "Fox squirrel dens," *Journal of Mammalogy*, 20:456–465 (1939).

Cahalane, V. H. "Caching and recovery of food by the western fox squirrel," *Journal of Wildlife Management*, 6:338–352 (1942).

Koprowski, John L. "Natal philopatry, communal nesting, and kinship in fox squirrels and gray squirrels," *Journal of Mammalogy*, 77:1006–1016 (1996).

———. "Sex and species biases in scent marking by fox squirrels and eastern gray squirrels," *Journal of Zoology*, 230:319–323 (1993).

Gray Fox

Grinnell, Joseph. "Gray fox," in *Fur-Bearing Mammals of California: Their Natural History, Systematic Status, and Relations to Man*. Berkeley, CA: University of California Press, 1937.

Hallberg, Donald L., and Gene R. Trapp. "Gray fox temporal and spatial activity in a riparian/agricultural zone in California's Central Valley," in Warner, Richard E., ed., *California Riparian Systems: Ecology, Conservation, and Productive Management*. Berkeley, CA: University of California Press, 1984.

Trapp, G. R. "Comparative behavioral ecology of the ringtail and gray fox in southwestern Utah," *Carnivore*, 1:3–32 (1978).

Trapp, G. R., and D. L. Hallberg. "Ecology of the gray fox: a review," in Fox, M. S., ed., *The Wild Canids: Their Systematics, Behavioral Ecology, and Evolution*. New York: Van Nostrand-Reinhold, 1975.

Gray Squirrel

Farentinos, R. C. "Nests of the tassel-eared squirrel," *Journal of Mammalogy*, 53:900–903 (1972).

Hall, J. G. "A field study of the Kaibab squirrel in Grand Canyon National Park," *Wildlife Monographs*, 75:1–54 (1981).

Ingles, L. G. "Ecology and life history of the California gray squirrel," *California Fish & Game*, 33:139–158 (1947).

Steele, Michael A., and John L. Koprowski. *North American Tree Squirrels*. Washington, DC: Smithsonian Institution Press, 2001.

Taylor, G. J. "The use of marking points of grey squirrels," *Journal of Zoology*, 155:246–247 (1968).

Gray Wolf

Ballard, Warren B., and James R. Dau. "Characteristics of gray wolf den and rendezvous sites in southcentral Alaska," *Canadian Field-Naturalist*, 97:299–302 (1983).

Burkholder, B. L. "Movements and behavior of a wolf pack in Alaska," *Journal of Wildlife Management*, 23:1–11 (1959).

Peters, Roger P., and L. David Mech. "Scent-marking in wolves," *American Scientist*, 63:628–637 (1975).

Peterson, Rolf Olin. "Wolf ecology and prey relationships on Isle Royale," Fauna Series 11, National Park Service, Washington, D.C. (1977).

Grizzly Bear

Craighead, Frank, Jr., and John J. Craighead. "Grizzly bear prehibernation and denning activities as determined by radiotracking," *Wildlife Monographs*, 32:1–35 (1972).

Green, Gerald I., David J. Mattson, and James M. Peek. "Spring feeding on ungulate carcasses by grizzly bears in Yellowstone National Park," *Journal of Wildlife Management*, 61:1040–1055 (1997).

Klein, David R. "Track differentiation for censusing bear populations," *Journal of Wildlife Management*, 23:361–363 (1959).

Mattson, David J. "Foot loadings and pad and track widths of Yellowstone grizzly bears," *Western North American Naturalist*, 63:72–79 (2003).

Ground Squirrel

Coss, Richard G., and Donald H. Owings. "Rattler battlers," *Natural History*, May 1989, 30–35.

Dobson, F. Stephen. "Agonism and territoriality in the California ground squirrel," *Journal of Mammalogy*, 64:218–225 (1983).

Evans, F. C., and R. Holdenried. "A population study of the Beechey ground squirrel in central California," *Journal of Mammalogy*, 24:231–260 (1943).

Linsdale, J. M. *The California Ground Squirrel*. Berkeley: University of California Press, 1946.

Loehr, K. A., and A. C. Risser Jr. "Daily and seasonal activity patterns of the Belding ground squirrel in the Sierra Nevada," *Journal of Mammalogy,* 58:445–448 (1977).

Kangaroo Rat

Bartholomew, G. A. Jr., and H. H. Caswell Jr. "Locomotion in kangaroo rats and its adaptive significance," *Journal of Mammalogy,* 32:155–169 (1951).

Behrends, Philip, Martin Daly, and Margo I. Wilson. "Range use patterns and spatial relationships of Merriam's kangaroo rats," *Behaviour,* 96:187–209 (1986).

Jones, W. T. "Dispersal distance and the range of nightly movements in Merriam's kangaroo rats," *Journal of Mammalogy,* 70:27–34 (1989).

Tappe, Donald T. "Natural history of the Tulare kangaroo rat," *Journal of Mammalogy,* 22:117–148 (1941).

Thompson, S. D. "Microhabitat utilization and foraging behavior of bipedal and quadrupedal heteromyid rodents," *Ecology,* 66:220–229 (1985).

Kit Fox

Egoscue, H. J. "Ecology and life history of the kit fox in Tooele County, Utah," *Ecology,* 43:481–497 (1962).

Rodrick, Penny J., and Nancy E. Mathews. "Characteristics of natal and non-natal kit fox dens in the Northern Chihuahuan desert," *Great Basin Naturalist,* 59:253–258 (1999).

Rodrick, Penny J., Katherine Ralls, and Robert A. Garrott. "Coyote-kit fox interactions as revealed by telemetry," *Canadian Journal of Zoology,* 72:1831–1836 (1994).

Marmot/Woodchuck

Armitage, K. B. "Social behavior of a colony of the yellow-bellied marmot," *Animal Behaviour,* 10:319–331 (1962).

——. Male behavior and territoriality in the yellow-bellied marmot," *Journal of Zoology,* 172:233–265 (1974).

Merriam, H. G. "Woodchuck burrow distribution and related movement patterns," *Journal of Mammalogy,* 52:732–746 (1971).

Van Vuren, Dirk H. "Predation on yellow-bellied marmots," *American Midland Naturalist,* 145:94–100 (2001).

Marten

Hargis, C. D., and D. R. McCullough. "Winter diet and habitat selection of marten in Yosemite National Park," *Journal of Wildlife Management,* 48:140–146 (1984).

Raine, R. M. "Winter habitat use and responses to snow cover of fisher and marten," *Canadian Journal of Zoology,* 61:25–34 (1983).

Spencer, W. D. "Seasonal nest-site preferences of pine martens in the northern Sierra Nevada," *Journal of Wildlife Management,* 51:616–621 (1987).

Spencer, W. D., and W. J. Zielinski. "Predatory behavior of pine martens," *Journal of Mammalogy,* 64:715–717 (1983).

Zielinski, W. J., and Richard L. Truex. "Distinguishing tracks of marten and fisher at track-plate stations," *Journal of Wildlife Management,* 59:571–579 (1995).

Mice

Bartholomew, George A. Jr., and Grant Reynolds Cary. "Locomotion in pocket mice," *Journal of Mammalogy,* 35:386–392 (1954).

Ecoscue, Harold J. "Laboratory and field studies of the northern grasshopper mouse," *Journal of Mammalogy,* 42:99–110 (1960).

Eisenberg, J. F. "A comparative study of sandbathing behavior in heteromyid rodents," *Behaviour,* 22:16–23 (1964).

Meserve, Peter L. "Three-dimensional home ranges of Cricetid rodents," *Journal of Mammalogy,* 58:549–558 (1977).

Randall, J. A. "Behavioural adaptations of desert rodents," *Animal Behaviour,* 45:263–287 (1993).

Mink

Ben-David, Metav R., Terry Bowyer, and James B. Faro. "Niche separation by mink and river otters: Coexistence in a marine environment," *Oikos,* 75:41–48 (1996).

Marshall, William H. "A study of the winter activities of the mink," *Journal of Mammalogy,* 17:382–392 (1936).

Williams, T. M. "Locomotion in the North American mink, a semi-aquatic mammal: The effect of an elongate body on running energetics and gait patterns," *Journal of Experimental Biology,* 105:283–296 (1983).

Moose

Bowyer, R. Terry, Victor Van Ballenberghe, and Karen R. Rock. "Scent marking by Alaskan moose: Characteristics and spatial distribution of rubbed trees," *Canadian Journal of Zoology,* 72:2,186–2,192 (1994).

Bubenik, Anthony B. "Behavior," in Franzmann, Albert W., and Charles C. Schwartz, eds. *Ecology and Management of the North American Moose.* Washington, DC: Smithsonian Institution Press, 1977.

Coady, J. W. "Influence of snow on behavior of moose," *Le Naturaliste Canadien,* 101:417–436 (1974).

Phillips, R. L., W. E. Berg, and D. B. Siniff. "Moose movement patterns and range use in northwestern Minnesota," *Journal of Wildlife Management,* 37:266–278 (1973).

Reeves, Henry M., and Richard E. McCabe. "Of moose and man," in Franzmann, Albert W., and Charles C. Schwartz, eds., *Ecology and Management of the North American Moose.* Washington, DC: Smithsonian Institution Press, 1977.

Scherrer, B., and R. Joyal. "Summer movements and feeding by moose in western Quebec," *Canadian Field-Naturalist,* 92:252–258 (1978).

Mountain Lion

Beier, Paul. "Cougar attacks on humans in the United States and Canada," *Wildlife Society Bulletin,* 19:403–412 (1991).

Beier, Paul, David Choate, and Reginald H. Barrett. "Movement patterns of mountain lions during different behaviors," *Journal of Mammalogy,* 76:1056–1070 (1995).

Cunningham, E. B. "A cougar kills an elk," *Canadian Field Naturalist,* 85:253–254 (1971).

Hansen, Kevin. *Cougar: The American Lion.* Flagstaff, AZ: Northland Publishing, 1992.

Logan, Kenneth A., and Linda L. Sweanor. "Interaction between pumas," in *Desert Puma: Evolutionary Ecology and Conservation of an Enduring Carnivore.* Washington, DC: Island Press, 2001.

Stoner, David C., et al. "Long-distance dispersal of a female cougar in a basin and range landscape," *Journal of Wildlife Management,* 72:933–939 (2008).

Mule Deer/Black-Tailed Deer

Bertram, R. C., and R. D. Rempel. "Migration of the North Kings deer herd," *California Fish & Game,* 63:157–179 (1977).

Leach, Howard R. "Food habits of the Great Basin deer herds of California," *California Fish & Game,* 42:243–308 (1956).

Linsdale, J. M., and P. Q. Tomich. *A Herd of Mule Deer—A Record of Observations Made on the Hastings Natural History Reservation.* Berkeley, CA: University of California Press, 1953.

Livezey, Kent B. "Home range, habitat use, disturbance, and mortality of Columbian black-tailed deer in Mendocino National Forest," *California Fish & Game,* 77:201–209 (1991).

McCullough, Dale R. "Sex characteristics of black-tailed deer hooves," *Journal of Wildlife Management,* 29:210–212 (1965).

Smith, H. Duane, M. C. Oveson, and C. L. Pritchett. "Characteristics of mule deer beds," *Great Basin Naturalist,* 46:542–546 (1986).

Stankowich, Theodore, and Richard G. Coss. "Alarm walking in Columbian black-tailed deer: Its characterization and possible antipredatory signaling functions," *Journal of Mammalogy,* 89:636–645 (2008).

Taber, R. D., and R. F. Dasmann. "The black-tailed deer of the chaparral: Its life history and management in the North Coast Range of California," *California Fish & Game Bulletin,* 8:1–163 (1958).

Taylor, W. P., ed. *The Deer of North America.* Harrisburg, PA: Stackpole Books, 1956.

Wachtel, W. A., M. Bekoff, and C. E. Fuenzalida. "Sparring by mule deer during rutting: Class participation, seasonal changes, and the nature of asymmetric contests," *Biology of Behavior,* 3:319–330 (1978).

Muskrat

Earhart, C. M. "The influence of soil texture on the structure, durability, and occupancy of muskrat burrows in farm ponds," *California Fish & Game,* 55:179–196 (1969).

Errington, P. L. *Muskrat Populations.* Ames: Iowa State University Press, 1963.

Sather, J. H. "Biology of the Great Plains muskrat in Nebraska," *Wildlife Monographs,* 2:1–35 (1958).

Steininger, Von Birte. "Beiträge zum Verhalten und zur Soziologie des Bisams," *Zeitschrift für Tierpsychologie,* 41:55–79 (1976).

Opossum

Fitch, H. S., and H. W. Shirer. "A radiotelemetric study of spatial relationships in the opossum," *American Midland Naturalist,* 84:170–186 (1970).

Gillette, L. N. "Movement patterns of radio tagged opossums in Wisconsin, USA," *American Midland Naturalist,* 104:1–12 (1980).

Ladine, Troy A., and Robert E. Kissell Jr. "Escape behavior of Virginia opossums," *American Midland Naturalist,* 132:234–238 (1994).

Petrides, G. A. "Sex and age determination in the opossum," *Journal of Mammalogy,* 30:364–378 (1949).

Ryser, Jan. "The mating system and male mating success of the Virginia opossum," *Journal of Zoology,* 228:127–139 (1992).

Pocket Gopher

Howard, Walter E., and Henry E. Childs, Jr. "Ecology of pocket gophers with emphasis on Thomomys bottae mewa," *Hilgardia,* 29:277–356 (1959).

Marshall, William H. "Thomomys as burrowers in the snow," *Journal of Mammalogy,* 22:196–197 (1941).

Reichman, O. J., Thomas G. Whitham, and George A. Ruffner. "Adaptive geometry of burrow spacing in two pocket gopher populations," *Ecology,* 63:687–695 (1982).

Reid, V. H., R. M. Hansen, and A. L. Ward. "Counting mounds and earth plugs to census mountain pocket gophers," *Journal of Wildlife Management,* 30:327–334 (1966).

Porcupine

Curtis, James D., and Edward L. Kozicky. "Observations on the eastern porcupine," *Journal of Mammalogy,* 25: 137–146 (1944).

Johnson, M. K., and A. B. Carey. "Porcupine pellet pH color and composition," *Southwestern Naturalist,* 24:544–545 (1979).

Marshall, W. H., G. W. Gullion, and R. G. Schwab. "Early summer activities of porcupines as determined by radio-positioning techniques," *Journal of Wildlife Management,* 26:75–79 (1962).

Roze, Uldis. *The North American Porcupine.* Washington, D.C.: Smithsonian Institution Press, 1989.

Pronghorn

Bullock, Robert E. "Functional analysis of locomotion in pronghorn antelope," in Geist, V., and F. Walther, eds., *The Behavior of Ungulates and its Relation to Management.* Morges, Switzerland: International Union of Conservation of Nature and Natural Resources, Pub. # 24, 1974.

Byers, John A. *American Pronghorn: Social Adaptation & the Ghosts of Predators Past.* Chicago: University of Chicago Press, 1997.

——. *Built for Speed: A Year in the Life of Pronghorn.* Cambridge, MA: Harvard University Press, 2003.

Kitchen, D. W. "Social behavior and ecology of the pronghorn," *Wildlife Monographs,* 38:1–96 (1974).

Raccoon

Gehrt, S. D., and E. K. Fritzell. "Resource distribution, female home range dispersion and male spatial interactions: group structure in a solitary carnivore," *Animal Behaviour,* 55:1211–1227 (1998).

Giles, L. W. "Utilization of rock exposures for dens and escape cover by raccoons," *American Midland Naturalist,* 27:171–176 (1942).

Schneider, D. G., L. D. Mech, and R. Tester. "Movements of female raccoons and their young as determined by radiotracking," *Animal Behavior Monographs*, 4:1–43 (1971).

Steuwer, F. W. "Raccoons: Their habits and management in Michigan," *Ecological Monographs*, 13:203–257 (1943).

Tevis, L., Jr. "Summer activities of California raccoons," *Journal of Mammalogy*, 28:323–332 (1947).

Zeveloff, Samuel I. *Raccoons: A Natural History.* Washington, DC: Smithsonian Institution Press, 2002.

Red Fox

Ables, E. D. "Ecology of the red fox in America," in Fox, M. W., ed., *The Wild Canids: Their Systematics, Behavioral Ecology and Evolution.* New York: Van Nostrand Reinhold Co., 1975.

Henry, D. J. *Red Fox, the Catlike Canid.* Washington, DC: Smithsonian Institution Press, 1986.

Macdonald, David. *Running with the Fox.* New York and Oxford: Facts on File Publications, 1987.

Scott, T. G. "Some food coactions of the northern plains red fox," *Ecological Monographs*, 13:427–473 (1943).

Seton, Ernest Thompson. "A chapter of fox life," in *Animal Tracks and Hunter Signs.* Garden City, NY: Doubleday & Co., 1958.

Storm, G. L. "Movements and activities of foxes as determined by radio-tracking," *Journal of Wildlife Management*, 29:1–13 (1965).

Red Squirrel

Hatt, R. T. "The pine squirrel in Colorado," *Journal of Mammalogy*, 24:311–345 (1943).

Koford, R. R. "Mating system of a territorial tree squirrel in California," *Journal of Mammalogy*, 63:274–283 (1982).

Shaw, W. T. "Moisture and its relation to the cone-storing habit of the western pine squirrel," *Journal of Mammalogy*, 17:337–349 (1936).

Smith, C. C. "The adaptive nature of social organization in the genus of tree squirrels Tamiasciurus," *Ecological Monographs*, 38:31–63 (1968).

——. "Structure and function of the vocalizations of tree squirrels (Tamiasciurus)," *Journal of Mammalogy*, 59:793–808 (1978).

Ringtail

"*Bassariscus astutus*. Ringtail," in Verts, B. J., and Leslie N. Carraway. *Land Mammals of Oregon*. Berkeley, CA: University of California Press, 1998.

Trapp, G. R. "Some anatomical and behavioral adaptations of ringtails," *Journal of Mammalogy*, 53:549–557 (1972).

———. "Comparative behavioral ecology of the ringtail and gray fox in southwestern Utah," *Carnivore*, 1:3–32 (1978).

River Otter

Liers, E. E. "Notes on the river otter," *Journal of Mammalogy*, 32:1–9 (1951).

Melquist, W. E., and M. G. Hornocker. "Ecology of river otters in west central Idaho," *Wildlife Monographs*, 83:1–60 (1983).

Reid, D. G., T. E. Code, C. H. Reid, and S. M. Herrero. "Spacing, movements, and habitat selection of the river otter in boreal Alberta," *Canadian Journal of Zoology*, 72:1314–1324 (1994).

Tarasoff, F. J., A. Basaillon, J. Pierard, and A. P. Whitt. "Locomotory patterns and external morphology of the river otter, sea otter, and harp seal," *Canadian Journal of Zoology*, 50:915–929 (1972).

Snowshoe Hare

Dolbeer, R. A., and W. R. Clark. "Population ecology of snowshoe hares in the central Rocky Mountains," *Journal of Wildlife Management*, 39:535–549 (1975).

Gilbert, B. S. Use of winter feeding craters by snowshoe hares," *Canadian Journal of Zoology*, 68:1600–1602 (1990).

Grange, Wallace B. "Observations on the snowshoe hare," *Journal of Mammalogy*, 13:1–19 (1932).

Krebs, Charles J., Rudy Boonstra, Stan Boutin, and A. R. E. Sinclair. "What drives the 10-year cycles of snowshoe hares?" *Bioscience*, 51:25–35 (2001).

Rongstad, Orrin J., and John R. Tester. "Behavior and maternal relations of young snowshoe hares," *Journal of Wildlife Management*, 35:338–346 (1971).

Spotted Skunk

Crabb, W. D. "Food habits of the prairie spotted skunk in southeastern Iowa," *Journal of Mammalogy*, 22:349–364 (1941).

———."The ecology and management of the prairie spotted skunk in Iowa," *Ecological Monographs*, 18:201–232 (1948).

Doty, Jeffrey B., and Robert C. Dowler. "Denning ecology in sympatric populations of skunks in west-central Texas," *Journal of Mammalogy,* 87:131–138 (2006).

Striped Skunk

Greenwood, Raymond J., A. B. Sargeant, J. L. Piehl, D. A. Buhl, and B. A. Hanson. "Foods and foraging of prairie striped skunks during the avian nesting season," *Wildlife Society Bulletin,* 27:823–832 (1999).

Nams, Vilas O. "Olfactory search images in striped skunks," *Behaviour,* 119:267–284 (1991).

Storm, G. L. "Daytime retreats and movements of skunks on farmlands in Illinois," *Journal of Wildlife Management,* 36:31–45 (1972).

Verts, B. J. *The Biology of the Striped Skunk.* Urbana, IL: University of Illinois Press, 1967.

——. "Mephitis mephitis," in Verts, B. J., and Leslie N. Carraway. *Land Mammals of Oregon.* Berkeley, CA: University of California Press, 1998.

Weasel

Fitzgerald, B. M. "Weasel predation on a cyclic population of the montane vole in California," *Journal of Animal Ecology,* 46:367–397 (1977).

King, Carolyn. *The Natural History of Weasels and Stoats.* Ithaca, NY: Cornell University Press, 1989.

Quick, Horace F. "Notes on the ecology of weasels in Gunnison County, Colorado," *Journal of Mammalogy,* 32:281–290 (1951).

Simms, D. A. "North American weasels: resource utilization and distribution," *Canadian Journal of Zoology,* 57:504–520 (1979).

White-Tailed Deer

Alexy, Karen J., Jonathan W. Gassett, David A. Osborn, and Karl V. Miller. "Remote monitoring of scraping behaviors of a wild population of white-tailed deer," *Wildlife Society Bulletin,* 29:873–878 (2001).

Anthony, R. G., and N. S. Smith. "Ecological relationships between mule deer and white-tailed deer in southeastern Arizona," *Ecological Monographs,* 47:255–277 (1977).

Hirth, D. H. "Social behavior of white-tailed deer in relation to habitat," *Wildlife Monographs,* 53:1–53 (1977).

Kile, T. L., and R. L. Marchinton. "White-tailed deer rubs and scrapes: spatial, temporal and physical characteristics and social role," *American Midland Naturalist,* 97:257–266 (1977).

Lingle, Susan. "Escape gaits of white-tailed deer, mule deer and their hybrids: gaits observed and patterns of limb coordination," *Behaviour,* 122:153–181 (1992).

Moore, W. G., and R. L. Marchinton. "Marking behavior and its social function in white-tailed deer," in V. Geist and F. R. Walther, eds., *The Behavior of Ungulates and its Relation to Management.* Morges, Switzerland: International Union for Conservation of Nature and Natural Resources, 1974.

White-Tailed Jackrabbit

Rogowitz, Gordon L. "Seasonal energetics of the white-tailed jackrabbit," *Journal of Mammalogy,* 71:277–285 (1990).

——. "Locomotor and foraging activity of the white-tailed jackrabbit," *Journal of Mammalogy,* 78:1172–1181 (1997).

Woodrat

Bonaccorso, F. J., and J. H. Brown. "House construction of the desert woodrat," *Journal of Mammalogy,* 56:518–519 (1972).

Eschenrich, P. C. "Social biology of the bushy-tailed woodrat," *University of California Publications on Zoology,* 110:1–132 (1981).

Horton, J. S., and J. T. Wright. "The wood rat as an ecological factor in southern California watersheds," *Ecology,* 25:341–351 (1944).

Linsdale, J. M., and L. P. Tevis Jr. *The Dusky-footed Woodrat.* Berkeley: University of California Press, 1951.

Stones, R. C., and C. L. Hayward. "Natural history of the desert woodrat," *American Midland Naturalist,* 80:458–476 (1968).

Thompson, S. D. "Spatial utilization and foraging behavior of the desert woodrat," *Journal of Mammalogy,* 63:570–581 (1982).

APPENDIX C: VISUALIZING HOME-RANGE SIZES

A mammal's home range usually has an irregular shape that is determined by terrain, available cover, food supply, and other animals' ranges. The best way to begin visualizing a species' general home-range size, though, is to picture a square with a certain side length. Then, in our mind we can modify the shape of this area according to the local terrain to get a picture of how far an animal might travel in its foraging or hunting.

In this book I've chosen to use square kilometers and hectares for home range examples, because acres and square miles are cumbersome to work with. A square kilometer is 1 kilometer by 1 kilometer, and a hectare is 100 meters by 100 meters (or 0.01 km²). The following chart helps depict what size square can be visualized for a given area. On the next page is a diagram showing the relative sizes of some of these areas.

Home-Range Size (examples)	Each Side of Square (metric)	Each Side of Square (English)
0.05 hectare (ha)	22 meters	24 yards
0.1 "	2 meters	35 yards
0.5 "	71 "	77 "
1	100 "	109 "
5 hectares	223 "	244 "
10 "	316 "	344 "
25 "	500 "	545 "
50 "	707 "	770 "
1 km² = 100 ha.	1 km	1,090 yds or 0.62 mi.
5 km²	2.2 km	1.4 mi.
10 km²	3.2 km	2.0 mi.
15 km²	3.9 km	2.4 mi.
20 km²	4.5 km	2.8 mi.
25 km²	5 km	3.1 mi.
30 km²	5.5 km	3.4 mi.
40 km²	6.3 km	3.9 mi.
50 km²	7.1 km	4.4 mi.
60 km²	7.7 km	4.8 mi.
75 km²	8.7 km	5.4 mi.
100 km²	10 km	6.2 mi.
500 km²	22.4 km	13.9 mi.
1,300 km²	36 km	22.4 mi.

Relative Area Sizes

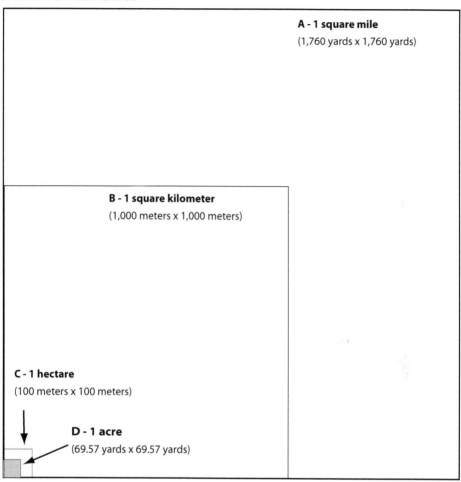

A - 1 square mile
(1,760 yards x 1,760 yards)

B - 1 square kilometer
(1,000 meters x 1,000 meters)

C - 1 hectare
(100 meters x 100 meters)

D - 1 acre
(69.57 yards x 69.57 yards)

Conversions:

1 hectare = 2.47 acres

1 acre = 0.4 hectares

1 km² = 100 hectares

1 km² = 0.386 mi²

1 mi² = 2.59 km²

1 mi² = 640 acres

1 kilogram = 2.2046 lb.

1 lb. = 0.4536 kg

1 lb. = 16 oz.

1 oz. = 28.35 g

APPENDIX D: RESOURCES

The following organizations are some of the many programs that are advancing the field of wildlife tracking. Other very good programs, too many to list here, can be found through Internet links and referrals from these organizations.

Earth Skills
Jim Lowery and Mary Brooks
(661) 245-0318
http://www.earthskills.com
and http://www.walk
withtheanimal.com
Classes and many tracking
resources

Tom Brown's Tracking,
Nature, Wilderness
Survival School
https://www.trackerschool
.com

A Naturalist's World, Jim
Halfpenny
https://www.tracknature
.com

Alderleaf Wilderness College
https://www
.wildernesscollege.com

Animals Don't Cover Their
Tracks
https://www.facebook.com/
groups/271764596196849

Beartracker Wildlife
Tracking, Kim Cabrera
https://www.bear-tracker
.com

Cascadia Wild
https://www.cascadiawild
.org

Deep Nature Guides
http://www.deepnature
guides.com

Earthwork Wilderness
Survival Training School
https://earthworkprograms
.com

Keeping Track, Sue Morse
https://keeping track.org

Lead with Nature
https://www.leadwithnature
.com

The Mindful Tracker,
George Leoniak
http://mindfultracker.com

Natural Awareness Tracking
School, Rob Speiden
http://www.trackingschool
.com

Nature Tracking, Jonah
Evans
http://www.naturetracking
.com

Ndakinna
https:///www.ndakinna
center.org

Point Reyes Tracking School
https://pointreyes
trackingschool.com

Practical Primitive
http://practicalprimitive
.com

Roots School
https://rootsvt.com

San Diego Tracking Team
https://www.sdtt.org

Tracker Certification
https://trackercertification
.com

Trackers Portland
https://trackerspdx.com

The Tracking Project, John
Stokes
https://thetrackingproject
.org

Vermont Wilderness School
https://vermontwilderness
school.org

Walnut Hill Tracking and
Nature Center
https://www.walnuthill
tracking.com

White Pine Programs
https://whitepineprograms
.org

Wilderness Awareness
School
https://www.wilderness
awareness.org

Wolf Camp & School of
Natural Science
https://www.wolfcollege
.com

GLOSSARY

agonistic. Being aggressive, defensive, or submissive in social interactions with members of the same species.

alternating track pattern. A track pattern in which the hind track on each side lands on top of the front track on the same side. See also **direct register** and **indirect register,** and see chapter 3.

bound. A gait in which the two front legs move simultaneously or in quick succession, followed by the two hind legs moving simultaneously or in quick succession. See chapter 3.

canid trot or canine trot. A trot that creates a track pattern in which the front tracks are on one side and the hind tracks on the other. See chapter 5 and the "Domestic Dog" pages.

dewclaw. A vestigial digit on a mammal's foot, especially occurring in pairs among most North American two-toed ungulates. Dewclaws may or may not register in a track depending upon the species, the gait, and the substrate.

diagonal walk. See **alternating track pattern.**

direct register. A walking, alternating track pattern in which each hind track is superimposed exactly over each front track on the same side. See chapter 3.

dish-fissure/disk-fissure. Pressure releases in the floor of the track that commonly indicate running gaits.

disk. A pressure release in the floor of a track that often indicates a medium-speed gait.

dispersal. The movement of a mammal from the home range of its mother to a new home range of its own.

estrus. The receptive period of female mammals (heat).

explode-off. An extreme pressure release outside the track that commonly indicates high-speed motion or rapid acceleration.

Glossary

gallop. A gait in which the two front feet land and then the two hind feet land beyond the front tracks. See chapters 3 and 5.

gestation. The period of development of a fertilized egg to parturition, or the period of embryonic development in the uterus to parturition.

group/intergroup. Respectively, the measurement of groups of tracks and the space between them in a lope or gallop track pattern. See chapter 5.

hectare. Area measuring 100 meters by 100 meters. See appendix C.

home range. The area used by an individual animal for feeding and breeding. Home ranges may be measured variously, considering either annual or seasonal use and considering overall or most concentrated use. See appendix C for help in visualizing an animal's home range.

indicator pressure release. A pressure release, usually small, that recurs in the identical place of every track made by the same foot (e.g., RF) throughout a trail. Indicator pressure releases may be caused by bodily functions, injuries, or deformities, or may be random.

indirect register. A walking, alternating track pattern in which each hind track covers only part of the front track underneath it. See chapter 3.

internal pitch. The sloping of the floor of a track that indicates weight shift toward the deepest part of the track.

lead. The first of a pair of front or hind legs to move in a bound, lope, or gallop.

lope. A gait that creates a track pattern either F-H-F-H or F-F/H-H. Also called a canter. See chapter 5.

overstep track pattern. A walking track pattern in which the hind track falls ahead of the front track on the same side, commonly created by a "pace walk." See chapter 3.

pace walk. See **overstep track pattern.**

parturition. The action or process of giving birth.

pitch. The inward or outward orientation of an individual track away from the direction of travel. See chapter 5.

plate/plate-crumble/plate-fissure. Pressure releases on the outside of a track that indicate fairly substantial sideward motion.

pressure release. A disturbance in the soil or other track substrate left behind by the moving foot. Pressure releases occur on the floor of the track and outside it and indicate an animal's body motion, including speed, change of direction, and head turns, among many others.

reverse disk. A pressure release in the floor of a track pushed toward the front, as in a braking motion.

ridge. A pressure release on the outside of a track that indicates slight sideward motion.

rotary gallop/rotary lope. Respectively, a gallop and lope that have different front and hind leads, for example, LF-RF-RH-LH. The resulting track pattern forms a C shape or backward C shape for each group of four tracks.

straddle. A measurement of the inside of a track pattern, especially in an alternating or overstep pattern. See chapter 5.

stride. A measurement of distance moved by an animal in a walking or running gait. See chapter 5.

substrate. The soil, sand, grass, leaves, snow, or other material in which a track registers.

trail width. Measurement of the width of a track pattern at its widest point. See chapter 5.

transverse gallop/transverse lope. Respectively, a gallop and lope that have the same front and hind leads, for example, LF-RF-LH-RH.

trot. A gait in which the two diagonally opposite legs move simultaneously; there is an airborne phase between each pair's landing. See chapter 5.

INDEX

CLEAR PRINT SUMMARY

(approximate hind track widths in inches)

CATS 4 (F) + 4 (H)

1⁵⁄₁₆	Domestic cat p. 42
1⁹⁄₁₆	Bobcat p. 34
3	Mountain Lion p. 46

DOGS 4 (F) + 4 (H)

1¹⁄₁₆	Kit fox p. 82
1³⁄₁₆	Gray fox p. 68
1⁹⁄₁₆	Red fox p. 90
1¹¹⁄₁₆	Coyote p. 56
2¹⁵⁄₁₆	Gray wolf p. 76
Variable	Domestic dog p. 64

RABBITS 4 (F) + 4 (H)

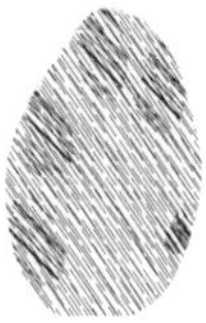

1¹⁄₁₆	Cottontail p. 108
1⅝	Black-tailed jackrabbit p. 100
2¼	Snowshoe hare p. 116
2⅝	White-tailed jackrabbit p. 122

RODENTS 4 (F) + 5 (H)

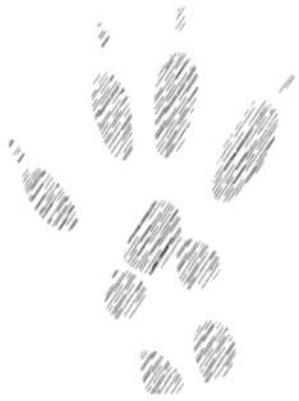

⅛–¼	Mice p. 184
⅜	Pocket gopher p. 198
⁷⁄₁₆	Kangaroo rat p. 170
⁹⁄₁₆	Vole p. 216
⅝	Woodrat p. 220
⅝	Antelope squirrel p. 128
¹¹⁄₁₆	Chipmunk p. 140
⅞	Ground squirrel p. 162
1¹⁄₁₆	Red squirrel p. 210
1⁵⁄₁₆	Gray squirrel p. 154
1⁷⁄₁₆	Fox squirrel p. 148
1⅝	Muskrat p. 192
1¾	Marmot p. 178
1¹⁵⁄₁₆	Porcupine p. 202
3⁹⁄₁₆	Beaver p. 132

WEASELS AND SKUNKS
5 (F) + 5 (H)

½–⅞	Weasel p. 278
⅞	Spotted skunk p. 262
1¹⁄₁₆	Striped skunk p. 270
1⅜	Mink p. 250
1⁹⁄₁₆	Marten p. 242
1⅝	Badger p. 230
2¾	Fisher p. 238
2⅞	River otter p. 256

RACCOONS, OPOSSUMS, & BEARS 5 (F) + 5 (H)

1⁵⁄₁₆	Opossum p. 304
1¹⁄₁₆	Ringtail p. 296
1⅞	Raccoon p. 288
4¾	Black bear p. 310
4½–7	Grizzly bear p. 318

INSECTIVORES
5 (F) + 5 (H)

¼	Shrew p. 324

UNGULATES
2 (F) + 2 (H)

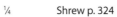

1⁷⁄₁₆	Mule deer p. 356
1⅝	Bighorn sheep p. 328
1¾	Pronghorn p. 364
1¹³⁄₁₆	White-tailed deer p. 370
2–3	Feral pig p. 348
2¼	*Burro p. 336
2¾	Elk p. 340
3¼	Llama p. 350
3⅝+	Domestic cow p. 338
3½–5	Moose p. 352

one-toed

TRACK PATTERN SUMMARY

ALTERNATING/DIAGONAL PATTERN (cats, dogs, ungulates; also opossums, ringtails, muskrats, marmots, and badgers, sometimes fishers)

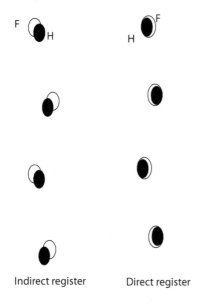

Indirect register   Direct register

BOUND PATTERN (long-tailed and short-tailed weasels, pine martens, river otters, mink, fishers)

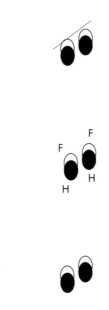

GALLOP PATTERN (rabbits and hares plus most small to medium-size rodents—mice, chipmunks, ground squirrels, tree squirrels, etc.)

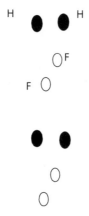

OVERSTEP/PACE PATTERN (wide-bodied animals including striped and spotted skunks, raccoons, bears, muskrats, marmots, porcupines)

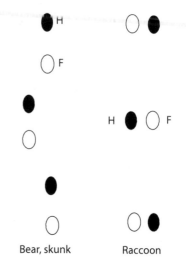

Bear, skunk   Raccoon

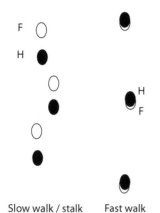

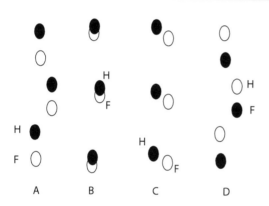

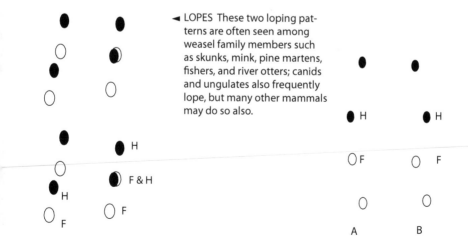

OTHER WALKS A slow walk and a fast walk create the patterns shown here; they resemble trots "D" and "B" below, but can be distinguished from trots from less extreme soil movement in the tracks.

Slow walk / stalk   Fast walk

TROTS These are four of the most common trot patterns. "A" is a normal-speed trot, "B" a fast trot, "C" a "canid trot," and "D" a slow trot. Cats, dogs, and ungulates often trot, but the "B" trot is also often seen among some rodents such as voles and pocket gophers.

A   B   C   D

◄ LOPES These two loping patterns are often seen among weasel family members such as skunks, mink, pine martens, fishers, and river otters; canids and ungulates also frequently lope, but many other mammals may do so also.

A   B

About the Author

Jim Lowery has taught wildlife tracking and wilderness skills since 1987 through his school, Earth Skills, including many special trainings for field biologists, teachers, rangers, schools, and nature center staff and volunteers, and has conducted lectures, webinars and workshops aimed at deepening the connection to nature for all ages. He has worked as a consultant and quality-control expert for mammal surveys that use tracking, and has taught numerous specialized workshops on particular mammal species. His broad approach to tracking meshes every element with the art: analyzing detail, understanding and visualizing movement and posture from tracks, knowing animals' biology and behavior, and applying natural intuitive skills, the latter a product of five years' study and teaching in his "Walk with the Animal" project. Jim has authored many monographs and articles about tracking technique and track interpretation, and compiled numerous videos available at his websites www.earthskills.com and www.walkwiththeanimal.com.